AN ENQUIRY INTO MORAL NOTIONS

AN ENQUIRY INTO MORAL NOTIONS

BY
JOHN LAIRD

NEW YORK: MORNINGSIDE HEIGHTS
COLUMBIA UNIVERSITY PRESS
1936

First published in 1935
American edition, 1936

All rights reserved

CONTENTS

PART ONE

VIRTUE; OR THE THEORY OF ARETAICS

PART TWO

DUTY; OR THE THEORY OF DEONTOLOGY

PART THREE

BENEFIT AND WELL-BEING; WHICH IN THE FORM OF WELL-DOING MAY BE CALLED AGATHOPOEICS

INTRODUCTION

MY intention in writing this book is to compare, examine, and cross-examine what I believe to be the three most important notions in ethical science, to wit, the notions of virtue, of duty, and of well-being in so far as morally relevant. If more learned terms seem appropriate, I should say that I wanted to discuss aretaics, deontology, and (in Plutarch's language) agathopoeics.

No other moral notions, I submit, can compare in importance with these three. Indeed, I should go so far as to say that if all these notions could be shown to be empty, ethics itself would be empty too. No doubt many writers on this subject, both to-day and in earlier times, have attempted to introduce a deflated, workaday ethic, and in the process of doing so have held that all the old-fashioned conceptions should be stripped of their metaphysical or totemistic phylacteries and should be dressed, inconspicuously, and without any amulets, in a sort of lounge suit. Such a view, I believe, implies the denial of genuine ethics, although it may provide several ethical dummies. But I do not want to argue the point directly. As it seems to me, if anyone complains that ethics makes extravagant, fantastic, or superstitious claims, the first thing to do is to examine what precisely these claims are. If that were settled, there should not be any insurmountable difficulty in discovering whether the claims were self-contradictory or inapplicable to our lives, and, again, whether an adequate substitute could be found and restrained from boasting. At any rate, this is the course I propose to pursue. I want to coax or to force the dominant vital and distinctive ethical notions to develop their meaning *vis-à-vis* one another.

It is the business of moralists to present as systematic a theory as the facts permit. Consequently it is usual to find that moralists, if not altogether one-sided, are prone to attempt the erection of a moral system upon a single principle, and either to ignore other moral principles or to include them

A*

in a sketchy and perfunctory fashion. Therefore, if I was right in selecting the notions of virtue, duty, and well-being as so very fundamental, it must follow that a great many moral systems are attempts to propound a *pure* theory of aretaics, or of deontology, or of agathopoeics; and history corroborates this inference.

I intend, therefore, to pay special attention to the question whether any one of these three notions is capable of being *the* foundation of ethics and of supporting the other two.

On the other hand, a smaller but still a considerable number of moralists have persistently maintained that ethics is governed by several distinct conceptions which either have nothing to do with one another (except that they commingle in morals) or at any rate are co-ordinate. In recent years, and especially in England, one form or the other of this perennial opinion has received fresh vitality from the writings of certain Oxford teachers who may be called the New Intuitionists. To use a political metaphor, these Oxford writers may be called either separatists or federalists in ethics. Their opponents, to abuse a political term in the usual way, may be called unionists, although of very different varieties.

Being one who was once an ethical unionist and who still inclines towards a form of that creed, I have naturally been deeply impressed by this New Oxford Movement in ethics, as the sequel will show. If I cannot agree with the separatists, I have at least become convinced that the arguments of the federalists are nearly if not quite as strong as the arguments of those unionists who belong to the persuasion to which I formerly adhered. But I want to renounce my past *in toto*, and to make no attempt to defend any opinion I formerly uttered. In my view the times are propitious for attempting an untendentious comparison of ethical ideas of the sort I have indicated, and I want to try to make this comparison with equity and some patience, despite my shady past.

PART I

VIRTUE

OR

THE THEORY OF ARETAICS

I

GENERAL CONSIDERATIONS

THE word "virtue," in its general moral signification, is used comparatively seldom nowadays, although its opposite, "vice," is still widely employed. I think, however, that "virtue" is a more convenient, as well as a more compendious, term than, say, "moral worth" or "excellence of moral character"; and since moralizing seems itself to have gone out of fashion, it is no great matter if some of the terms of the discussion have a slightly old-world flavour. I should also explain, perhaps, that I mean to use the word in the traditional way as a designation for all commendable qualities of moral character and not exclusively or usually as a name for what is shining and saintly and superlative. In this sense, even the respectable bourgeoisie might conceivably be virtuous.

It would be generally agreed, I suppose, that a man's virtues are features of his personal character; and I shall assume that they are. If confirmation were needed, it might be found in quite unexpected quarters. Thus Hume is commonly and correctly regarded as, in the main, a utilitarian moralist, that is to say, as one who holds that an action should be approved or condemned in proportion as it tends to confer personal or social benefit. Indeed Adam Smith censured Hume for excessive devotion to the principle of utility (although it must be conceded that Bentham was of opinion that Hume was not utilitarian enough). In Hume, however, we find a most explicit assertion of the view that it is *character* that we approve when we approve morally. "Actions," he said (*Treatise*,* p. 411), "are by their very nature temporary and perishing; and where they proceed not from some cause in the characters and disposition of the person who performed them, they infix not themselves upon him, and can neither redound to his honour,

* Selby-Bigge's edition.

if good, nor infamy, if evil. The action itself may be blame-able; it may be contrary to all the rules of morality and religion. But the person is not responsible for it; and as it proceeded from nothing in him, that is durable or constant, and leaves nothing of that nature behind it, 'tis impossible he can, upon its account, become the object of punishment or vengeance." Again he said (*ibid.*, p. 477): "'Tis evident, that when we praise any actions, we regard only the motives that produced them, and consider the actions as signs or indications of certain principles in the mind and temper. The external performance has no merit. We must look within to find the moral quality."

Hume, as usual, put his case as clearly as it could be put. He claimed, as these quotations show, that it was *evident* that morality referred to disposition, character, and motive, and that it did so primarily because it was concerned with what was *durable* and *inward* in the moral agent. Indeed, as he explained, since a "motive" although inward is perishing, motives like actions are but signs of virtue, although they come nearer to virtue on account of their inwardness.

Accordingly, it seems essential to ask, in the first place, whether the moral character in general (and also more specific moral dispositions) is a reality of which we can give a clear and adequate account.

Here, it must be confessed, there are difficulties of at least two kinds. (1) Terms like character, disposition, or tendency seem largely to be names for potentialities, and it is always puzzling to raise questions about the nature and actual status of a potentiality. (2) Again, it may not be readily apparent how a non-moral or sub-moral "disposition" differs from a moral disposition.

(1) The first type of difficulty may be conveniently illustrated by the current distinction, in popular, semi-medical slang, between "organic" injury or disease, on the one hand, and "functional" disturbances on the other. The difference is that if there is something "organically" wrong, it is possible

to show the existence of a definite and stubborn pathological condition of the relevant organs, and hence to infer the effects of this condition with as good reason as can be found in any other instance in which definite effects are assigned to definite causes. If, on the other hand, nothing organically wrong can be discovered, all that can be said is that particular "functional" disturbances have occurred. We can give a name to such disturbances and may discover, by experience, which of them are likely to recur and which are likely to clear up. Giving a name, however, is very different indeed from assigning a cause; and although it may be reasonable to say that we can infer the presence of an *unknown* cause or set of causes for these disturbances, it is not very creditable to our intelligence if we give this unknown cause a name, and it is altogether discreditable if, having baptized the infant *in absentia*, we go on to speak of it as if we knew it had real existence, and were wholly comparable to known causes whose existence can be independently verified.

It is to be feared, however, that if "character" and "disposition" are regarded as the permanent "causes" of perishing thoughts, emotions, and deeds, our explanation is similar to a pseudo-explanation of "functional" disorders and not to the honest explanation that can point to an organic cause. If we knew more about the nervous system we might literally be able to distinguish an enduring "organic" cause for untruthfulness or some other moral defect. If, again, we could discern a permanent "soul" additional to those psychic experiences of passion, imagination, or cogitation that recur and perish but do not visibly endure, we should have discovered a durable psychic organ and might conceivably have independent evidence of its lasting moral condition. In fact, however, we can do neither of these things. Therefore if we are to use terms like "character" and "disposition" significantly we must be very careful indeed to avoid the fallacy of treating an *unknown* "cause" as something that we know very well.

On the other hand, it is clear that when we think of "things"

---

in ordinary life, whether bridges or tea-cups or hardened arteries, a good deal of what we mean is properly and necessarily expressed in terms of capacities. "This bridge is lightly constructed"—that is to say, it is a bridge that would not support a ten-ton lorry, that will support light cars and motor cycles, that might have supported a platoon of marching Russians had they crossed it (which they didn't). Since what we want to know about such things is how far we can rely on them in the proximate future, we have a very special interest in these hypothetical propositions about what *would* happen under this or the other condition; and the logic of the situation entitles us to make assertions about what would have happened in the past as well as about what would happen in the future.

Potentiality, then, enters into our conception and knowledge of ordinary things. This "knowledge," indeed, may be conjectural, but it is matter of reasonable conjecture; and similarly we have the right to ascribe potentialities to persons as well as to things. The surveyor gives the bridge a certificated character, informing whoever may be concerned that it may be trusted to support horses and carts and light cars. The mistress gives her cook a "character," informing whoever may be concerned that the cook may be trusted to boil plain potatoes adequately, and also not to thieve. There is no essential difference in principle between the cook's "character" and the surveyor's certificate for the bridge. In either case, on the evidence of past and present actuality, we are entitled to assert potentialities of a distinctive kind, usually respecting the future, but, if we like, respecting past and present also.

Nevertheless we should exercise a certain caution in making these entirely reasonable statements. The bridge would have supported the Kaiser; but it need not therefore be credited *ad hoc* with a mystical Kaiser-bearing "virtue." The cook's capacity for boiling plain potatoes is not an inner mystery having an explanatory profundity of an entirely different order from the actual occasions on which she *has* boiled potatoes. Similarly, so far as I can see, there is no good reason for regarding a man's moral character as a deep and holy well in which all that really matters is a secret sediment at the bottom. If the moral character were a name for the *unknown* cause of his moral thoughts and actions, it would indeed be secret and mysterious by definition; for it would be an unknown quality. But if it is essentially a statement of our knowledge about what *would* happen as well as an account of our knowledge about what *has happened* in the moral way there is nothing more mysterious about virtue and moral character than about anything else that concerns morality.

Hence it is necessary to interpret, perhaps even to qualify, the explanation Hume put so well. According to him, actions and even "motives," being transient, are but the signs of an enduring moral character. If this statement means that the man himself, in his integral and enduring personality, is the subject of moral responsibility and that virtue or wickedness should be ascribed to the *man*, most of us would agree with it; and, very probably, it is correct. If, on the other hand, Hume's statement is taken to mean that actions and motives are not themselves a part of the personality that is morally judged, and that the genuine subject of moral consideration is, so to say, behind or beneath these superficial "signs," it is, I should say, most thoroughly exceptionable. Statements about what a man *would* do or feel do not characterize him in a profounder or more scientific way than statements about what he *has* done or felt. Certainly he endures. Certainly there is an intelligible sense in which there is "more in him" at any given moment than the particular actions or thoughts that occur "in him" at that moment. But what in this sense is "actually in him" at the moment in question is not, on that account, negligible or merely superficial. It is part of what is morally judged, and it may very well be the part of the man that, morally speaking, is of greatest account.

(2) The other difficulty of a general kind, to which I have referred (i.e. that which concerns the proper boundaries of the moral character), is apt to arise wherever we draw dis-

tinctions rather for our own purposes than (it would seem) for Nature's. Plants, for instance, would appear to be very definite entities of Nature's contriving; and so are robins or men. *Per contra*, a theme like pathology or therapeutics seems to indicate a sort of criss-cross between Nature's ways and ours. It deals with a selection of Nature's habits with special reference to what human beings want or fear. And this, in a different way, seems also to be true of the theme of virtue, vice, and moral character. Aristotle said that conditions of the soul that were praised were just what we meant by the virtues (N.E.I. 13 at the end). More adequately, he said repeatedly that in treating of virtue we were treating of that which is noble. Others would assert that moral character had exclusive reference to moral responsibility, and that moral responsibility was primarily a juristic conception, a man being accounted "responsible" precisely in so far as he is legally presumed to be capable of understanding and obeying the laws of the courts. In short, the boundaries of moral character have to be defined by conceptual cross-currents.

For the present, I prefer merely to indicate this difficulty, not to discuss it in detail. We shall meet it again.

Let us turn, then, from these highly general preliminaries to a somewhat closer examination of the two points Hume underlined, viz. (*a*) the *durability*, and (*b*) the inwardness of virtue and moral character.

(*a*) As we saw, the assertion that the moral character is durable cannot avoid the general difficulties concerning potentiality in an acute form. In an ethics based on character we put the emphasis upon what is supposed to be permanent, although our evidence is drawn from what is intermittent; and we may puzzle ourselves without end about the simple problem whether the good man really is good when he is asleep. There are also, however, more determinate ethical difficulties.

In the first place, it seems clear that instability of character frequently occurs and receives moral censure. An unstable moral character, however, is "a" character that is *not* an enduring character. It is either *several* "characters" or a fluctuation within what is called by courtesy "the" character.

In the second place, there are grave and manifest difficulties regarding the actions which, as we say, are "out of character," or out of keeping with a man's usual character. While a good character may reasonably be pleaded in mitigation of an offence, it affords no sort of denial that the offence actually occurred, and is no proof that a grave offence was morally speaking trivial, although serious in other ways.

Such instances, it is true, fall into different classes. *Imprimis*, the moral personality is very complex. Consequently we should not be surprised to find that everyone has an Achilles heel, that a boxer who is very courageous in the ring might nevertheless show a yellow streak during a shipwreck, that generous people have odd little specialized meannesses. Such examples show that complete moral consistency in a man's moral character need not be expected, but they do not even suggest that the "character" does not have *durable* inconsistencies. *Secundo*, in certain types of delinquency, we conceive ourselves to have ample evidence for inferring that an offence that has occurred but once may nevertheless demonstrate the existence of a long-continued vicious trend of character, possibly unsuspected but certainly not absent. It is, for example, difficult to suppose that sexual vices of the sort that, when discovered, bring shame and infamy could be committed by men of standing and of high reputation unless they really did indicate something vicious and stubborn in the offender. *Deinde*, as in the common saying that *everyone* is a potential murderer, it might be argued that certain offences (not all) would be committed by anyone who was *very* deeply provoked—that is to say, that while certain impulses (say towards homosexuality) either do not exist in many people or, if they exist, can always be controlled, others (say towards brutality and violence) may become irresistible in anyone. If so, there would be no contradiction in the circumstance that a man, in most respects meek and amiable, should murder his wife, although other men, not so meek and much less amiable, would either find life with such a woman not unbearable or if they did find it unbearable would resort, not to deeds of violence, but to a legal separation.

We do, then, draw these distinctions, and we are seldom content with the formal statement that if a man has wittingly done something wrong the wrong action must have proceeded from *him*, and therefore must be evidence of his durable moral character. Such a formal inference, I think, would be as nearly as possible empty and dead. It would have vitality only if it were much more intimately allied with what we habitually mean by moral character.

The conclusion, therefore, is that certain actions are evidence of settled virtue or vice, while other actions, not morally negligible, give little evidence of the kind. Hence virtue and vice (if defined as *durable*) do not exhaust the whole domain of morals, or at any rate do not obviously do so. On the other hand, it may intelligibly be contended (whether or not it is true) that a moralist's *principal* business is with the theory of virtue and vice. If we cannot say of some given action, or vagrant thought, that it is morally characteristic of some particular man, we regard it very differently from one that is morally characteristic; and many would be disposed to regard the former as a sort of regrettable accident situated on the extreme periphery of the moral sphere.

When we say that the moral character is durable we do not mean that it is irrevocably fixed. On the contrary, we usually hold that character grows, and that it is pliable, to some extent, even in its maturity. We are also prepared to admit that it may degenerate during senescence, although we believe that normally the moral character wears better than the memory, than many passions and even than the intellect. We may also be prepared to admit that character may be reborn or "converted," not always towards celestial food; and that the converts may revert, either towards the flesh-pots of Egypt or alternatively towards spiritual manna. There is no greater theoretical problem here than in any other instance of persistence through change.

It should be noted, however, that the persistence of the character is not simply an affair of habit. There is, indeed, very old and very good authority for the truth that the moral virtues develop by habit and exercise; but we need not infer, in consequence, that virtue is always an acquired thing, the offshoot of training and discipline. Even if it were, its response to such nurture would imply a nature, and a virtuous *naturel* need not be supposed to be present at birth or before it, but like many other human powers may be supposed to become effective during a latish phase of development.

As we shall see, there have been many theories on this point, some philosophers maintaining that all our natural impulses and other powers are capable of being developed in a morally healthy way, although all are also capable of reaching a pathological diathesis, others that all are naturally good although a few may be forcibly turned to evil, others that some are originally evil (if indeed the whole fleshly and vainglorious part of us is not originally and ever afterwards a mass of corruption having a natural period in complete spiritual death). I mention these matters here only to show that the "particular go" of the moral character has to be examined as well as the general fact of its persistence. We need not suppose that a man's moral character is an acquired knack or skill similar to skating, cycling, or high diving; but there is likely to be at least as much knack about it as, say, about ordinary walking.

(*b*) The other main point in Hume's analysis is the *inwardness* of virtue. This characteristic of inwardness is not, of course, peculiar to virtue since it applies to all secret thoughts and imaginations, and (many would say) to what is sub- or un-conscious as well. Such inwardness need have no special relationship to virtue or vice; but a man's virtue, at any rate in an essential part of it, belongs to what is inward, covert, and secret in his heart and mind.

What is "outward" as opposed to "inward" is what is

public in two senses. It is public because it gives evidence to the public, and also because of its public effects—that is to say, its effects on the ordinary course of Nature and on the lives of others. If we assume (as we usually do) that nobody is acquainted with the mind and heart of another person except by means of certain physical manifestations, it follows that anything in the mind and heart that is not so manifested cannot be "outward" and must be "inward."

Such inward principles might be unknown to the person who has them; but all except a few psycho-phobiacs believe that *some* "inward" principles are apparent, introspectively, to the person they inwardly move. Since all physical motion is public in principle, what is "inward," in the relevant sense, cannot refer to mere internal changes in anyone's physical body. It must refer to the mind and the feeling; and that is the current opinion, although if it were held that nothing mental occurs without a correlated bodily change, nothing would be completely secret or altogether inward in the sense alleged. In the present state of our knowledge, however, such doubts are but faint and distant clouds; for we cannot ascertain the minute physical changes alleged to be precisely correlated with our secret thoughts, feelings, and (perhaps) sub- or un-conscious selves. It should be noticed, however, that it is more accurate to speak of physical manifestations than of physical expressions; for the word "expression" suggests an intention to communicate, and we derive much of our knowledge of other people, not from what they say or from what they mean to convey to us by any sort of gesture, but from their silence, their nervous movements of an unintended kind, and similar signs.

This being understood, there is an obvious and quite inescapable moral difference between "outward" and "inward," for the simple reason that the same outward manifestation may proceed from very different inward principles, and that much that is inward appears to occur without any relevant outward manifestation at all. Since on any moral theory a *mere* physical deed without any inward purpose, intention, or motive (conscious or subconscious) is not a moral fact at all, and since many thoughts and desires (which yield no public indication of their particular nature) *do* pertain to morality, there is no way of dodging the force of this contention.

Thus (to keep to the first type of instance) it is clear that two persons may perform the same deed (commonly considered right) with very different ulterior purposes; and similarly with regard to deeds commonly considered wrong. A's candour, for example, may be part of his native or established probity, B's an attempt to gain confidence with a view to subsequent fraud. Even if the proximate candid deed be said to be "right" in both instances, we should certainly form a very different moral judgment regarding A and B; and the distinction must be inward since there is no outward difference in the proximate act, and since there would never be any subsequent outward difference at all if B, let us say, abandoned his fraudulent purposes.

This distinction has the closest relevance to our subject, for nearly everyone who opposes morality to mere legalism does so on the ground that morality looketh on the heart, while the law looks only to the outward performance; and even Herr Hitler, although of opinion that "traitors should not be punished according to the extent of their actions, but according to the state of mind they have shown" (as reported July 14, 1934), dealt drastically with what was said to be *shown* in order to prevent later public consequences. On the other hand, the truth contained in this doctrine of inwardness should be freed from certain misconceptions that may easily attend it.

Firstly, it should not be inferred that the outward manifestation is morally irrelevant. The public effects of an action are not negligible, and the agent may be morally responsible for these public effects. Even if a murderous spirit is sometimes morally worse than an actual murder, some attention should surely be paid to the standpoint of the murdered person.

Keeping to the standpoint of the moral agent, it should be noticed, secondly, that there may be a very relevant moral difference between an inward motive that remains secret and one that does not. No doubt if our criminal, fully resolved upon murder, sets out with his loaded pistol, but is knocked down by an omnibus, or finds that his intended victim has sailed for Patagonia, there may be no relevant moral difference (as respects *him*) between his impotent deed and the deed he had resolved upon, unless we include the nebulous possibility that he might have been converted by some evangelist during his journey. His resolve was fixed, and only an accident stopped him. In this case, however, he had resolved *to act*—that is to say, had resolved that his resolution should not remain a mere secret resolution. If he merely harboured murderous thoughts without actually deciding upon murder, or were but half in earnest about his decision, or never intended to do more than imagine murderously, our judgment of him would be very different indeed from our judgment of an actual murderer.

In consequence, thirdly, we should remember most scrupulously that those who talk about the secret springs of action mean to refer to streams that ultimately *gush*. They speak, for example, of generosity, affection, and modesty, and call them inward; but they mean to refer to impulsive dispositions that begin inwardly but proceed outwards. There is an apparent exception, it is true, if the moral injunction be to quiescence, to a life of inward contemplation; but even in that case the forbearance from overt action is itself an action publicly manifested.

Fourthly, it should not be inferred that the inner moral life is not to be judged by public standards. On the contrary, if that inner life is right and good, it *is* right and good, and is not affected by the agent's opinions about such a matter except in so far as right and good moral opinions (or principles) are part of the rightness or goodness of the opiner. Indeed, many of our most secret thoughts, for example, shame, may have a public origin and a public reference. They may not be publicly manifested, and yet be regarded by those who have them in secret as the sort of thing that would lead our fellows to despise us were the shameful characteristic known.

II

CLASSIFICATION OF THE VIRTUES

Mr. N. Hartmann, who among recent moralists has made by far the most serious and the most valuable attempt to classify the virtues, admits that his enterprise has to remain tentative and unsatisfying. As he says (*Ethics,** ii, p. 226), "we can only pick out what the consciousness of the age has elaborated and has to a certain extent made palpable. . . . An historical survey shows that several specific groups of virtues can be distinguished, but that between them the intermediate members are evidently still lacking. We must seize upon the values, where and how we can, at the risk of losing their unity in their variety and of making mistakes as to their gradational order."

These questions of unity and of gradational order are likely to remain perplexing. Regarding the former, it is tempting to be frankly pluralistic. A just man need not be generous. A bold man need not be truthful. A lewd man may be bold. As soon as we embark upon this disintegrating course, however, we begin to perceive that it has no end. A man who is generous where large sums are concerned may be very niggardly indeed regarding petty cash. The courage that mocks at calumny may whine at the threat of a bayonet.

Accordingly, being alarmed at this indefinite proliferation of our classifications, we snatch at the monistic antidote to our pluralism. Often it takes courage to tell the truth. Therefore (forgetting that it may also take courage to tell a lie) we tend to suppose that courage must permeate all the virtues, not because it is always present, but because it *may* be required in any other virtue, even in the virtue of refusing an alms.

Thus we approach a limited pluralism of the cardinal virtues, regarding each such virtue as a pervasive spirit that

* English translation. (London: George Allen & Unwin, Ltd.)

permeates all virtuous conduct; hereafter, perceiving that these cardinal virtues are themselves interdependent (for it takes courage and wisdom to be temperate or just), we tend, like Plato, to hold that the cardinal virtues are really one. As soon, however, as we try to grasp their unity we find it as elusive as quicksilver. Plato found it in the principle of doing one's proper work, or making the best of one's powers. Christian ethics found it either in an intarnishable personal purity, or in the deep and moving philanthropy of invincible charity towards one's neighbour, or in the theological virtues of faith and hope. Others, like Nietzsche and M. Bergson, look for a union between the Apollonian and the Dionysiac in virtue—that is to say, for a subtle commingling of formal stability with romantic adventure. And so we oscillate with little hope of finality.

The idea of a gradation of the virtues may seem more promising, for many have asserted that there are well-marked stages in the spiritual pilgrimage of a soul that develops as a soul should. Thus if we knew, as Plotinus believed he knew, both the start and the goal of such a pilgrimage, we might indicate with some precision how we should strip ourselves of all that occludes the vision of the One and by ascending a well-trodden spiritual path attain fulness of life in a rarer atmosphere. Even if a definite ascent were not always to be expected, as in the "noble path" of the Buddhist which appears to stretch precariously between the morass of sensuality and the abyss of complete other-worldliness, virtue would at least follow a definite road. Similarly a mystical rationalist like Spinoza could indicate levels of virtue where, at the top, union with Nature came through the understanding of her principles and acquiescence in them, where reason was always strength and stronger far than the crude physical strength which nevertheless had the basic virtue of tenacity.

Something, therefore, perhaps much, can be done along these lines; and such attempts may be none the worse because there is as much metaphysics or theology as ethics in them. In the main, however, it can hardly be said that we know very much more about the gradation of the virtues than we know about their unity. We produce lists of commendable small manners and of commendable great manners, counting some of the former and most of the latter among moral virtues, and what we usually commend in all such instances is some highly complicated pattern of mind, heart, and action in particular types of situation. The qualities of soul that we commend are not at all simple, and few if any of them are restricted to the good manners that are appropriate to the situation in question.

It seems clear, however, that a great part of what we commend in the mind and manners that we believe to be appropriate to some type of situation is usually commended in terms either of duty or of benefit and well-being. Thus (if truthfulness be a duty), the habit of veracity is commendable because it facilitates the duty of truth-telling. If, again, we commend the family system on the ground that parents who are faithful to one another and to their children are likely to care better for their children than nurses, schoolmasters, or others who do not have the same special and natural interest in these particular children, the virtue of parental solicitude is commended (rightly or wrongly) on the ground of its probable benefit. In either case, virtue would be commended, not for itself, but either for its good consequences or for its conformity to right rules; and any classification of the moral virtues based on duty or benefit subordinates virtue to these other moral notions. Yet in a consistent theory of moral aretaics, the classification of the virtues should *not* be based upon duty or benefit, although it would be legitimate and might even be necessary to indicate the principal ways in which duty or benefit flowed from or accompanied the virtues.

Pretty clearly, if permanence and inwardness be the essential notes of virtue, a sound classification will be seriously concerned with these notions; and I propose to indicate how a serviceable although imperfect classification may reasonably be attempted on these lines, if it be remembered, firstly, that attention to what is inward in virtue does not exclude attention to the commendable relations between inward and outward; and, secondly, if the limited characteristic of duration or stability be subsumed under the wider notions of integrity and of order.

Nothing within the universe is wholly self-existent or entirely self-sufficing. Nevertheless it is a convenient and permissible exercise of abstraction to consider certain entities by themselves as well as in their interrelationships; and this logic justifies the attempt to distinguish (a) between those inward characteristics that are primarily (and may be exclusively) inward, on the one hand, and, on the other hand, (b) those that being inward are also other-regarding. Since I do not want to affright the reader by coining too many terms from a dead language, I shall call virtues of the former class "personal," instead of calling them, let us say, essentially endo-psychic; and I shall call virtues of the latter class "other-regarding," meaning by the term, not merely that these virtues regard other persons, but that some of them may regard birds and beasts and man's attitude to Nature as a whole. Among the "personal" virtues I shall further distinguish between those that are specially concerned with order of some kind (a. 1) and those that are not (a. 2). A similar subdivision might be attempted in the case of the "other-regarding" virtues, although there it is of less importance.

(a. 1) Even a slight acquaintance with the history of moral theory would be sufficient to show that much in the nature of moral virtue has often been held to consist in a certain balance proportion or harmony within the human soul. Plato said so in the *Republic* when he said that the virtue of temperance consisted essentially in the limitation of each of the major divisions of the soul to its proper ambit, and that "justice" was the positive principle whose negative aspect was temperance. Aristotle's unconvincing doctrine of the "mean" seems to have been based upon the ideal of a proper attunement of the passions (as bodily health, according to Alcmaeon of Crotona, was a balance of powers within the body) although

Aristotle developed his doctrine with reference to manners, e.g. to princely giving, aristocratic demeanour, moderation of statement, tact, agreeable conversation without buffoonery or smuttiness. Bishop Butler's celebrated theory, similar in many respects to Shaftesbury's, was that the soul of man is a system or hierarchy "made for virtue" by the Great Designer, and achieving virtue when the governing parts of man's nature exert themselves magisterially. On all these theories, and on many others, virtue is an inner harmony and order.

They all, of course, sheltered a nest of assumptions. According to some of them, Nature was an ideal conception, being a name for the orderly arrangement of things; and man's "proper" functions were determined with reference to this ideal. According to others, God designed man for certain purposes, and man's essential moral virtue was to fulfil these purposes, although it was also held that a matter-of-fact examination of man's distinctive nature would disclose what he was made for, without the need of any supernatural revelation. Nevertheless moral virtue, in many essential particulars, was the retainer of metaphysics or theology. And perhaps it is.

In a subject so disputable as moral theory, it need not occasion surprise (although it may arouse disappointment) that those who believe moral virtue to be a balance, hierarchy, or harmony of the fundamental powers of the human soul may differ profoundly in their accounts of the nature of these powers and of what they consider the due and proper hierarchy. According to a long tradition "reason" is at the top, and its proper function is to guide and govern; and certainly moral virtue, if it existed at all, would be sub-human if it were not a thing that could be pondered by a reflective being who could look before and after, and if it could never become an affair of intelligible principle. Many, however, to whom this rationalistic tradition makes a general appeal would jib at the intransigence of the more confident rationalists. Admitting that many of our passions have to be curbed and mastered as well as directed in a reflective way, they would strenuously deny that feeling, sentiment, and impulse are, morally speaking, the slaves of a despotic reason, and they are sceptical about the numerous attempts to interpose some semi-rational amalgam of "rational desire" between "reason," the overlord, and "passion," the vassal. They would further point out that according to many rationalists in ethics, the function of "reason," morally exercised, is to discern duty (duty, on this theory, being an affair of rational insight) and consequently that a rationalistic ethic of this type is essentially an ethic of duty and not of virtue.

Others rush to the opposite extreme, maintaining that the sweetness of impulse not the rigours of "reason" are the authentic substance of virtue. Like Rousseau they would hold that the human heart is tender, fine, and true if it is not perverted by the head (and, more dangerously, by other people's heads); or they would assert, like Lord Russell, that morality is poisoned by habitual overdoses of principle and reflection, making men weary and paralysing their natural joys. They might even maintain like Hume that reason *ought* to be the slave of the passions, its sole conceivable function being the discovery of means to ends—that is to say, of the various ways in which passion and desire may be satisfied. If there is rule in us, they say, it is the rule of a ruling passion. And here it should be noted that the usual ethical defence of such views is in terms of *benefit*. If rational mastery is possible it is hurtful; if it is not possible it is useless.

In addition to these acute differences of moral opinion we should notice a further source of perplexity in the very idea of order as the essence of virtue. Orderliness, perseverance, consistency, and other such properties seem to be dubiously virtuous since it is not at all impossible for them to characterize wickedness and sin. A careful, persevering, methodical swindler is surely the worst kind of swindler as well as the most dangerous; and so in a crowd of other instances.

This observation certainly does not prove that order, perseverance, and consistency have nothing to do with virtue;

for although their presence does not ensure virtue, their absence might very well destroy it. The circumstance, however, seems conclusive proof that orderliness cannot be the whole of virtue; and although certain writers appear to maintain that these apparently convincing instances of methodical villainy are misleading, on the ground that they can occur only on a very small scale or are but the parasites of union and solidarity of a greater species, I can see no good reason for believing that the retort is relevant, or that it could have any important bearing upon the characteristics of *personal* virtue.

(*a.* 2) The other subdivision in the class of what I have called personal virtues does not contain very many members since the great majority of the virtues (other than those already considered) have an essential social reference. The clearest instances, I think, are those that are described in terms of purity and beauty, although the virtues that have to do with a clear inner wisdom, with self-culture, with personal freedom and independence, and with self-content and inner acquiescence —the peace and joy of the spirit—might also be included. Such virtues, although other-regarding in many aspects, would certainly be misconstrued if their own inward features were subordinated to these outward relationships; and self-culture for its own sake, irrespective of its utility or the honour that other men may accord it, is probably a notable virtue. On the whole, however, it seems best to pay special attention to purity and beauty.

When we speak of purity we frequently think of chastity and of modesty, that is to say, of purity in matters of sex. These matters, it seems plain, are primarily other-regarding; for when a man speaks of "reverencing his body," the honour he accords it is principally based upon the dignity of its natural office, and modesty is a name for the way in which purity should comport itself in a nasty world. On the other hand, purity of heart and mind, the purity that remains unspotted, not from ignorance but from an unconquerable personal cleanness, is the name for an authentic personal virtue however difficult it may be to describe the virtue with accuracy.

Part of our meaning pretty certainly is that many sins are simply *dirty*, and hard-headed moralists, particularly those who look for the clarities of duty or for some demonstrable social gain, are apt to look askance at this conception of moral dirtiness. Without denying the existence of profound personal repugnances they prefer to consider such feelings as of little account, particularly in the moral way, and are inclined to dismiss the subject with the reminder that doctors and nurses, for example, have to unlearn such repugnances, and are supposed to take no hurt from their unlearning. A morality of this order, they would say, is based upon superstition and taboo; and dirt is only matter in the wrong place.

Such arguments, however, cannot prove that there is no dirt, or that the right or the wrong place makes no difference to the matter, or to us in relation to the matter. In short, there is force in the contention that however superstitious and ignorant many of our applications of the conception may be, the conception of moral cleanness itself has an inexpugnable place in ethics, and consequently that, if any moral theory cannot find a place for it, that moral theory is demonstrably inadequate.

Another objection that might be raised is that our admiration of purity is aesthetic rather than moral, although purity is shown in the moral sphere; and I think the objection has substance, for I would not conceal my opinion that it is difficult, if not impossible, to distinguish moral beauty-or-ugliness from other forms of beauty-or-ugliness except by saying (very uninstructively) that moral beauty or ugliness is shown in moral conduct or character. And certainly we consider modesty decorous, and chastity a beautiful virtue.

Nevertheless it might reasonably be urged (although the statement would be absurd according to *some* aesthetic theories) that it is impracticable and wrong-headed to attempt to excise the bloom of beauty from its site. Could it be an accident that moral beauty *is* moral? And if it is no accident, how can we deny that the beauty is itself moral? According to this way of arguing, we should distinguish between the beauty intrinsic to and inseparable from certain features of the character, and the sort of beauty that a detached observer may discern in the great majority of the virtues. Mr. Lascelles Abercrombie, for example, professes to find self-sacrifice beautiful (although I do not know what he means by saying so); and most of us would say that heroic virtue has an aesthetic quality (although we would not deny the same to heroic wickedness). In such instances, I submit, it is easy to distinguish between the aesthetic and the moral attitude; despite the fact that it is morality that is judged to be beautiful. In other instances, however, it is difficult, and it may be impossible, to do so.

Here, I fear, I must abandon the topic of moral beauty, and also what I have called the (predominantly) personal virtues.

(*b*) Within the other-regarding virtues, the most convenient division, I think, is between the social virtues (*b*. 1) and those (*b*. 2) that have a wider purview. Let us examine the social virtues first.

(*b*. 1) "The sum of virtue," said Hobbes, "is to be sociable with them that will be sociable, and formidable to them that will not" (*De Corpore Politico*, iv, 15); and we need not quarrel with the formula even if we do not consider it altogether unexceptionable. We should, however, examine its distinguishable forms.

The rudiments of friendship are to be found in the associative or co-operative spirit, and this spirit, by very general consent, is accounted virtuous, unless it is a strictly business arrangement unsentimentally restricted to private benefit (as Hobbes thought it always was, and hence was censured).

This co-operative spirit inevitably takes different forms. In all instances it implies mutual fidelity, readiness for mutual aid, and tenacity in such assistance; but its applications vary. Among equals it implies a sense of *full* partnership, each man regarding his fellow as an end as well as a means; and there can be no comradeship without *something* of this spirit. Among unequals, however (whether the source of the inequality be "natural" or political), it may require the spirit of allegiance and obedience on the one hand, and, on the other hand, the spirit of leadership and command.

I do not say that duty and well-being do not enter into these matters. On the contrary, they include the substance of justice and of loyalty, and these are the inner shrine of duty and are also notable for the effects upon human welfare and misery. Nevertheless it may reasonably be contended that neither duty nor benefit exhaust what is morally admirable in these affairs, and even that the virtue in them is prior, both logically and historically, to the obligation or to the manifest advantage.

Again, it must be conceded that the generality, the pervasiveness, and the inclusiveness of these virtues proves that they are very largely non-specific. They are broad spiritual patterns, impressionistically not analytically discernible, a breath not a chemical root. Within any of the patterns, features may be discerned that are similar to the features in other patterns, not necessarily admirable; and this comment has to be made upon the treatment of nearly all the virtues. It need not, however, be a damning comment; for patterns do exist, and so does impressionistic vision.

In a general sense, then, the spirit of association is a moral virtue; but sociableness is a pallid name for the distinctive loyalties of friendship, mating, compassion, and love. These virtues are the names, in general, for specialized forms of kindness and affection, not for something thin and watery, but for something close and deep. Their charm and their fervour are too obvious to need rhetoric. It is better to appreciate them with sincerity and abandon the hunt for superlatives. But it is necessary to remember also that although, when we speak of love or friendship, we commonly think of a peculiarly close relationship between a very few persons, there is no intrinsic reason for these spiritual restrictions in all the aspects of these virtues. The virtue of Christian charity goes out to all mankind. It is a burning philanthropy for Scythian and barbarian, bond and free. And it need not be a god only who has the countenance of one that pities men.

Although love and affection reciprocated yield the deepest personal satisfaction that any of us can experience, we commend and admire them when they are not reciprocated, and account them non-existent (or very nearly so) when the prospect of reciprocal personal benefit preponderates. Similarly, in a type of virtue closely connected with them, namely, generosity and gratitude, we repudiate the "generosity" that is a sort of insurance against possible future indigence, or the "gratitude" that is obsessed with the favours to come. (But these virtues are not simply the outpourings of affection, since there may be great generosity with little affectionate feeling, and since gratitude presupposes some definite service in the past.) In this sense, therefore, love and affection are "disinterested," not because the lover is not benefited by his love, but because he does not look for benefit from his loving. In the same way, self-renunciation and self-sacrifice, in so far as these are virtues—as frequently they are not, but instead a sulky insult to natural joy—are congruent, in principle, with such disinterestedness.

It is usual to join love and sympathy by the straitest ties; but sympathy is a highly ambiguous word, and some of its varied aspects should be clearly distinguished. Mere contagiousness of emotion, for example, is fellow-feeling but not sympathy. I need not be sympathetic with my neighbour if both of us are startled by an explosion; but I *am* sympathetic if the sight of his distress disposes me to make common cause with him, and to reassure him when I am not greatly reassured myself. Sympathy must be consciously transitive, and at least presumed to be interpenetrating if it is genuine sympathy and not a mere similarity of feeling. In the main, however, when moralists speak of sympathy they have in mind something much more intellectual than this transitive, inter-

penetrating emotion, although the emotion and the actions
to which it commonly prompts may be the seed and even
the root of the virtue. They mean, to be brief, the power of
putting oneself imaginatively and even intellectually in the
other man's place; and sympathy, in this sense, is a rare and
difficult as well as a very precious virtue. It can be attempted
by all, it can be instilled very generally by a liberal education
in life's humanities, but at its highest it is an exceptional
thing, like any other great imaginative achievement. Martyrs,
saints, and prophets may have it, and these not always.

So regarded sympathy merges into justice and duty, but it
may be prior to both of these, and also to the wider aspects of
the moral search for human welfare. Indeed, in a general way
and with some misgivings, we are disposed to commend love,
compassion, and sympathy when they seem to be at odds
with social benefit and even when they run counter to duty.
Few would blame a wife for attempting to conceal her husband's crime. Many would blame her if she did not attempt
to conceal it, and although we may deplore the waste of treasure
when affection is showered upon a worthless object, we also
commend the love of inveterate publicans and hardened sinners.
Love may work great mischief if it is foolish, blind, com-
plaisant, partial; but we admire it in a moral way when it is all
these things.

For this among other reasons (some may hold) virtue is a
greater thing morally than either duty or benefit, and not the
virtues of affection only but also the virtue, say, of courage. For
courage, we sometimes think, redeems what would otherwise
be a very sordid affair.

This virtue of courage (which tends to defy classification
since it is really a temper implied in all the virtues although
capable of existing where other virtue is absent) may serve
at least as a reminder of the hardness of virtue, and of its
formidableness to the unsocial in Hobbes's formula.

According to Hobbes's theory, the association of men into
social groups (which, in his view, would speedily disintegrate

unless they were cemented by the political device) implies the dissociation of each such group from other groups, since the groups are supposed to cohere for all the essential purposes of stable human existence. Social virtue was therefore held to be as terrible in war as it was kindly in peace. Indeed, in war-time force and fraud became the cardinal virtues so far as the "gladiators" were concerned. Again, within the body politic, the patriot's virtue was always formidable to rebels, traitors, outlaws, and law-breakers.

If it were held, as I suppose the most belligerent peoples would usually concede in theory, that organized war, as an instrument of social policy, is flatly opposed to moral virtue it would also be agreed that individual association and concord does not necessarily imply political dissociation and enmity, and that the warlike virtues have their place, not as an essential ingredient in a noble life, but as an occasional and contingent necessity. On the other hand, even if wars should cease, police work would not cease with them; and, apart from organized police work, men would have to be hard with themselves and with their fellows if their virtue were a serious thing at all. According to some moralists there is even a place for anger in virtue. They call it "righteous anger"; and other moralists, like Adam Smith in his *Theory of the Moral Sentiments*, make the distinction between the awful and the amiable virtues the the basis for the most fundamental ethical classification.

On the whole, it seems wiser to make no such attempt. *Any* virtue, even the virtue of loving-kindness, may have to be firm and stern. It should not be simply soft. The virtuous man has to be firm with himself, accepting hardship and obloquy when they come, and resisting alluring seductions. What may be harder, he may have to struggle with obstacles in other men as well as in himself and in physical Nature. He may hope, indeed, that the obstacles he encounters in others may be overcome with their eventual consent, and he may have very strong reasons for circumspection when he is opposed to most of his fellows. For they may be right and he wrong. Nevertheless no virtue is always easy or merely amiable, and it is unwise, in principle, to make an absolute separation between the awful virtue of a Regulus and the gentle virtues of angels in petticoats, like the heroines in *Little Women*.

Again, while it is tempting to make an absolute separation between the social virtues and such virtues as a free and independent spirit, pride as opposed to vanity, self-respect, and personal honour, this temptation, I think, should be resisted. Personal pride and self-respect may indeed be contrasted with the regard for others, but the contrast is within the same category. Their standards are essentially social standards, the very meaning of the standards is interpersonal, a way of describing a man's virtue *vis-à-vis* his fellows. This is obvious in the instance of honour, scarcely less obvious in the instance of pride, at least tenable in the instance of self-respect, and undeniable in the instance of liberty and independence where the independence in question does not mean the absence of an interpersonal attitude and standards but the recognition, on the part of social groups, that they consist of individual men and women, each of whom is a member of the group and not its mere instrument, and each of whom, facts being what they are, has an independent personal claim to self-direction, freedom from degrading constraints, a mind and will of his own, a claim to privacy and frequently to a certain aloofness of spirit. Freedom, independence, and other such virtues, so far from being anti-social or unsocial, are implications of sociality in so far as a society is a genuine partnership.

A brief reference to the difficult virtue of humility may serve as a bridge between the examination of these social virtues and the account of another group. Even with respect to his fellows a proud man may commendably be humble. He is not great, but he is not negligible; and if there be greatness in him, he may still commendably be humble, if he thinks of human achievements that are greater still, or has aspirations towards what human nature might be yet hitherto has never become. He may reverence man's powers including his own, and yet be profoundly aware of human imperfection. In the main, however, humility seems to have its place, not so much when a man compares himself with his fellows, and worships heroes fantastically over-praised, as when his standards are superhuman, that is to say, cosmic or theistic; and it should never be assumed that such standards are either irrational or unethical. Morality need not be "all too human."

(b. 2) If we turn, then, to other-regarding virtues not specially concerned with our attitude to other *men*, we have to give our attention to man's relation to other living things, to physical nature, and to the entire universe, whether or not that universe be theistically conceived.

As regards other living things, while man's need for natural nourishment and his necessary antagonism to beasts of prey, venomous animals, and even plants, spirocetes, and tape-worms are the source of obvious ethical difficulties that I cannot pretend to resolve, it seems to me to be utterly immoral to hold, with Kant and Spinoza, that there are no ethical limitations to man's dominion over all else that lives, and that the moral virtues have no reference at all to non-moral or non-rational beings. Even if some sort of fellowship is presupposed in the scope of all moral action, there is surely a fellowship of joy and suffering between man and other animals, and it is not apparent why man's side of this fellowship should alone have ethical importance (as if wild and beautiful things could not concern him although his cat and his canary did).

As regards physical Nature, it is commonly held that a virtuous man can dispose entirely as he chooses of things that can neither think nor feel, and that any apparent exceptions, such as a reverence for natural beauty, are due, not to physical Nature, but to what physical Nature can bestow, the wicked destruction of natural beauty, for example, being wicked because of *man's* loss. Some, however, would maintain, ostensibly without metaphor, that if man's spirit be not interfused with dancing daffodils and stately trees, man cannot be truly at peace with himself and with the world. His virtue would be too uncreaturely to be stable. And they may be right.

According to some great moralists acquiescence in oneself and in one's universe is not only man's blessedness but also his proper virtue; for what every man has to learn is ultimately to accept the universe and himself. According to others, any such view is notably deficient, since it tells us nothing about the relevant type of acquiescence, and would be consistent with a patient fatalism or a flaccid resignation where unconquerable aspiration and bold adventure would point the better way. Similarly, when it is said that a man's virtue consists in making his life "square" or "tally" with the order of his universe, it would seem that such a view, unless accompanied by the explanation that man's universe is itself very good and that man's adaptation to its goodness has itself a high and significant level, is compatible with the meanest accommodation to the meanest environment. The emphasis in all such cases must be on the excellence of the universe, not on the mere fact of conformity with it, and if the note of excellence be muted, we should expect and approve quite a different doctrine, the view, namely, that even if a man's life be fleeting, and his environment senseless and imperturbable, it is still man's moral business to live nobly so long as he may.

Nevertheless, although this matter may need a great deal of explaining, it is useless to deny that virtue has a cosmic aspect, and that this cosmic aspect (whether or not it implies a theological cosmism) might prove, on thorough inspection, to belong to the very stuff of moral virtue. Hence faith and hope, for the Christian, are among the cardinal virtues, and pantheists would hold that a certain loyalty towards the nature of things, a love of all being *qua* being, a reverence for existence as such, and the sort of optimism (not uncritical) that is born of this loyalty, love, and reverence are at the very heart of moral human virtue. These metaphysical virtues, therefore, should be included along with the others, with the explanation that although metaphysical in their nature they need not, in their common existence and exercise, show any traces of academic subtlety or learned solicitude. There may be a profound natural metaphysic of the human soul, distinct from school-philosophy and from all the eddies of learned dust.

At the beginning of this attempt to classify the virtues I pointed out that from the nature of the case only a very partial success could be expected; and this disappointment (I suspect) has been very amply fulfilled in the present discussion. It seemed advisable, however, to explore the territory of the virtues with a particular aim in view, and that aim was itself a serious obstacle in a task that, without any special obstacles, was quite sufficiently perplexing.

The main general difficulties were that most of the moral virtues are very complex patterns rather than distinguishable single elements analytically distinguishable, and that the patterns themselves intermingle and form grades and hierarchies; that what is virtuous in one respect or aspect need not be virtuous in another; that (probably) we cannot speak of virtue at all until a certain delicate and complicated level of mind, heart, and personality is reached; that this level has to be examined in the light of its value as well as in the light of psychological fact; and that, although some such word as "pattern" best describes the general character of most of the moral virtues, certain virtues (like courage) seem to be parts of virtue rather than virtuous patterns, while characteristics like firmness and, in certain cases, radiance seem to have a certain correlation with virtue but themselves are too general even to be called a pattern.

The more special obstacles encountered in our own enterprise depended principally upon the circumstance that we were trying to give some account of moral virtues without making use of the notions of duty or of benefit, not, of course, because these notions had nothing to do with moral virtue (for an ethic of virtue would usually maintain that duty and benefit flow from the virtue of the moral character) but because an ethic of virtue would not be a distinctive moral theory in

B*

any way if virtue could be represented simply as a means of benefit or as a disposition to do one's duty. I have therefore omitted such a duty as prudence (which seems wholly concerned with benefit) and have said very little about wisdom or about specific duties like veracity or promise-keeping. I have further attempted (although not always, I fear, with success) to avoid the illusory satisfactions of a mere subterfuge. It is not unusual to say that virtues are "situational," and that they describe what is "fitting" or "appropriate" in a given moral situation. If, however, virtue is essentially inward (and if it is not there is nothing distinctive about an ethic of virtue) we have to try to examine, not the occasions for the exercise of virtue, but the spirit of virtue itself; and if what is "fitting" or "appropriate" is so on account, not of duty or benefit only, but also of something fine and precious in the character, it seems necessary to look beyond duty and benefit as well as beyond the mere situation or occasion.

III

THE SPRINGS OF VIRTUE: AND THEIR EXPRESSION

As we have seen so very frequently in the preceding discussion, a theory of aretaics, that is to say, an ethic of virtue, sets itself to explore man's inner personality with the object of discovering the well-springs of morality in that secret place. It looketh upon and it trieth the heart. Its method, in Martineau's* language, is idio-psychological, a searching of the individual mind and soul. On the other hand, as we have also seen, these inward springs need not and should not remain merely inward. They are, in the normal case, springs of action; and action, in the relevant sense, is public, not private.

Hence the partisans of aretaics commonly maintain—as Martineau certainly did—that ethics (as they conceive it) has to do with these springs of action, not simply at their source but in their development, that is to say, has to do with what flows from them. The virtues express themselves in action, and when we think of them we think of them in their natural expression. To examine the "expression" separately, as is the habit of many moralists, is really, they say, to depersonalize it, in short, to demoralize it. On the other hand, they are equally firm in maintaining that virtue could not be the spirit of the moral life if it were not, like all else that lives, a spirit of active response.

It is of the nature of a friend, they say, to show himself friendly. Without the inner friendly spirit, friendship, indeed, would be meaningless; but the friendly spirit, if it exists, is also a disposition towards friendly deeds, and it expresses itself in these deeds, unless, by some calamity, it is rendered impotent. Friendly deeds, therefore, in the normal case, *belong* to the virtue. They are not merely superadded to it, or acci-

* *Types of Ethical Theory.*

dentally allied with it, and the principle of this explanation should include not only the "natural" and "spontaneous" expression of a friendly spirit but also its planned and astute expression if the friend be intelligently prospicient. An intelligent man evinces his intelligence in his actions. A reflective man thinks before he aims and aims before he shoots. Consequently intelligence and reflection, in this sphere, are to be regarded, in M. Bergson's phrase, as prolongations of the more impulsive forms of action, but they are just as clearly an expression of character as any impulsive action. A friend may show himself friendly by some spontaneous gesture. He may also show his friendship by taking infinite trouble about his friend's investments. But in both cases he gives what we call "practical expression" to his friendship.

It seems clear, however, that this line of argument may be dangerously facile. Thus it seems reasonable to urge that without a certain fundamental decency, fairness, and good will in the citizens even the simulacrum of social health could scarcely be expected. On the other hand, these properties, although necessary in a healthy society, do not of themselves suffice to cure social ills; and even if, in some remote and vague sense, everything else that is requisite may be said to be some sort of "expression" of these virtues, we might have to conclude that the "expression" played at least as great a part as its stimulus. Any tolerable legal system, for example, is largely based upon "natural justice"; and this vague conception itself frequently occurs in legal decisions. But anyone who compares the methods employed in some private enquiry by a Discipline Committee (whose members cannot be accused of bad faith) with the procedure of an experienced court of justice must see, with a pained surprise perhaps, but all too clearly, that centuries of patient solicitude, as well as long personal training, are required before the simplest matters can be dealt with in a way in which even a colourable imitation of systematic justice is shown.

No doubt it may be argued that a distinction of this kind is largely the distinction between skill and efficient technique, on the one hand, and moral qualities on the other. Hence the inference might be drawn that *morality*, although necessary for social health (perhaps its prime requisite), can never of itself cure social ills; and similarly in other instances. This view, I think, is important and, in the end, sound; but I cannot think that it settles the matter. Take, for example, the Augustinian maxim, *Ama et fac quod vis*. Can it seriously be contended that even in moral matters a strong affection for one's kind or a genuine love of all existence can of itself provide complete insight into moral duty or into ethical benefit, that assassinations are necessarily and always to be commended if they are prompted by a great love of one's country or of one's class, that it is impossible to love unwisely both for the lover and for the beloved? Quite apart from all questions of skill and mere technique, it is surely apparent that the strongest and the most genuine affection may prompt to actions that in any ordinary sense are morally wrong.

I submit, therefore, that we should enquire more closely into the question of the relation between the springs of moral action and their "expression."

For the most part, the writers who deal with such matters give a sketch of what is now called the hormic psychology, or, more accurately, the hormic psycho-physics. Such *hormai* are variously called propensions, *prima secundum naturam*, instincts, impulses, appetites, "urges," and "drives," these terms, of course, permitting of certain minor individual differences, largely according to taste. Some of the *hormai* are relatively specific, others much more general. Thus in a well-known and courageous, if somewhat arbitrary, classification of the principal human instincts, the dispositions to suckle, to escape, to mate, and to herd are said to belong to the former class, while dispositions like curiosity, acquisition, and construction are much more general. Again, the discussion of these questions is nearly always rendered difficult to follow through its espousal of incompatible aims.

The human species has, in the main, pretty definitely characteristic ways of going about its biological business, in its courtships, say, or in the way in which it tends its young.

If so, the emphasis is upon a type of racial routine that is learned, as we say, by Nature's teaching. On the other hand, especially when it is held that instincts or other *hormai* are the raw material of human action, a place has to be found for an almost indefinite plasticity and educability of the *hormai*.* In that case systems of property are ascribed to an "acquisitive" instinct, the writing of *Woodstock*, the building of the Simplon Tunnel, and the Soviet system of government are ascribed to a primitive "constructive" instinct, and the *Critique of Pure Reason* to the instinct of "curiosity," although the primitive forms of these instincts in man are at the most a tendency to collect small objects, a certain native interest in manipulating pliable material, and a kind of wary attention in the presence of something novel. If, in addition, a theory of the "sublimation" of the *hormai* is offered, the effect of the additional explanation is that any *horme* whatsoever may be held to account for anything human; and sometimes we are presented with classifications, such as that of egoistic versus altruistic, in which there can be no serious attempt to describe typical *hormai*, but, instead, an attempt to distinguish between the ethical results of hormic behaviour.

All this may seem to be highly unsatisfactory; and truly it is so. Its logical difficulties, however, are of the same order as those we have already encountered in the classification of the virtues; and there *are* typical natural propensities in the human species of the sort described in some of these theories.

According to certain authors the essential part, if not indeed

---

* One is reminded of Falstaff's explanation of the sad affair at Gadshill: "Why, hear you, my masters: was it for me to kill the heir-apparent? should I turn upon the true prince? why, thou knowest I am as valiant as Hercules: but beware instinct; the lion will not touch the true prince. Instinct is a great matter; I was now a coward on instinct. I shall think the better of myself and thee during my life; I for a valiant lion, and thou for a true prince."

the totality, of instinct is an inherited and racial mode of behaviour, scarcely distinguishable from a chain of reflexes; and they say this without reference to the "conditioning" of reflexes that according to the modern materialists in biology is the reality that in our superstition we misname mind and consciousness. If so, mind and intelligence would be in the van if it directed our instincts, in the cart if the instincts bore it along. Others, however, would maintain, like Dr. McDougall, that all instincts are psycho-physical from the outset. They are always minding and feeling as well as simply behaving.

There are many reasons why it is unnecessary for present purposes to take sides in this dispute. In the first place, Dr. McDougall's theory refers ostensibly to *instinct*, not necessarily to all *hormai*. In the second place, when we are dealing with the moral character, we have necessarily to deal with processes not merely physical but also psychic, and, as we shall see, at a certain high level of the psyche. On the other hand, the particular point at which Dr. McDougall makes a start with his celebrated theory of the "instincts" concerns us very nearly; for McDougall begins with an emotional "motive," and treats each instinct as a unity in which the emotion is canalized into a pretty definite channel of action. Charles Darwin's book on *The Expression of the Emotions* indicates, with great precision, the sort of theory that McDougall and William James elaborated, each in his several way. It is also congruous with most of the newish theories of aretaics, as for example with Martineau's; for a virtuous "motive" according to these theories is an affair of the heart, that is to say, of emotion; each such motive gives rise to a typical chain of reactions; and moralists are concerned with the ensemble of motive allied with its "natural" reactions.

It must be confessed that any such theory leads to serious difficulties in its application. The very distinctive emotion we call fear, for instance, seems to be correlated with *several* modes of response. It may startle into flight, paralyse into immobility, rouse to desperate pugnacity. Yet many writers, particularly Dr. McDougall, reckon "escape" and "pugnacity" among the fundamental instincts. Contrariwise, it seems difficult to imagine *what* specific emotion is at the root of the "constructive" or the "acquisitive" instincts except the excitement of these activities themselves, or the turmoil and unease that may arise when they are balked. A one-one correlation between a specific emotion and a specific channel of response, consequently, seems very unplausible. Nevertheless a certain qualified assent may reasonably be given to the theory. A single hormic "motive" may indeed have several behaviour-channels into which it may flow; but it always has a limited number; and when different motives flow into the same channel of behaviour, the truth may very well be that commingled emotions jointly seek an outlet that either of them might have sought separately. In short, it seems clear that most emotions, if not all, do have a "natural" physical expression, and that this physical expression may be a prolonged series of typical reactions.

To grant this, however, is rather to start than to put an end to perplexity, and we should do well, I think, to sharpen our wits by recalling a sceptical comment of Hume's. "According as we are possessed with love or hatred," he said (*Treatise*, II, ii, p. 7), "the correspondent desire of the happiness or the misery of the person, who is the object of these passions, arises in the mind, and varies with each variation of these opposite passions. This order of things, abstractedly considered, is not necessary. Love and hatred might have been unattended with any such desires, or their particular connection might have been entirely reversed. If Nature had so pleased, love might have had the same effect as hatred, and hatred as love. I see no contradiction in supposing a desire of producing misery annexed to love, and of happiness to hatred. If the sensation of the passion and desire be opposite, nature could have altered the sensation without altering the tendency of the desire, and by that means made them compatible with each other."

Hume's treatment need not have been so very "abstracted." It is a matter of common knowledge that lovers may be, and

often are, very cruel to one another. Even if these cruelties
were but the storms of courtship, a kind of experimentation in
mutual power and influence in a highly charged atmosphere,
it would surely be doubtful whether all the quarrels and
jealousies and misunderstandings were wholly admirable in
the lovers, not to speak of their effect upon other people. It is
not in fact the truth, however, that these cruelties are but
cruelties of courtship, vanishing when union has succeeded
approach, and restricted to affairs of mating. They may occur
in all cases of love and friendship in which there is high
excitement; and what would love and friendship be if they
were never excited, but always tranquil conditions? Certainly
love and friendship seldom include *settled* cruelty or hurtful-
ness. If love turned to that we should not call it love any
longer. But even if the hurt and cruelty are tempestuous and
short they are *meant* at the time; and they may be very terrible,
as anyone may note who considers crimes of jealousy in which
there seems no doubt that genuine affection between the
parties had never ceased.

In the concrete, then, a "desire of producing misery,"
although not a settled desire of that kind, may be "annexed"
to love. The paradox is a paradox of fact, not of whimsical
metaphysical speculation. But what should we infer from the
circumstance?

While the cruelties of love may yield a short and defiant
satisfaction (not always *very* brief) their general effect is a
swift, sympathetic reversal. The lover, therefore (unless his love
has been mingled with pride or foolish policy, and perhaps
even then), is struck with instant remorse. Accordingly, unless
we hold that this sympathetic union is itself only arbitrarily
"annexed" to love, it seems clear that love could not grow
in the way in which it does grow if hate were its usual fruit.
If it persistently had the effects that we ascribe to hatred, its
evil results would react upon the emotion itself. Its exercise
would be pain and torture for all concerned, its joys (if it had
any) would be despicable and furtive. In short, it would be

a very odd sort of "love." Nevertheless, since love's cruelties are also very odd, we should not deny *all* meaning to the conception.

In the main, I think, two conclusions follow: (*a*) The first is that writers on aretaics commonly ascribe to the inward motive properties to which it has no sound logical claim. (*b*) The second is that in consequence of this oversight they frequently advocate, not aretaics, but an ethic of well-being, although they do not think so. I propose, therefore, to develop these matters.

(*a*) Regarding the first of them, Hume's argument essentially was that a motive and its expression are distinct realities having no logical interconnection. To this the obvious reply is that no one need suppose that there should be a logical connection. There is a logical connection, no doubt, between an *intention* and its fulfilment. If the intention is frustrated, it is not fulfilled. If it is fulfilled, the agent does what he meant to do. What is generally meant by a motive, however, and what is relevant to these arguments, is not simply an intention to do so and so, but primarily an inward feeling which "naturally" and, it may be, unconsciously, initiates or prompts a certain" expression" (as the perception of incongruity is "expressed" in a smile). In such matters the connection is causal not logical. The relaxation of mental tension may be followed (causally) by a relaxation in the neighbourhood of the lips; and fear may lead to flight.

To deny a *logical* connection, therefore, is not necessarily to deny *all* connection; and, according to most hormic theories, the actual nature of the causal connection that really exists is, in certain of its aspects, plain enough. In broad outline, although not always in detail, an instinct survives if it is profitable. It is strengthened by exercise if, instead of being in principle self-defeating, it attains the sort of result that favours it retroactively.

Since envy and hatred may flourish according to such theories (indeed since some old men may have kept themselves alive in order to spite their heirs) it is clear that these general and largely biological considerations cannot suffice for a theory of ethics. Nevertheless they may very well suffice to indicate a certain type of genuine causal connection. As we have seen there is a sort of virtuous circle in loving, since for the most part the actions that are prompted by love stimulate and encourage the affection. And similarly in many other cases.

Nevertheless causes are *different* from their effects, even when the causes and the effects support one another in what I have called a virtuous circle. There is no justification for confounding between the unity of a causal process and the unity of an identical thing. In particular, it is quite unjustifiable to commend a motive when the reason for the commendation properly belongs to the expression and the results and scarcely at all to the motive. Indeed, Hume's argument was timely precisely because it forced attention to the distinctions within these causal series.

(b) Regarding the second point, it is to be noted that moralists who argue in terms of benefit are apt to confine their attention to the good that the agent *intends*. This intention, combined with the qualities of will that are necessary to make the intention effective, implies a certain inwardness. If it did not, there would be *only* benefit and not morality, as there is in sea breezes and gentle rain. This attenuated inwardness, however, seems to be definitely emaciated in comparison with what we commonly account a moral motive, and lends itself to an over-intellectual and too nicely calculating theory of morals, repugnant to those who believe (and with justice) that a certain gracious profusion of spirit is a great part of moral virtue, and is often better far than cautious reckoning. Let the heart but echo the "voice of nature."

Therefore it is important to observe that an ethic of benefit and well-being need not confine itself to such benefits as are strictly intended. No doubt when we have had experience of the usual fruits of motives like affection and generosity we know something about the beneficial results of such actions (in their common exercise) without consciously naming them or making enquiry into them. We also exercise them without any restraints due to the memories of past disaster, and it is conceivable, although perhaps more plausible than authentic, that these motives themselves sharpen our insight into what is good. In the main, however, an ethics based on the natural virtues of the heart, that is to say, upon certain laudable motives-in-their-typical-expression, need not refer at all to the *thought* of benefit. What is essential is that such natural virtues should (normally) *be* beneficial whether those who exercise them have thought about the matter or not.

It seems to me that an ethics of the "voice of nature" is most plausible when it is argued on these lines. On the other hand, the theory seems manifestly insufficient, for the voice of nature seems to speak in very similar accents to many of the higher mammals as well as to man. For the most part a female cat is a good mother, although a few cats seem frankly to be bored with their offspring and are very neglectful of them, and although a very few eat their kittens. If, then, a good mother in the human species is morally admirable and a good mother in the feline species is denied moral admiration, the reason must lie in certain qualities that the human mother possesses and the feline mother lacks, unless, indeed, we hold, quite arbitrarily, that morality is simply a human affair, and so make an end of the problem.

Here the differentiating qualities cannot be a parental instinct, experienced with emotion, and beneficial to the offspring and to the species. For the feline mother shares these qualities with the human mother. Nevertheless if the "voice of nature" theory, interpreted in terms of beneficial natural instincts and other propensions, does not suffice for morality in the full sense, it may constitute a great and significant part of human morality; and I have tried to indicate that there are strong reasons for holding that it does.

I have also tried to show, however, that any theory of aretaics has little solid ground (although it might have some aesthetic justification) if its commendations are confined strictly to the inward motive without regard to the expression and the consequences of such inwardness; that the expression and the consequences must be distinguished from the inward motive, however true it may be that all of them together form a continuous natural process; and that the benefits that flow from such a motive are and ought to be included among the principal reasons why it is commended. Indeed, an ethic of benefit seems to be strong enough to deal even with the instances in which, *prima facie*, aretaics makes its strongest case. According to an ethic of virtue, we retain a certain moral admiration for a generosity that is clearly unwise, that is to say, *not* beneficial in the particular instance. "Quite so," rejoins the ethic of benefit. "In the particular case we may very well commend the motive, although we cannot commend its foolish or mischievous exercise. The reason, however, is clear enough. The motive is usually beneficial, and its comparative rarity enhances its value. Therefore we are always very loth to condemn it, although in egregious instances we have no serious alternative. Substantially, however, our very reluctance to condemn is itself tutored by the idea of benefit. The virtue is a very tender plant, easily made to wither by the faintest chill of criticism or ridicule. Therefore we spare it when we can in order that, unfortunate in some particular instance, it may not be hampered in its normal beneficial exercise. The *prima facie* objection is not a real objection; and the whole matter is assessed in terms of benefit."

I do not say that this rejoinder is altogether successful, but surely it is forcible and pertinent.

IV

THE HEART AND THE HEAD

THERE is no indigenous reason why an ethic of virtue should inevitably be unintellectual. Virtue, it is true, is a habit, and we sometimes contrast habit with thinking, but the contrast cannot be absolute since there are habits *of* thinking, since the habit may be the product of thinking (on the teacher's part if not on the pupil's), and since there is no contradiction (but, on the contrary, great utility) in habits that are reflectively regulated.

Anyone, indeed, who has studied the great Greek moralists would be inclined to assert without the least hesitation that a commendable moral disposition must be in accordance with right reason, and that, although this "right reason" need not be the agent's (since the intelligence behind it may emanate from the Director of Spiritual Education and his predecessors) it should generally be assumed that the agent's reason and reflection accept the rightness in question.

Such a student, therefore, may be seriously perturbed when he finds that Christian ethics does not readily respond to the dominant note of reasonableness. Christian ethics, in its Oriental way, has other aims, and these may seem rather to subvert than to supplement the classical spirit. No doubt it is possible to argue that what Christianity inculcates is not the absence of reflection but the need for altering the direction of human reflection. Certain profound simplicities that the wise and prudent may have forgotten should be recalled to everyone's mind. Worldly and political wisdom should be subordinated to a higher wisdom, and this higher wisdom should not be the unworldly wisdom of Plato or Aristotle but an unworldly wisdom of a different kind. It is knowledge of the *truth* but not in the Greek way. The new truth is communion with an infinitely compassionate deity, not intellectual affinity with a god who eternally geometrizes.

These explanations, however, seem rather to aggravate than to diminish the gulf between an ethics of right reason, in its ordinary sense, and an ethics of the heart; for the heart is likelier to reach the truth of such communion than the head.

No doubt it should not be assumed that because our knowledge of our fellow-men does not lend itself to mathematical treatment (and in that sense is to be judged unscientific), it is therefore not effective knowledge; and if spiritual forces direct and encompass the universe, an ungeometrical knowledge of them is knowledge all the same. Still, it is not reflective knowledge in the ordinary sense; and although the *rapport* of civic friendship was certainly not overlooked in Plato's *Republic* or absent from Aristotle's *phronimos*, it was different from intellectual contemplation. We have therefore to enquire into the extent to which reflection, and the intellectual understanding of principles, belongs to the substance of moral virtue; and we may begin by examining the extreme view that the truest morality need not even be *conscious*, not to say articulate or reflective.

Superficially it might appear that since our conscious processes are intermittent, any moral theory that is based on the permanent moral character is, by that very fact, committed to a belief in the existence of what is sub- or un-conscious. If, however, we hold fast to the view indicated in our first section, viz. that "character" is *unknown* except as a statement about what would happen in the moral way under this or the other circumstance (as well as for what is happening and has happened in the moral way), there is no need to accept either of the two most disputable assumptions in the common theory of the sub- or un-conscious, viz. that we can speak of unconscious toothache or unconscious despair *in the same sense* as of conscious anguish, and that we *know* what is happening in secret when something is done or thought that looks as if it were the result of intelligent process, although there is no memory or other introspective evidence of *any* train of thought.

Nevertheless it is correct to observe, firstly, that if (say) the solution to a problem flashes suddenly into our minds in an idle moment long after we definitely abandoned all conscious effort to struggle with the problem, there is the same formal relation between the puzzle and its solution as there would have been had we consciously solved it by excogitations of which we had been continuously aware. Similarly, while it seems absurd to assert confidently that there *is* an infantile "self" irresponsibly following the "pleasure principle" and disturbing the adult "self" (which warily follows the "reality principle"), although there is no consciousness of the tension, it may be legitimate to say that certain psycho-pathological cases do exhibit the sort of disturbance that might be expected if there were distinct psychological organizations having this sort of conflict in their aims. The dramatic merits of psychoanalysis are considerable.

In the second place, the word "consciousness" seems to be the name for a very complex event in which various properties and offices may be distinguished, and there may well be conditions under which the faintness or absence of some of these properties may make us hesitate to speak of "consciousness" *pur sang*. Thus when we speak of our "consciousness" we usually signify by the term a certain luminousness, togetherness, and reflexiveness, each of a peculiar kind. We are awake and alert, not asleep or anaesthetized; and this is the property of luminosity. There are, however, degrees of sleepiness or of anaesthesis, and according to the late Sir Henry Head there are various degrees of physiological "vigilance." It is difficult, therefore, to be certain where the "luminosity" of consciousness begins. The "togetherness" of consciousness, again, is an intricate affair. What we mean by it, roughly speaking, is that our immediate experience is continuous in its essence. The time-scattered luminosity of twilight sleep or the scurry of a dream gives us, in William James's phrase, "sciousness" rather than consciousness even when the sciousness is vivid. We are "conscious" in the ordinary sense when we are aware

of the continuity of experienced passage, have the memory
prompt if tentative, and have a certain connected grasp of
our situation, temporal, spatial, and, it may be, social. In all
this, obviously, there are different levels of effectiveness, and
consequently a necessary dubiety about the precise boundaries
of "consciousness." Furthermore (and principally) there is, in
all *con*sciousness, a necessary element of *reflexiveness* or self-
acquaintance, not indeed of a pure self, or, as M. Bergson
would say, of a self that is "put in the corner," but a grasp of
our past, *our* present, *our* situation, in a word of *our*selves as
agents.

It is at this point, I suggest, that the ethical problems regarding this matter become most considerable. What is meant by
the "heart" in moral philosophy is a thing of emotion and
sentiment, a sensitive heart that experiences joy and bitter-
ness, that throbs in sympathy with others. Processes still more
secret than this, if they can ever legitimately be said to occur,
are interpreted on analogy with the "heart" thus understood,
and are an extrapolation of it. On the other hand, this level
of emotional experience, although "conscious," need not be
reflexive in any discriminating way. It has the warmth and
intimacy of *personal* togetherness of experiencing; but it need
not be accompanied by explicit introspection, that is to say, it
need not be reflexive at the subtler, more articulate levels of
reflexiveness.

The whole subject of the nature of introspection has been
debated in many psychologies; but if it is assumed (as I have
assumed) that there is such a thing as self-acquaintance, it has
to be admitted that the attitude of express and deliberate
attention to ourselves is difficult to sustain, and that the art
of self-description is one in which very few excel. To search
one's heart, and to reveal it either to ourselves or to other
people, may even be a work of genius, and is never the work of
an ingenuous tyro. Yet a certain ingenuousness of the spirit
may be the finest flower of morality; heart-searching may be
an affront to virtue; and even if these statements were false

or exaggerated, the articulate recognition and description of the heart and its sentiments seems to be an affair, not of moral virtue, but of literary skill. What is wanted morally is that a man should *be* virtuous, not that he should be self-consciously virtuous; indeed, virtue may be forgone if it does not go unself-consciously.

Introspection of this explicit order is an affair of the head; and it indicates one of the ways in which the head may be opposed to the heart. In the main, however, the contrast between head and heart is not the contrast between self-consciousness and unself-consciousness, but the wider contrast between feeling and thinking. The dispute is about reflection in general rather than about reflexiveness in special; and so we should address ourselves to the more general question.

As we saw in the last section we commonly regard man's reflective capacity as part of the essence of his morality; for we commonly deny morality to the animals, even when their emotions and behaviour are of the type that would be moral in men; and similarly we are of opinion that young children are only moral in the making. No doubt it would be possible to argue that a greater delicacy of emotion and of sympathy is the genuine distinguishing characteristic even here, but this greater delicacy seems itself to be allied with knowledge and reflection. The *knowledge* of good and evil is in question, and this knowledge, it seems plain, is the sort of capacity that only a reflective being could have. Both directly and indirectly, therefore, it is at least highly probable that morality, as we mean and intend it, could not exist in an unreflective creature.

This being granted, however, it might be maintained, and in fact is maintained by a very large number of moralists, viz. by all who are sentimentalists, and indeed, by all anti-rationalists, that although reflection and the use of general ideas may define the distinction between man and the other mammals, man's morality, admitting it to imply reflection in certain subordinate ways, is primarily and fundamentally emotional. If so, an unreflective and even childlike emotional disposition might exist and be the core of morality in a human being, although human beings would also be capable of using reflection in the service of these emotions, and so of acting morally in a way very different from the other animals.

The main questions to be considered in this connection concern (*a*) the relation between means and ends, together with certain other debatable matters incident to that relation, (*b*) the rationalistic implications of moral principle and of moral duty. These questions should be examined separately.

(*a*) If the end of an action were simply its result, all questions of this order would be questions of benefit, and need not be examined at this stage of our discussion. A conscious end, however, is, at the least, a result that is intended; and the conception of an unconscious end seems unsound in principle. It could mean, at the most, that certain types of process can be satisfied in certain ways only, whether or not the agent knows what would satisfy them. More generally, when an end is regarded as the fulfilment of a unitary process, or as the completion of a tendency, its consideration falls within the scope of an ethic of virtue. Benefit, no doubt, may be the true and final explanation, in terms of arguments already adduced; but if, as in an ethic of virtue, we profess to hold that the initial quality of the impulse is the relevant consideration, all "means" may be regarded, quite legitimately, as the devices we adopt for developing and furthering such impulses.

Although means and end very often intermingle, a means, if it is just a means, is an instrumental thing, and discussion concerning it is discussion concerning matter-of-fact instrumentality. The knowledge of means, therefore, is matter-of-fact knowledge, and the use of them is simply skill. It may therefore reasonably be enquired whether skill and matter-of-fact knowledge are ethical at all. How is it *moral* to be deft or to be knowledgeable?

One of the reasons, no doubt, why we apply such very different moral standards to adults and to children is that we know or presume that grown-up people have an adequate understanding of the ordinary consequences of ordinary actions. This in itself is an important matter ethically; for we hold that a man is morally culpable if he neglects to acquire the sort of practical knowledge requisite for a useful citizen or if, having acquired it, he forgets it at the useful moment.

This principle, again, is not confined to what I have called the "ordinary knowledge of ordinary consequences," i.e. to a certain minimum of practical common-sense knowledgeableness that may be legally presumed to be the possession of everyone, not an imbecile, who has attained the age of twenty-one. It is not, indeed, the moral duty of everyone to have the special practical knowledge and skill that is required for doctoring, seamanship, or any other particular calling, and it may not be everyone's duty to acquire any special skill at all. But most of us should apprentice ourselves to some calling, at any rate in modern conditions of society; and it is the moral duty of anyone who enters a calling to acquire the skill and the knowledge necessary for that calling, to improve that skill and knowledge beyond the necessary minimum (if he can), and to use his skill and knowledge to the full extent of his powers. The principle, moreover, applies out of business as well as in business. It is not doctors only who have the duty of considering the ways of health. And the principle is not restricted to unpsychological matters-of-fact. In great measure we should be our own spiritual physicians, and have some notion of how to bring spiritual first-aid to our friends.

We may therefore affirm with confidence that matter-of-fact knowledge and skill are not irrelevant to morality. A moral person is a moral agent who *directs* his agency; and he cannot direct his agency unless he is aware of the bent of the agency. Again, it is a moral duty to make oneself effective, and to improve one's efficiency, provided that the efficiency is not efficiency in wrong-doing.

As the proviso shows, however, it is clear that efficiency need not of itself be moral. An ethic of duty presupposes efficiency in fulfilling obligations, an ethic of benefit or well-being commends beneficial efficiency in the moral agent. Our present question, however, is what an ethic of virtue has to say on the matter.

When wisdom is included among the moral virtues, the knowledge of means as well as the knowledge of ends, together with all calculation and reasoning that has a bearing on either of these, must also be included; and if it be said that the moral virtue of wisdom is concerned with ends rather than with means, and with ways of living rather than with physical science, this change of emphasis (for it is not a complete restriction) does not very seriously affect the above statement. Efficiency must be included in wisdom, if the wisdom is genuine.

An ethic of the heart, however, need not include wisdom among the moral virtues, unless on the theory that our emotional or instinctive nature possesses a sort of divination into the true and the good, and consequently is wiser than reflection; and if the substance of this ethic be that the growth and fulfilment of the finer native impulses and dispositions is the core of virtue, a knowledge of matter-of-fact would be strictly subordinate to the impulses and dispositions.

Such an ethic would further argue (and here its contention would be very plausible) that morality *never* includes skill. What morality does enjoin in such matters (we might be told) is care and diligence, the treating of serious things seriously; what it condemns is sloth, negligence, and misplaced levity. From these virtues, in conjunction with our inborn talents, skill and knowledge result; and the result is praiseworthy, provided again that the care and diligence is not exercised in a bad cause. But virtue explains what dispositions are good (or else is out of court); and the degree of skill that anyone possesses is not a moral matter except in so far as it is an indication of care, diligence, scrupulousness, and other such virtues.

When we pass from means to ends, reason (if it enters at all, which is often denied) has a critical and judicial office, readily distinguishable from matter-of-fact knowledge about means and ends; and this critical office, if rational, deals with questions of principle. To this we must therefore turn.

(b) If our acquaintance with good and evil were not itself an instance of rational insight, the question of moral principle would come in only as an affair of consistency, and would necessarily be subordinate in principle since consistency in wicked, mischievous, or foolish ways seems to be entirely possible. The principal question at issue, therefore, is whether we do apprehend good and evil by a rational apprehension; and I propose to postpone discussion of this part of moral theory until a later part of our enquiry. Here I shall only say that if there truly is *knowledge* of good and evil, such knowledge can scarcely be denied to be of a rational kind.

Some writers hold, it is true, that our acquaintance with good and evil is akin rather to perception than to reasoning. We divine the good, they say, in particular cases, and beyond these we cannot safely go. If we attempt to classify, compare, and systematize such instances, or in other words, reflect about them, the delicacy and sinuosity* of our apprehension of the good is blunted and irremediably damaged. *No* law, not even a moral law, can care for the little things; and the little things are precisely what is delicate and sinuous in morality. Arguments of this type (of which much more anon), however, could not even if they succeeded (and their success in fact is very doubtful) do more than indicate a certain insufficiency in all general moral laws. They would not even suggest that there are no such laws, that the laws could not be discovered by reflection, or that reflection is irrelevant to the discovery of the partial insufficiency of moral laws, or to the reasons for that insufficiency.

These questions concerning good and evil, however, do

* Cf.

> He who binds to himself a joy
> Does the winged life destroy,
> But he who kisses the joy as it flies
> Dwells in eternity's sunrise.

not exhaust our present topic; for some moralists* maintain that duty and moral goodness are utterly distinct in all significant respects, while others, more moderately, maintain that duty and right are not identical, in conception or in fact, with any form of goodness, and that they cannot be derived from the good.

If so, the greater part of what we call moral principle plainly concerns principles of duty and of moral rightness, for that, by very general consent, is the sphere of the judicial office of the moral reason. It is difficult to suppose, however (although Martineau supposed it), that this judicial office could legitimately be regarded as something that a virtuous disposition carries along with it in its stride. It is not, in any sense, the simple, natural expression of a virtuous disposition, and it is not simply a piece of relevant information that the memory has pat for the purpose of fulfilling a disposition. The judge is above the disposition. And if criticism in terms of moral principles is held to be either implicit or explicit in moral virtue, such virtue is necessarily reflective.

These questions are most conveniently discussed in connection with the analysis of an ethic of duty, and should therefore be postponed. There are two points, however, which should receive preliminary attention now.

The first of these is the problem whether all moral action should be made a matter of principle. According to Kant, human action is moral only if it is performed from duty; but if this statement means that duty should consciously be part of the motive (or the whole motive) of righteous action, it is surely mistaken. Suppose a man gives generously, or saves a comrade under fire, or is friendly to his companions, or considerate to his servants without any thought of his duty. Is it to be inferred that such actions are not right, or have an inferior sort of rightness, although if the man does these same actions with the additional persuasion that they are his duty, they *then* become his duty?

* E.g. some of the New Intuitionists.

It is surely clear that the answer is negative. If these actions are right they could be shown to be right, that is to say, they could be seen to be duties because they are so. And most of us would hold that moral agents are capable of passing such reflective judgments, and would not be moral agents in the full sense if they were incapable of doing so. But it does not follow that everyone who does his duty is morally bound to consider the matter of duty every time he performs a right action; and an intolerable condition of moral priggishness would result if it did follow.

The second point is a variant of the first. It is the simple fact that the sense of duty is not the only moral motive. We should not, I think, go so far as Hume when he said (*Treatise*, p. 479), following Cicero and Hutcheson, that "no action can be virtuous or morally good unless there is in human nature some motive to produce it distinct from the sense of its morality"; for to say such a thing would be to affirm that every ethic of duty is fundamentally mistaken, and that it is *never* true that to perceive the rightness of a certain action and therefore to do it for *no* ulterior or other reason is the path of righteousness. On the other hand, it seems to me just as false to maintain that duty can never be done without the sense of its accomplishment as to hold that there could never be virtue without the sense of virtue.

V

THE HEART AND THE WILL

It is often said that an adequate theory of the will was unknown to the ancients. That view seems hard on some of them, particularly on Aristotle; but it is also possible to raise the question whether the modern or scholastic-modern theory of the will is really a signal discovery. For the moment, however, I shall suppose that we know quite clearly what we mean by our "wills," and shall examine the relation of voluntary action to an ethic of virtue, particularly to virtues of the "heart."

Certain authors define moral virtue in terms of will. Thus, according to Kant (Preface to the *Metaphysical Elements of Ethics*, xiv), moral virtue is strength of will in doing one's duty and resisting temptation. It seems plain, however, that many of the Christian virtues are not in any ordinary sense voluntary. Purity of heart, for instance, could scarcely be attained by trying; for the effort itself presupposes the sense of impurity, and the heed that is given to the avoidance of impurity seems contradictory to the virtue of purity. Again, the Christian virtue of brotherly love cannot be summoned at will, and Kant's exegesis, according to which the command to love one's neighbour is not a command to feel affection for him (since affection cannot be commanded), but, instead, a command to treat him *as if* we felt such an affection, is plainly *not* what was meant in the Scriptures. Indeed, it is rather amusing to see how easily moralists who profess to agree with Kant on this point contradict themselves flatly. Mr. Webb, for example, accepts Kant's exegesis on page 23 of his Calcutta lectures*; but on page 103 he says that the command to love our enemies means that even when we turn machine-guns on them we should not have hatred or malice in our hearts—in other words, that we should treat them as foes, but still feel

* *The Contribution of Christianity to Ethics.*

c

affection for them, precisely the opposite of the Kantian view.

This question seems to me to be altogether fundamental. There is a very general modern tendency, not at all confined to those who advocate an ethic of duty on Kantian lines, to say that ethics, in Sidgwick's language, is "the study of what ought to be, so far as this depends upon the voluntary action of individuals" (*Methods of Ethics*, I, i, summary)—although Sidgwick (ibid., p. 3) cautiously added the qualification "in some degree"—and it is clear that this legal or ecclesiastico-legal view fits in very readily with our usual modern notions concerning merit and liability to punishment. Thus there is something perturbing in the plain circumstance that many Christian virtues are not voluntary in this legal sense; and moralists should consider, with special care, what they are prepared to affirm on this very fundamental issue.

It seems necessary, then, to avoid initial hasty assumptions, and, as our current ideas about the "will" may be one of them, to examine these current ideas.

For the most part we reach our conception of the "will" by noting and classifying certain deeds. I "will" to raise my arm, or to wind my watch, and lo! the watch is wound or the arm raised (unless I am paralysed, or the mainspring of the watch is broken). The usual and the fundamental conception of a *willed* action, therefore, is that of the sort of deed that, if we decide to do it, is *straightway* done; and we readily contrast actions such as raising the arm with, say, the action of secreting saliva, which does not, in general, respond instantaneously to our decisions (if any) concerning it. Physiologists would probably add that such willed actions pertain to the skeletal muscles whose contractions depend on the central nervous system, but this additional explanation is irrelevant to our present purposes for two reasons. The first of these is that this physiological view has to be based on the experience of willing, and is but an elaboration of the physiological conse-quences of such evidence from experience. The second is that *thinking*, to an appreciable extent, is one of the actions that can be willed in this fundamental sense, and thinking has no obvious connection with the movements of the skeletal muscles.

Hence the conception of a "voluntary" action may be readily derived. An action, we say, is voluntary if it *could be willed*, or, more accurately, could be willed or inhibited, supposing that the agent so decided. It would occur, if he willed it. An action is non-voluntary if it would not occur if the agent willed it (unless by sheer coincidence through the operation of some other cause); and an action is involuntary if it occurs in spite of the agent's contrary decision. We further say that voluntary actions are "under our control," and, for legal or ethico-legal purposes, that laws and commandments are restricted to voluntary actions, since actions that an agent cannot control are beyond the influence of threats or other persuasions. Such "control" is usually ascribed to the higher or "magisterial" part of the self, since every voluntary action implies a certain degree of foresight, and may be an instance of deliberate planning, faithfulness to principle, and critical self-examination.

So regarded, everything seems to be simple. The voluntary level or control of action refers to actions that could be willed-or-inhibited (whether or not they actually are willed-or-inhibited), and a *willed* action is one that, in the vulgar phrase, is "on tap" whenever the agent decides to perform it. There may indeed be difficult borderline cases. It is easy to raise a finger, and to go on raising a finger, but not indefinitely; for a point will come at which the finger refuses to budge until it is rested. That is a trivial illustration; but it would be easy to multiply illustrations that are not trivial. For many moral decisions are hard, and even if it is plausible to hold that any ordinary man *could* perform his moral duty in the same fundamental sense as that in which he *could* wind his wat of an evening, we may have doubts about the matter. S so, let us say, shirks the unpleasant duty of admitt He *could*, of course, write the note or say the have done so, in private, dozens of time

the note along with the other letters that he *has* posted. Nevertheless he may really be unable to say the words or to post the letter when he knows what the effect of such an action would be.

The existence of such borderline cases, however, is obviously no sort of denial of the manifest truth that there are authentic instances of willed action nowhere near the borderline, cases that are no obstacle to the admission of a voluntary level of action, that is to say, of potential willing. It is also clear that if the voluntary level of action is restricted to the account we have hitherto given of it, that is to say, means *simply* the possibility of *immediate* successful response to a decision, purity, brotherly love, and many other moral virtues are not, in that sense, voluntary. Therefore we have either to accept the fact or, doubting it, have to ask whether there is not some further legitimate sense of the term "voluntary" in terms of which the contrast may be diminished or even annulled.

It is clear that the actions that can be performed at will (in the above sense) vary from person to person, although many such actions are, as we say, in everyone's power. A practised speaker can speak in public at will; an unpractised person may be tongue-tied with the best will in the world. Most people can jump over a three-foot ditch; but some could not, even if the leap meant safety. And so forth. What we can do at will, in short, is not a fixed possession of the individual person, or a common possession of the race. It is largely the effect of training and experience at any given time, and our powers in this particular vary gradually as we reach maturity and then decline.

The time factor in willing, therefore, is to be carefully noted, and I think we should say that there is no proper warrant for limiting voluntary action to what at any moment can be immediately effected. Longer views can be and ould be taken. In a great part, it is true, these longer views contradict the shorter; for much that we include in adequately described as a series of immediate volitions, just as the orator's speech is a series of articulations. There is reasonable doubt, however, whether all that we mean can be sufficiently described in this way. For by practice we acquire capacities which enrich our powers of immediate voluntary action, and it seems very doubtful indeed whether this acquirement of new capacities can itself be said to be willed, even when it is the result of repeated voluntary application at a different level of possible immediate achievement. We may know, or suspect, from other people's history, that we ourselves, by practice, could learn to keep three balls up in the air at once. When we become competent jugglers we can perform this feat at will; but granting that all the efforts in our apprenticeship are voluntary, it would appear that the acquired skill is acquired (in part) *through* willing rather than actually willed.

This consideration leads to another point about the "will." While in the main we think of *willing* as the decision to perform followed by the immediate performance of some particular action (with certain reservations, easy to include in principle, regarding what we call a "resolution" to perform a particular action at a future date without any further deliberation or choice at that future date), we also think of it in other ways. For sometimes we think, and profess to know from experience, that many of our most important decisions do not have a date, but have become insensibly dominant to such an extent that the process of deliberating and choosing, or, for that matter, of choosing without deliberation, is out of place. In this sense a man's will is his settled mind regarding certain types of objects of his activity, and we go so far on these lines as to use a people's "will" as a synonym for public opinion, even to the extent of supposing that such a will may be inarticulate and opposed to what the people think they want and are aiming at. Such a conception may indeed be lacking in clarity. But we do employ it.

In this last sense of "willing" it seems clear that there is no marked contrast between such willing and conditions of soul like purity or human kindness. There may indeed be a shift of emphasis, the "willing" referring to aim and activity (as when pirates are deemed such if they act *animo furandi* even if they do not successfully rob*) the other conditions of soul being a more "inward" affair. Again, the reference to a "settled mind" may be directed to the head rather than to the heart. Substantially, however, there is only a difference of emphasis, and no rigorous distinction of principle.

The question, then, is whether "willing" is a thoroughly ambiguous word (with the conclusion that in one of its senses many of the virtues do not pertain to the will, although in another sense they may and do) or whether it always designates the same property, in different applications (with the consequence that Kant and other moralists have been mistaken in drawing the distinction that seemed to them so important).

Obviously there is a great *prima facie* contrast between what can be directly accomplished by deliberate effort and what cannot be accomplished and should not be attempted in this way. Equally obviously, there is great *prima facie* importance in the distinction that Kant noted, the difference, namely, between what can and what cannot be commanded. And, further, it seems plain that these distinctions cannot reasonably be accounted superficial.

If so, the most we could say legitimately by way of deprecating the finality of the difference would be that there is a continuity of meaning in the various senses in which we speak of willing, and consequently that although the extremes differ very much there is not a total disparity. In that case the connecting link must be found, I think, in the considerations we adduced in connection with the time-factor in willing. If long-range willing is not merely a series of vigilant, short-ranged decisions, but also implies, or may imply, the acquirement of new powers, themselves indirectly not directly willed, there is an approach towards "willing" regarded as a settled

* See *The Times*, July 27, 1934, *in re* piracy *jure gentium*.

mind and disposition; and it might be difficult to deny that the approach was very close indeed.

A similar conclusion might be reached by other routes. Granting that purity, affection, and many other virtues cannot be summoned at will, or learned like reading and writing by a succession of express volitions, it could scarcely be contended that, in Sidgwick's quiet phrase, already quoted, they are not amenable to volition "in some degree"; for if we held such a view we should really be holding that self-mastery and self-control, in their ordinary senses, had no application to these virtues at all. Certainly, a poise and balance of the personality may be attained without the will or volition to attain it (whether the explanation be found in "nature" or in "grace"), and when this happens the unity of the mind may be sweeter and stronger than if a resolute will were the perpetual task-master. To hold, however, that voluntary self-control *never* can have anything to do with any of these moral virtues seems a gross over-statement which ought to be strenuously disputed. The control may indeed be indirect. If a man cannot banish his rage by deliberately willing to be calm—and I do not see why he cannot use the imperative "Steady now" with effect in his own case as well as in the case of others—he may allay it appreciably by resolutely thinking of something else, by some childish symbolical gesture (as some golfers used to break a club in the days when clubs were wooden and cheap) or, in many cases, by deliberately repressing the usual expression of rage. And if such repression is dangerous he can voluntarily undergo treatment by some priest or by some psycho-analyst.

In any case the mere fact that certain virtuous motives cannot be summoned at will, and have a spurious look if they (or the look of them) is sedulously cultivated, is quite insufficient to show that they are altogether outside the range of volition. It would seem, indeed, that a friendly spirit towards someone we initially dislike may be induced by comradely action, by letting proximity do its usual work, by refusing to entertain suspicions, and by exercising tolerance about obvious faults. Even if it were not so, however, it is surely clear negatively that we can and should exercise some control over our emotions (as well as over their expression), and even more importantly that, if we *have* the virtuous emotions, it is our business to use them for virtuous ends. Even if Kant were right in saying that it was nonsense to *command* anyone to love his neighbour, it is not nonsense to command anyone who *does* love his neighbour to go on loving him in the expectation and indeed in the knowledge that the love itself will grow if it is encouraged to express itself.

It must be conceded, then, that we have, in fact, considerable voluntary control over our emotions, and some power of intentionally stimulating as well as of repressing and directing them. No emotion, I think, is exempt from this, although some may respond to volition more readily than others; and if the highest virtue in certain kinds should be regarded rather as a gift than as a voluntary achievement, volition enters into the more imperfect forms of these virtues, that is to say, enters into the lives of most of us so far as these virtues are concerned. The difficult case of purity in general and of chastity in particular may illustrate the point. It is neither impossible nor foolish for most of us to try to cleanse our hearts as well as to mend our ways. If we cannot succeed altogether unless we are spiritually reborn, we can at least get rid of a great deal of nastiness, and prevent further nastiness from intruding and accumulating. In short, it is an exaggeration to hold that any virtue or moral goodness is entirely and inevitably non-voluntary, although it is clearly a mistake to hold that ethics is wholly concerned with "the voluntary action of individuals" if a voluntary act, as Mr. Moore suggests (*Ethics*, p. 15), should be defined as one which could be accomplished if the agent decided "just beforehand" to do it.

In an ethic of duty, and in the deontological part of the theories of the New Oxford intuitionists and others, the conception of "will" is all-important. The topic will therefore be be prominent in later pages of the present book. Its connection with an ethic of virtue, as I have tried to indicate, is that neither habits nor emotional dispositions (which are commonly regarded as the foundations of aretaics) are exclusively voluntary, and that the latter are sometimes falsely said to be necessarily non-voluntary. Hence it is frequently said that an ethic of virtue either necessarily omits or, at the least, blurs and boggles over a very essential part of ethics, viz. duty itself.

My contention has been that it is easy to obscure these questions by introducing a false glitter of apparent clarity. Neither Christian nor Greek aretaics need be at all dismayed by the contention, if it be true, that all morality must be "in some degree" voluntary, although Christian ethics in particular emphasizes virtues that, if semi-voluntary, are voluntary in a very slight degree. There is no sharp boundary between what is voluntary and what is not. Therefore I do not think we should infer that an ethic of virtue is inevitably partial and incomplete on the mere ground that it is not based, exclusively or even predominantly, upon the "will."

Obviously if there are moral virtues, or instances of moral virtue, that are not, in the main, matters of "will," the conclusion is that much in morality is not a matter of will. The moralists I have called "separatists" and "federalists" in the introduction to this book frequently accept this consequence, although I imagine that few of them (especially among the New Intuitionists) would agree in detail, or even generally, with the arguments I have advanced.

VI

MORAL AND NON-MORAL VIRTUE

THE word *virtus* in the Latin signified such moral virtues as *gravitas*, continence, and loyalty, and indeed all moral perfection; but primarily, manly strength and efficiency. As in the transferred sense of old-fashioned English chemistry, it also meant the specific power of any substance. The Greek *arete*, again, while primarily suggesting manliness in Homer, was applied to human excellence of every kind, indeed, by Hesiod to high rank, and by Sophocles to that which was famous.

I mention these matters, which are sufficiently attested by any reliable classical dictionary, to show that aretaics, or the theory of virtue, might at one time have suggested a wider theme than morality, whether in our sense or in an older signification. Such etymological considerations, no doubt, may be as irrelevant as the recollection that the word pagan once meant a rustic. They need not affect the present meaning of terms; and except in the rare and transferred sense in which we might speak of the "virtues" of opium, it would seem that "virtue" with us does always have moral significance. If, however, we compare moral with other personal excellences, we may find that the distinction is not very easy to draw, and that the classical tradition in our language and thought tends to induce a certain carelessness and nebulosity at the very point where clarity is eminently desirable.

We may conveniently approach our problem by considering its connection with duty and with good or benefit, despite the differences between these conceptions and the theory of virtue. If there is a problem even on an ethic of these types there is likely to be a problem, not less considerable, in an ethic of virtue.

At first sight it might seem that an ethic of duty could not possibly be encumbered with any difficulties of this order. For "duty" is moral duty, and therefore excludes any sort of non-moral duty. If anything becomes matter of duty it *ipso facto* becomes a moral matter.

The question, however, is not quite so simple. For suppose, as many would grant without hesitation, that there are duties of self-culture, self-realization, and duties also to aim and aspire greatly (if there be greatness in us), to produce beauty (if we have any capacity for producing it); and so forth. In that case anything great, fine, noble, or beautiful may be included under duty, and the "artistic conscience" is a genuine application of the moral conscience.

Some such view, I say, is commonly held, and I do not see why it should be condemned. Its implications, however, are obviously rather perplexing. "Art for art's sake," no doubt, may be a foolish idol, and would be if the meaning were that nothing but art should count in any man's life, or in the life of any people. But if the meaning be that art and beauty are things worth cultivating for their own sakes, although not the only things of this kind, then we do have the difficulty that, in and for themselves, these objects of endeavour are not merely autonomous but unmoral. Artistic excellence may indeed have affinities with moral excellence, as ordinarily understood, and so, indirectly, be moral in that way; but, essentially, it has its own standards; and it is frequently claimed (I do not say correctly) that if a great artist (or perhaps a lesser artist) could improve his art by acquiring experience in ways commonly condemned by morality, he ought, for the sake of his art, to be regarded as exempt from many of the customary moral rules. We should not, indeed, be disposed to give him a licence to murder on these grounds, but we might be disposed to grant him much artistic licence in his conduct; and similar arguments are frequently adduced regarding the great dictators of history, although, as we all know from contemporary experience, they are also very bitterly disputed.

At the moment, I do not suggest that these apparent difficulties should seriously perturb exponents of an ethic of duty, although I do not think they are contemplated in the cruder forms of such an ethic. A sophisticated deontologist might affirm (I suppose) that what is moral is always the endeavour after such and such an end, not necessarily the end itself; that there is no contradiction in the moral endeavour after an end not itself moral, but that moral endeavour is quite usually of this species, as it would be, for example, in a charity whose object was simply and solely the health and happiness (not the morals) of poor children at the seaside in summer; that if Romney or some other artist found his marital or paternal conscience in conflict with his artistic conscience he would have to deal with a conflict of duties, as other people, who are not artists, might have to do in other matters, and that the artists (including Romney) may not usually be very successful in such conflicts; and that, although this particular conflict is in terms of a conflict regarding possible benefits or spiritual achievements, it does not follow that *all* duties are of this type.

These contentions, so far as I can see, are consistent and may be true. They have the effect, however, of relating and perhaps even of subordinating many moral duties to a wide variety of goods, some of which, like beauty or happiness, need not themselves be moral at all; and the mutual relations between such goods may well be very intricate. This may be seen by a fuller consideration of an ethic of benefit.

In general an ethic of benefit is an ethic of doing one's best, or, in other words, of bringing about as much good as possible, such good to include, not the effects of any action only, but, along with these, all the good in the action itself. Such a theory implies that all goods are comparable *inter se* or, in a word, a theory of general axiology. Indeed, the morality of doing one's best is an application of this general axiology, the theory being, in essentials, that if x is good, an agent who can bring x about ought to bring it about.

It is apparent that in such a general axiology much is good

(or has worth, value, or dignity) that is not itself moral. Thus beauty ought to be brought about by anyone who can bring it about. So should happiness. So should health. And although there may be moral beauty, moral happiness (when virtue is its own reward) and moral health, nevertheless beauty, happiness, and health need not be moral at all and still be proper objects of moral endeavour. Anything that we admire and approve is good; and admiration and approval are not confined to ethics. Worth, nobility, dignity, fineness, value, excellence, perfection, and similar terms all describe something that although it may be, need not be moral.

As we have seen, it is likely that much in an ethic of virtue coincides with an ethic of benefit, although the benefits of virtue are usually regarded as the natural expression of a virtue rather than the express object of a will or intention to produce benefit. Such an interpretation of virtue, therefore, is more naturally allied with a wide axiology than with a narrow moralism; and if there be anything in virtue distinct from its intrinsic goodness (in the widest sense) and from its beneficial results, it is at least possible that the same wide standards should apply. Indeed, a well-known ethical school—I mean the advocates of a specific "moral sense"—enquired into beauty and virtue *together*, and understood the object of their research to be the fitting or decorous in its widest meaning, morality referring to what was fitting and decorous in the more serious affairs of life, but, except for the seriousness, similar in principle wherever there was appreciation or approval. Whatever was charming and amiable was the subject of their investigations. Thus Hutcheson frankly affirmed that "we seem to have a natural relish for certain qualities distinct from moral approbation," instancing such "natural abilities" as "a penetrating judgment, patience of labour, pain, hunger, a contempt of wealth, rumour, death," and in general anything that "naturally indicated a good temper" (*Enquiry* II, iii, 10); and Hume said that although our approbation of such abilities might be "inferior and somewhat different" from moral approbation, it was a grammarian's rather than a moralist's task to draw such distinctions, since natural and moral abilities "agreed in the most material circumstances" (*Treatise*, pp. 607 *sqq.*).

If there are moral and also non-moral virtues, it should be possible to distinguish between them by some general criterion, but it is not so easy to indicate what that criterion should be. Let us, however, make the attempt to discover it.

One possible suggestion would be that morality deals with the serious affairs of life, with the dispositions that pertain to the great manners not with those that pertain to little or trivial manners. Such a criterion, however, would seem to indicate a difference of degree rather than of kind, and its application would be at least as arbitrary as the legal distinction between a misdemeanour and a felony, or the theological distinction between sins that are "deadly" and sins that are not deadly.

Again, and perhaps more importantly, there might be endless disputes concerning the precise sense in which an alleged triviality was trivial. Is it a trivial thing, for instance, to prevaricate about trivial matters. According to Cardinal Newman, to "steal one poor farthing without excuse" is a worse thing than all the natural agonies of a miserable world, and these agonies could scarcely be accounted trivial, even if *morally* they are as naught. We should often suppose, indeed, that moral offences in small matters—the stealing of a brother's postage stamps, a lack of truthfulness when the gains of untruthfulness are tiny, a tendency to share unfairly when the things that are shared are of little account, is a surer indication of a morally defective character than similar moral offences on graver occasions where genuine fear may lead to unusual, uncharacteristic deviations from rectitude. In short, the triviality of the occasion is not an adequate criterion, and if the reference be to a trivial disposition or type of behaviour, it may not be entirely plain that our customary classifications of this kind are very well-grounded. Politeness, for example, is commonly accounted a minor virtue, and, possibly, not a moral virtue at all; but rudeness, in many strata of society, is a serious fault, very damaging to social relationships, very much of a stigma to anyone who has the reputation of being rude. If moralists account it trivial, they differ from most other people; and if they say that it is *morally* trivial although serious in many other ways, they are using, not the criterion of serious versus trivial, but a new standard of their own, viz. the *morally* serious and the *morally* trivial.

A second possible suggestion would be that the difference is really between part and whole. It may be, so far, virtuous to develop a part of one's nature, say the artistic part, but it is a moral virtue to cultivate this part of one's nature only if due regard is paid to the other parts, and to develop that part in a specialist's way only if that way is the best a man can follow on the whole.

This point of view is natural to an ethic of doing one's best, although it is more plausible, even on that ethic, if the reference is not to a man's own "good on the whole" but to the whole good he can perform. It is not clear, however, that it should be accepted on any other ethic. According to an ethic of duty, morality is but a part, not the whole, of a man's life; and although if anything in a man's life conflicts with his duty, duty ought to prevail without any question, there is much on which duty has no say one way or the other (this would be true even if duty settled the broad outlines of what everyone should do, provided that it did not settle everything in detail). Similarly, most of the admitted moral virtues, such as fairness or generosity, seem to be specialized activities, indeed, to be quite as clearly specialized as the artistic virtues. The entire conception, therefore, seems to be dubiously founded, unless, indeed, "doing one's best" is the only genuine ethic.

A third suggestion would be the simple one that moral virtues are those which are socially very desirable; but it is obvious that this criterion contains at least as many difficulties as the others. We might hold, for example, that the duties of self-culture need not be obviously social and that, even if they are social, it is seldom clear how far and when they should be subordinated to other social virtues whose direct benefit to contemporary humanity is usually considered greater. An artist, perhaps, should serve his country rather than his art during a great war, or during some great wars. If so, it would not follow that he should not serve his art in peace-time, or in a little war, or in a great war that is not the sort of great war in which patriotism must come morally before his art; and the mere statement of the artist's unfortunate case under such conditions, without any special arguments about the morality of patriotism or of the ethics of artistry, is enough to show that the whole moral question is almost indefinitely complicated.

Again, to revert to an earlier point, politeness is obviously a social affair; yet it is usually accounted a very minor part of morals, although socially of indisputable importance. If the common view of it is right, therefore, it is a mistake to say that any question is moralized precisely in proportion as it is socialized. And we might multiply such objections almost indefinitely. Both politics and economics, for example, are social sciences, but each is distinct from ethics; and if it were said that what is desirable in economics or in politics is also desirable morally, the reply would be (a) that any such view tacitly assumes the all-sufficiency of an ethic of benefit, and (b) that the usual meaning of such a statement would be that no application of economics or of politics could be morally desirable unless they conformed to certain moral standards of fairness, benevolence, and the like, i.e. that their moral excellence, if any, must be governed by ethical standards not their own.

A fourth suggestion would be that morality is an affair of voluntary endeavour or of the "good will"; but as we have already argued that an ethic of virtue is distinguished from other ethical systems because it is *less* voluntaristic than they, we could not define it by this criterion.

There may, of course, be other criteria; but I cannot think of any as important as these, and I am consequently disposed to think that all attempts along these lines are likely to fail.

Let us therefore approach the subject in another way. Virtue, we say, is commendable. Can we then distinguish it from everything else that is commendable?

At the present stage of our argument it should be sufficient to examine only those things that are usually commended for their own sakes. These include moral virtue, righteousness (or moral duty), and such beneficial action as is moral. They also include, or may include according to most philosophers, beauty, truth, happiness, and fulness of life.

Now there may be moral beauty; but in general we distinguish the aesthetic from the moral attitude fairly simply by saying that morality is always practical whereas the aesthetic attitude is not. Art, to be sure (that is to say, the making of things that have aesthetic appeal), is practical, but aesthetics, unless we fall into the common confusion between aesthetics and artistry, is not practical. There would, however, be a difficulty in distinguishing art from morals in this way; for both are practical, and although art for the sake of aesthetics would be an apter maxim than art for art's sake, an aesthetic interest seems intrinsic to artistry, and therefore art would seem to be both practical and commendable for its own sake as a type of activity.

Truth in the sense of sincerity, or of looking facts in the face, as well as in the sense of truthfulness or veracity, would seem to be a moral virtue; and we have already discussed the extent to which knowledge and well-informed belief are essential to morals. There are other senses, however, in which truth may not even be a good at all, not to say a moral good. What is good about truth in the sense in which we say that it is true that 2 and 2 make 4? And how is a libel or a piece of gossip good simply because it is true?

We might indeed compare the spirit of scientific curiosity with the moral spirit, and this, I think, is what most people would do if they compared truth with ethics. If so, we should again say that ethics was practical and science not, on the assumption, of course, that science is not studied for the sake of its power but for itself, and that it is not to be accounted "practical" simply because it employs and may exhaust the energies of its votaries.

Since so much in ethics is concerned with a man's care for his own soul, this last explanation makes the contrast between ethical and other "practice" rather threadbare in a part of it. Still, it might be contended, not unreasonably, that curiosity, like the impulse to create and to enjoy aesthetically, was fundamentally non-moral although self-repaying and therefore worth seeking for its own sake. If so, we should reach the conclusion that the conception of a self-repaying activity did *not* define moral virtue; although, as we have seen, it would also be reasonable to hold that an artistic (and we may now add, a scientific) conscience *was* moral in its own way. Another view that might be held would be that curiosity is not necessarily commendable at all. It need not be morally blameless. Indeed it frequently is not; and there may not be anything more commendable in the solving of puzzles than in a dog's sniffing and pricking up its ears.

The relation between happiness and ethics has been much discussed. We are all familiar with the questions whether happiness and pleasure are identical, whether there may not be an ignoble happiness or a despicable pleasure, and the like. In other words, the inevitable goodness of happiness may be challenged. Few would deny, however, that certain types of happiness are good and that it is a moral duty to try to obtain these, at any rate, for other people (and still more obviously to diminish needless pain).

This being granted, almost anyone would agree that we have to distinguish between the mere occurrence of happiness and its moral occurrence. There is nothing particularly moral in a lizard enjoying the sun, but there may be something decidedly immoral if little wanton boys hunt the lizard. As we saw, the usual device of moralists is to say that the intentional pursuit of happiness is a moral matter, its mere occurrence non-moral. We also saw, however, that this view might be challenged on the ground that it lays too much stress upon the *thought* of happiness, and indeed that an ethic of virtue might well be preferred to an ethic of intentional benefit (happiness being regarded as a possible benefit) on the ground that the natural expression of the "heart" (and "virtue" so regarded) was likely to be more beneficial than a calculated pursuit of happiness.

If so, the line between commendable natural abilities and commendable moral qualities becomes very hard to draw, as the examples cited from Hutcheson very clearly attest. A natural contempt of "wealth, rumour, death" is something we greatly admire in most of its applications; and we do not admire it the less if it is (as we say) "natural," that is to say, if it is not acquired by painful self-discipline and sedulous heed to moral precepts. In other words, it *is* a virtue, even if it is "natural"; and it is not, as Hume suggested, "inferior," at any rate, if the man who contemns wealth, rumour, and death be supposed to know what he is contemning, and not merely assumed to contemn them because he seems to ignore them. We might say, indeed, that a man who has overcome avarice, undue sensibility to other people's opinion, or the fear of death, is superior to one who has never known these disquietudes, on the ground that his success in this difficult exercise attests a general strength of character whose value could not be confined to these particulars; but that seems to be the only sense in which it is sensible to talk about "inferiority."

There remains "fulness of life," a most dubious member of this company, since it is not clear that *none* of our impulses should be starved (on moral, aesthetic, or any other reputable grounds) and pretty clear that the "fulness," if it be a frantic zest for novelty and versatility, might well be at odds with any tolerable harmony of existence. Again, it might be argued that unless this "fulness" reported itself in happiness, it would be worthless. Suppose, however, that a certain zest and gusto in living and a certain opulence of experience as such is genuine inward wealth and so an intrinsic good. In that case the ideal of fulness would suggest an ethic of trying greatly and of living boldly, but would not clearly distinguish itself from ethics. It would rather suggest a revaluation of current ethical standards; and it would not be likely to separate moral from natural abilities.

I do not think, then, that this way of approaching our problem has been much more successful than the other; and if success eludes us by all routes we have to make the humiliating confession that no short formula will express the difference between moral and non-moral with complete precision, and that it may be doubtful whether a longer formula would do so either. Is there, then, nothing to guide us on this question? I think guidance is possible, although not a formal definition.

In the first place, we can affirm that intentional benefit is always a moral matter, provided that the intended benefit is, in the agent's opinion, the greatest benefit he can bring about by the action. The agent may of course be wrong, for various reasons. What he means to do may be incapable of achieving the benefit aimed at. There may be certain benefits (e.g. scientific or artistic) which, according to some moralists, ought not to come into the reckoning at all, if that reckoning is strictly moral. (I think these moralists are mistaken, provided that aesthetic or scientific goods really are goods.) Again, some moralists would say that in certain cases the right action need not be the most beneficial. If so (although I suspect they are often mistaken) the most beneficial action might not be the one that a true morality would inculcate. Nevertheless all actions of the type I have indicated pertain to the sphere of morality. The very mistakes in them, if they occur, must be moral mistakes.

In the second place, we may say provisionally that wherever there is duty there is morality. No doubt there may be a question whether (e.g. in the so-called artistic or scientific conscience) there really is duty or not; and, again, it might be objected that duty is another name for morality, and consequently that there can be no solution of our problem by simply renaming it. This objection, however, seems to me to be mistaken; for much that we regard as moral virtue is not, strictly speaking, duty, since it lacks the complete voluntariness that is customarily attributed to duty.

These suggestions have been devised in terms of deontology or of agathopoeics, and may be subject to a certain revision, as well as to a certain extension, when the time comes for a fuller discussion of an ethic of duty and an ethic of benefit respectively. In a provisional way, however, I think we should be prepared to allow that a voluntaristic ethic of duty or of benefit and well-being may at least come near to giving a comprehensible simple definition of ethics.

It also seems to me to be plain, however, that ethics is not confined to the field defined by either of these ethical systems. What they include always pertains to morality; but what they exclude may also pertain to it, and does so in fact in so far as moral virtue is neither a matter of express intention nor of completely voluntary duty. This additional region is what is so difficult to define; and perhaps it cannot be defined. It is *connected* with volition and self-control, as we have seen, but only in the sense that it involves directly or indirectly a certain development of personality which is usually considered at the voluntary level. Provided that "natural abilities" are to some extent integrated at this level, we cannot say outright that they are not moral; and if the natural expressions of the "heart" are beneficial we also count them moral, provided again that they are not completely disconnected from voluntary control. Further than this, I think, we cannot go in the way of formal definition.

It might even be maintained that however highly we rated morality we should be profoundly mistaken if we thought that nothing else counted, and that if it does in fact commingle with other excellent things we should not jib at the circumstance. I have pointed out that there was a certain commingling of this kind in the Greek conception of virtue. I may now add that this view was St. Paul's also. For we read in Phil. iv. 8, "whatsoever things are true, whatsoever things are *honest*, whatsoever things are *pure*, whatsoever things are lovely, whatsoever things are of good report; if there be any *virtue* and if there be any praise, think on these things." Yet of these high things only the three I have italicized are exclusively moral.

VII

OUR KNOWLEDGE OF VIRTUE

MOST sciences, if they are at all advanced, investigate the nature of their own evidence; and the sciences which have not emancipated themselves from philosophy long ago, occupy themselves with such matters to an extent that often seems and sometimes may really be futile. There may be a question whether moral science would be better or worse if the great majority of professional moralists were not also professional philosophers; but it is inconceivable, even if the two branches of study agreed to a permanent separation, that problems concerning the special character of moral evidence would not obtrude themselves upon the least philosophical moralists.

Deontological moralists usually claim that the precepts of duty, either in the form of general rules or in the form of moral behests regarding the particular case, are instances of direct rational insight, and many of them have compared this insight to what they believed mathematical insight to be, although, to be sure, they were, for the most part, very indifferent mathematicians. In that case it would be competent for such moralists to examine the nature of this alleged insight into duty, just as it is competent for Hilbert, Brouwer, Russell, or other mathematicians to investigate the nature of mathematical principles and reasoning; but it would also be permissible to neglect such enquiries, as many mathematicians do in their own enquiries, believing, in the vulgar phrase, that they can deliver the goods without perpetually preoccupying themselves with the state of the edge of their tools.

Other theories, however, are in a different plight. An ethics of benefit or well-being may indeed assume that everybody can distinguish between benefit and hurt, or, regarding means, between utility and disutility. It has in fact been very often assumed that the only genuine benefit is pleasure, and that pain is the only real hurt. This assumption, however, is violently opposed to common belief upon the subject. Therefore it has to be defended, and with the defence of this or of any other interpretation of the nature of true benefit, or of genuine success comes the inevitable question of the nature of the evidence. Is it true in the last resort that a benefit is simply what we like, or what we want, or what we desire, or what satisfies us? Is it what we want, or like, or desire in a special way? Or do we have insight into the goodness of benefit in the same fundamental sense as we have insight into any other property of any other thing? These questions, plainly, are not negligible. If goodness were simply a property of a good thing, as redness is a property of a cherry, why should there be an obligation to promote it, why should it even attract us? If, on the other hand, a thing's goodness is a name for the way in which it entices us, how can it claim authority, or be the basis of standards that are hard, not easy?

These questions, in so far as they concern duty or benefit, may be relinquished until we come to examine these particular ethical theories. We have concluded, however, that virtue is not simply identical either with duty or with benefit although it may be very closely connected with both; and we are therefore at liberty to consider whether our evidence concerning the presence and the character of virtue raises any special points in this department of moral theory. I am inclined to think that it does.

In the first place, there is a very general belief that moral insight is itself dependent upon moral character. Evil ways, it is said, blunt, corrode, or even extinguish the understanding of goodness; good ways have the opposite effect. A certain remote and aloof comprehension of the difference between good and evil may indeed be credited to the depraved. It is said that the devils believe. In the main, however, we are confronted with the fact that conscience, in its cogitative as well as in its other aspects, itself degenerates or becomes atrophied as the moral character deteriorates. It becomes shameless or even rejoices in its shamelessness. An appeal to conscience is an appeal to a man's better nature. If he has no better nature, the appeal is vain.

It seems clear that a view of this kind does correspond, roughly at any rate, to the common findings of moral experience. It may, indeed, be question-begging, since the charge that abandoned living begets an abandoned set of moral principles (or pseudo-principles) is frequently brought against conduct and principles that, very likely, are judged to be abandoned only by those whose morality is unconscionably narrow. To say this, however, is only to say that a mistaken ethics applies its principles mistakenly, and that is a trivial statement unless indeed *all* ethics is just as likely to be mistaken as not.

Again, the view may beg many questions in another way. "Remorse and gnawings of conscience," to use Spinoza's phrase, may occur in over-sensitive souls or among those who are too ambitious in their moral aspirations. They regard every sin as infinitely horrible, and consider themselves viciously presumptuous if they do not discern a trail of sinfulness in their daily conduct. For the most part, however, such remorse and despair occur in the morally weak rather than in the morally abandoned or in the morally dull; and in that case it is usual to beg the question by employing the apparent subtlety of saying that the existence of a troublesome and remorseful conscience proves that the morally weak are not so very bad, or, in other words, that this particular defect of moral character does not have the deleterious effect upon the conscience that, according to the argument, moral defects of character do necessarily have.

Let us suppose, however, that the facts are as the argument states, that is to say that there is a very intimate correlation between the level of moral character and the level of moral insight, and examine, in consequence, whether any important consequences follow regarding the nature of moral knowledge.

Here it might be argued with a good deal of plausibility that the phenomenon in question is precisely what might be expected in any practical affair. Let a man deal with cattle, dogs, or motor-cars and the same type of fact will emerge. His interests will be roused, and his intelligence sharpened. What is more, it is, in general, easier to acquire knowledge, or something very like it, through practical experience, than by any other study or instruction. Again, faulty methods in practice are usually an obstacle in the way of understanding what is not faulty, partly from misdirection of interest, partly from a sort of acquired heedlessness, where heed is most essential. It is all quite natural and just what we might expect.

This account of the matter, I think, is accurate in what it asserts, and I see no way of proving that the connection between moral character and our acquaintance with what is good and fine is closer than in other instances of the stimulation of interest through practice. What cannot be definitely proved, however, may sometimes be reasonably suspected; and therefore it seems expedient to consider certain (perhaps inconclusive) suspicions that the circumstance may occasion.

In general we have to examine the very plausible, if not, indeed, the indisputable conclusion that appreciation or approval is an attitude of mind entirely *sui generis*. Moral approval, it is true, is not the whole of such appreciation. There is at least aesthetic and there is probably scientific appreciation as well. On the other hand, moral approval is at any rate a species of approval in general; and if this species of approval has features that are consonant with a general theory of aretaics, and are hard to reconcile with any other theory, the case, if not proved, could be said to be strongly supported by the peculiar facts that are in question.

Let us, then, examine the general contention.

According to Professor Moore (*Philosophical Studies*, p. 274), "if you could enumerate *all* the intrinsic properties a given thing possessed, you would have given a *complete* description of it, and would not need to mention any predicates of value it possessed." This statement, I think, puts the question as clearly as it could be put. A thing's "intrinsic properties" are just the properties the thing *itself* has. Thus my tobacco-tin is yellow, cylindrical, has a certain cubic content, and so forth. If it is agreed, then, that the value of anything cannot be a property of that sort, we have, in the main, to deal with two questions, viz., firstly, whether it is a property of anything at all, secondly, if it is a property, what other sort of property it could be than simply a descriptive property.

If we say that value is not a property of anything at all, our statement has again two possible meanings. It might mean that value is not a property in any intelligible sense whatsoever, or it might mean that value, although a property, cannot be a property of any given thing. In the former case, unless value has no meaning at all, it must express what is not a property; in the latter case, it might express a property although it could not express the property of any *thing*.

The word "property" as I understand it, and as I believe it to be used in these arguments, is not in the least mysterious. It is intended, quite simply, to be a name for anything that can be truly said of anything. Thus it is a "property" of my tobacco-tin, that it is yellow, that it has representations of medallions upon it, that it exercises weight upon the table, that my wife bought it for me when I was too lazy to go and purchase it for myself; and so forth. In short any attribute or relational attribute is a "property"; and it seems improbable that anything could be significantly said of the tobacco-tin that was not a "property" of it. An "intrinsic" property would be either an attribute or proper adjective of the tobacco-tin, or else some characteristic of the tin of the sort that would warrant a relational assertion, e.g. that it was purchased by my wife.

In this wide sense of "property" (which is the sense in which I use it, and, I believe, correctly) it is difficult to see how "value" could be anything *but* a "property" unless "value" were entirely meaningless. The strongest suggestion to the contrary, I think, is the view that value is an "emotive," not a descriptive predicate (which is a modern way of putting a very old view, viz. that value expresses an emotional or appetitive attitude towards something, and does not directly express anything that the valued thing *is*). To value anything, in short, is to say "Hurrah!" To disvalue it is to say "Pooh!"

If we accepted such a view, however, it would surely be plain that we *were* expressing a (relational) property of the valued thing. At the very least we should be saying, "This thing makes me exult" or "makes me turn up my nose," as the case might be, and, in order to make our theory of value at all plausible, we should soon find ourselves asserting, if not that we *ought* to exult or to turn up our superior noses at the thing, at any rate that the thing is of the type that any man of respectable taste or attainments would rejoice in or, negatively, would scorn. In short, we should indirectly assert some sort of appropriateness or inappropriateness between the thing and our emotions or desires, that is to say we should assert a relational property between the thing and our emotions. Such an assertion would be *about* the thing, but need not describe the thing *itself*, much as the assertion that the books on my shelves are over a hundred miles north of Edinburgh tells me something true *about* my books but does not, in any ordinary sense, describe the books themselves.

In short, even an "emotive" theory of value would describe a *relational* property of the thing said to be valuable, and would also describe a property of our minds in relation to the thing in question. Otherwise the theory would be entirely meaningless. We may therefore reject the view that emotive or any other phrases express no property of anything. For plainly they do. What we could affirm, however, is that such theories express a relationship between an emotional or appetitive state of mind and the things that induce such emotions or appetites (perhaps in some special form). If so, they need not describe any property of the thing itself, although the thing might contain special intrinsic properties in virtue of which the relationship aforesaid became possible.

This, however, would not be necessary. It would be quite possible (as Kant held in his aesthetic theory) that things are valuable (as Kant said they were beautiful) because of their general conformity, in *all* their properties, to human faculty or to its joyful exercise. In that case, value would not depend upon any special property of any special thing, but would be our response (or a part of our response) to a thing's totality; and this would involve the conclusion that value was no part of the description of anything valued since the complete description would describe the very totality that was valued. Nothing less would be valued, and we could not regard the value as a distinctive feature of the thing valued if in fact the whole thing were valued. The value would be a relational property of the entire thing valued, but it would not be a constituent property of the thing itself. It would describe *something*. Every predicate that is not meaningless does so; but it could not be included among the several descriptions that enumerate a thing's make-up. It could not tell us what anything is, and would therefore be useless for any descriptive science. On the other hand, it might enable us to draw inferences about ourselves and about our relations towards the things we say we value.

If value were a constituent property of a thing (when the word "thing" is used as widely as possible to include any possible object of our contemplation or inspection, and in particular to include all *persons*) it would be impossible to give a complete description of the thing without including its value, although, no doubt, a description that omitted value might be sufficient for certain descriptive purposes, just as, say, a description of a "wanted" man might be quite sufficient for police purposes although it did not mention the man's blood-pressure. If, again, relational properties are distinguished from constituent properties, there may be some question whether such properties are or are not descriptive of the thing; for it seems plain that nothing could be sufficiently described if its reactions towards other things and its place among them were wholly omitted. Indeed, the "field" may be the genuine unit and "things" but centres of stress within the "field." If, however, the meaning of saying that anything has value is that it stimulates, charms, or soothes something other than itself, or that it would do so were the other thing in a right condition, it seems clear that the thing's value describes the thing to a vanishingly small extent if at all, since the brunt of the explanation falls upon the approver not upon the approved.

As I remarked at an early stage in the discussion of this section, I do not intend, now, to examine all theories of moral knowledge, but, in the present place, those only which seem specially connected with aretaics. And here the argument must essentially be that the heart is knowledgeable in its own distinctive way. Such knowledgeableness, as we have seen, might mean only that love and sympathetic interest quicken our moral perceptions. We are now concerned, however, with the view that the heart does know in a special way.

Such a view, I think, could have little plausibility unless it were allied with what I have called an emotive theory of value, i.e. that all our approval or appreciation (and our moral approval or appreciation in particular) in the end expresses some variety of our sentiment or emotion. That is good which moves the heart in a certain way or—a dangerous qualification —*should* so move it. "Good" so understood need not describe the intrinsic properties of things, but it does yield a certain knowledge regarding ourselves in relation to other things and persons.

Such knowledge, it might be held, is quite different from the perception of things by sense, and from those inferences and apprehensions of logical connection that we call "reason." All these may be called descriptive knowledge; and emotive knowledge, if there is such a thing, is not in this sense descriptive. The question is: What are the characteristics of emotive knowledge, if it exists?

Much that is currently written about emotive speech—the phrase emotive *knowledge* is unusual—seems to me to be definitely erroneous. It is pointed out, quite correctly, that the function of speech need not be to describe. Even the speech that is intended to persuade need not do so by describing a fact or a principle. On the contrary, it may attempt to induce a certain attitude of mind; and this may sometimes be done by rousing our passions—with the usual consequence that we ignore evidence that does not square with our emotional prejudices and linger on anything that supports preconceived opinions. Again, speech may be used simply to please and not at all to instruct; and to convey an atmosphere instead of conveying information.

These obvious truths must be granted; but they give only partial support to the emotive theory. The instance of persuasion, for example, makes against the theory almost as much as for it, because the argument is not that pure emotion is the same thing as persuasion, but that, if an emotion is roused, our apprehension of fact and of principle is thereby biassed. In other words a certain blending of emotion and description, not something purely emotive, is the lesson we should be asked to learn. Similarly, if speech is used to please or to convey atmosphere it does not in general do so without description. It may indeed employ words that are like the infantile babblings of lovers—mere sympathetic noises—but it could not thrive on such language, and (except in so far as it charms by the beauty of its own sound and rhythm) it commonly delights and conveys atmosphere by a certain type of description, that is to say, by describing that and that only that rouses our sentiments by its congruence with our emotional moods. In such cases the end need not be descriptive but the means very frequently are.

A purely emotive use of speech, therefore, is very unusual; but the rousing of emotion is certainly one of the functions of speech, whatever means may be employed. On the other hand, it is not at all obvious that the arousing of emotion either conveys or *is* knowledge at all, and if knowledge is connected with it—e.g. the knowledge that the speaker is excited whether he is aware of the circumstance or not, or, again, that we, when we hear him, have similar emotions to his—it is not plain that *such* knowledge is in any way peculiar; for it may simply be the apprehension of certain emotions in ourselves or in other people. No doubt, if either self-knowledge, or our knowledge of other people's minds, is itself of a special kind, this variety of the knowledge must have such special features; but the fact that emotion is aroused, or spreads by a sort of contagion is no evidence of any such peculiarity in our knowledge of our own minds or of those of other people.

What may be contended, however, and what, very frequently, is contended, is that descriptive knowledge is always the knowledge of an outside observer while our acquaintance with ourselves is always an inner acquaintance—an instance of genuinely inside information. If, then, there is self-acquaintance (i.e. knowledge) and if inside knowledge must differ radically from external observation, it follows that self-acquaintance is non-descriptive and yet is genuine knowledge. Hence it is natural to maintain that we know ourselves not by looking but by feeling, and although the word "feeling" is conveniently ambiguous, it is at least not preposterous to hold, on these assumptions, that our "heart," sentiments, and emotions are or are a part of, the "feeling" on which this view relies. In short, to feel emotionally may be to know, although it can never be to describe (in an external fashion); and the heart may be an organ of knowledge, although not a scientific organ of descriptive knowledge.

I do not suggest that this view is correct, and I am strongly of opinion that it is frequently asserted on very inadequate grounds, viz. that knowing is always a kind of being, and consequently that if anything *is* such and such there is a presumption, that it should be able to know it. I can see no such presumption. Why should a stone, being a stone, be able to know its lapideity? And if the reply be that the doctrine holds only for things that are knowledgeable, I can see no contradiction in the view that knowledge is always at bottom a sort of inspection implying a certain aloofness between knower and known, with the consequence either that we can only know what is not ourselves or that (if we do know ourselves) we do so by performing the not impossible feat of looking at ourselves. Being such and such need not be knowing, and it need not be propitious to knowing. It might even be an obstacle, although not necessarily an insuperable obstacle, in the way of knowing.

The view before us, therefore, has often been held on wrong grounds; but it might be true nevertheless, and if it were true it would lend support to the doctrine that the heart could know, and in particular to the theory that the heart's knowledge may lie at the root of what we call value, if value be non-descriptive and, in the main, emotive. I propose therefore to suggest briefly some of the ways in which such a view could be further elaborated.

It is commonly held that emotions can be neither true nor false; but if there is emotional *knowledge*, this view would have to be abandoned. For knowledge presupposes truth, and if the heart be not infallible there will be the possibility of error also. Thus a theory of right and wrong feeling or emotional valuation would be required; and philosophers like Brentano have attempted to evolve one. "Our love and our hatred," Brentano said (*The Origin of the Knowledge of Right and Wrong.* Eng. trans., p. 20), "are qualified as right," and a rightness or wrongness of this sort belongs to all the higher forms of emotion, as opposed to mere natural impulses. The good itself is what is loved rightly or nobly.

A second point is at least equally important.

Up to the present the suggestion has been that, through feeling, we have an inner acquaintance with ourselves quite different from the knowledge of an external observer and that through the wisdom of such feeling we may discern all values (including moral values) in relation to ourselves. But what of others? Is not morality principally concerned with inter-personal relations? And how can a doctrine of personal inward-

D

ness, of *being* ourselves intensively and very consciously, instruct us on this important aspect of the question?

The answer is usually given in a single word: Sympathy. We sympathize with our fellows, not merely because we may feel as they do when, for example, both are startled by the same shot, but (it is said) because we enter into or share their feelings. We participate in their being, and thus the doctrine that "being" implies "knowing" (at any rate in some of its forms) may be extended beyond the personality of the experiment.

This view is very widely held, whether in doctrines of empathy (Einfühlung) or in some other form. Its critics say (and I agree with them) that it is impossible, literally, for two selves to mingle in one another's being, and hence that the doctrine is completely metaphorical. But if it could be accepted literally, it would be able to include the main interpersonal relations in the wide territory of "sympathy," and so to make the heart the organ of a great many virtues.

But I do not think highly of these conjectures.

PART II

DUTY

OR

THE THEORY OF DEONTOLOGY

VIII

DISCUSSION OF CONCEPTIONS

THE principal terms we have now to consider are "duty," "obligation," "ought," and "right." Except for the difference, say, between an auxiliary verb and an adjective, these terms, in their moral usage, are very nearly synonyms. There is a considerable distinction, however, if anyone holds that a man's duty, in any given situation, is the *one* thing he ought to do; for, in that case, alternative ways of behaving might conceivably both be right, and, much more importantly, the man's duty would be the *decisive* obligation in the situation. The decisive obligation might very well conflict with other moral obligations, as when Gibbon, sighing as a lover, obeyed as a son, that is to say, might conflict with what would have been a moral duty had a more peremptory duty not over-borne it.

In this sense of "duty" it is plain that the current phrase a "Conflict of duties" is nonsense. Hence there are grounds for inferring that "duty" is frequently understood in a wider sense. To avoid misconception, therefore, I shall use the term "obligation" without any implication of decisiveness; and shall employ the term "duty" to mean the *one* thing that ought to be done. The same object might be attained by speaking with Mr. Ross of "*prima facie* duties" (i.e. what I propose to call "obligations") as opposed to duties *simpliciter*, but I dislike the phrase "*prima facie* duty" very much more than Mr. Ross does (*The Right and the Good,** p. 20). It suggests that what seems to be an obligation at the first look may turn out not to be an obligation at the final inspection; and that is not what is meant. Again, it is perfectly natural to speak of several obligations attached, let us say, to some human association, and these obligations need not pull together.

* Hereafter cited as *R.G.*

All the terms I have mentioned may be used either in an ethical or in a non-ethical sense. A duty may be a customs duty or the "humble duty" at the end of a formal epistle, or the job for which one reports. "Right" is a protean adjective. It may mean "straight," it may mean "thorough," it may simply be opposed to "left." "Obligations" may be legal, and only moral in so far as it is moral to be law-abiding. So also the terms "ought" and "obligation" may be used in a logical or in an aesthetic context without any obvious moral implications. "From the evidence you ought to conclude that Byng was not a coward." "You ought to prefer Paul Potter to Landseer."

In the latter instances it might perhaps be said that the auxiliary verb has at least a semi-moral implication, indeed that what it asserts is that one's dignity as a thinking being or as a man of taste demands in the first case a logical process and in the second case a certain aesthetic attitude. I should agree that a logical or an artistic conscience is in its own way moral, but have to observe that these instances might appear to avoid the semi-morality (if it is such) of the word "ought." In the first of them we might just as well speak of logical necessity as of logical obligation, and we might just as well say "the evidence shows." In the second of them we might just as well say that Potter's work attained a much higher standard than Landseer's. Nevertheless, it would seem reasonable to hold that although we might just as well say these other things, we should not be saying the same thing if we said them, for we should be giving the logical or aesthetic grounds for a certain process rather than indicating that process itself.

In any case the idea of a logical or aesthetic obligation resembles the idea of a moral obligation, and such resemblance may even be instructive. Similarly it may be profitable to ask whether the boundaries between the moral and the non-moral senses of "right" and of "duty" are entirely distinct or whether, on the contrary, there is a debatable hinterland in which the debate may be instructive.

Take the adjective "right." Colloquially, "that's right" is an ugly way of saying "yes," and, generally, the adjective indicates precision or correctness, as in the "right" answer to a sum in arithmetic. What is right is "it," plumb in the middle of the target and therefore appropriate or fitting in the highest degree that is possible.

As it seems to me, this general sense of the adjective has a plain ethical application. What is morally right is what is morally "it," and is so without any restrictions whatsoever. This statement is less banal than it seems, for sundry moralists of repute prefer to use the adjective in a much narrower way. They would say, for instance, that right desires, right aspirations, right ideals or rightness of heart were phrases in which the word right was not used in what they regard as its sole legitimate (or convenient) moral sense, their reason being that anything morally right must, in their opinion, be directly and immediately an affair of volition, and that desires or the state of one's heart cannot be directly obtained by willing them. The view I have sketched, on the contrary, would maintain that if anything is "it" and is also moral, it is, quite plainly, morally right in any ordinary sense of ordinary language. To restrict the term "morally right" to any narrower signification is to use it as a technical term, and to use it cumbrously since the usual and perfectly legitimate meaning is almost certain to remain in the reader's if not in the writer's mind.

Take, again, both "duty" and "ought." Etymologically a duty is what is due, and what ought to be done is what is owed. Are these facts just an interesting piece of gossip about the history of the words, or is there a perennial flavour of them on every occasion in which the words are used significantly?

If the second alternative were true, every obligation would be a kind of requital, and in a wide sense of "justice" or of "treating on the merits of the case" this view has a certain plausibility. It seems hard to believe, however, that the relation between debtor and creditor can really determine all moral obligations, even when it is carefully explained that "of course" debts and credits are being understood in a much wider sense than bankers or borrowing countries are accustomed to use. The relation between debtors and creditors seems essentially to be a relation between determinate persons. Hence, as a matter of definition it would follow that a man could not owe anything to himself, and it would be doubtful whether he could owe anything to humanity, say, or to any nebulous public body. Yet it seems plain that we do have duties towards ourselves, and that even if all other duties must be duties towards others, it need not be clear who precisely the others are. Accordingly we should be encumbering ourselves with needless perplexities if we insisted that every duty must be owed, and it may be doubted whether there is any intelligible meaning in such rhetorical phrases as that a man "owes" a certain kind of conduct to his own self-respect, to the dignity of the rational spirit within him, to the reputation of his ancestors or to the divine spark in all human breasts.

An essential part of the conception of an obligation is that it is *binding*, and in the same way we speak of our "bounden duty," or feel that the right "constrains us," or say with Luther "Ich kann nicht anders." It is necessary, therefore, to examine this "binding force," what it is and whence it comes.

An ancient theory revived and made notorious by Hobbes was that men bound themselves morally, and also legally, by an explicit or tacit contract. This contract was an artificial but very sensible device in terms of which men, however greedy and unscrupulous they might individually be, perceived that they could have no security without a policy of mutual forbearance and therefore engaged themselves under penalties to restrain their intemperate and predatory impulses and so, within any community, to pursue the ways of peace. The "binding" in question, therefore, was a voluntary bond, a self-imposed restraint made secure by collective constraint, having abundance of life for its object. Each man bridled his desires, for there was no limit to what every man coveted; but each obtained far more by pursuing this policy of mutual forbearance than by remaining an outlaw and a mere gladiator with his hand against every other. It was better for men, merely on the score of self-interest, to stick together than to be stuck separately.

This literal and contractual sense of being "bound," together with its account of the executive machinery, or "sanction" for enforcing it, had the advantage of being readily intelligible, at least upon the surface, and did not really require the Hobbian premiss, that man, in the concupiscent part of him, was utterly selfish. It would be enough for the theory if man's selfishness were sufficiently prevalent to wreck society unless he bound himself, under penalties, to act peaceably. On the other hand, these legal notions of contract and its sanctions seem themselves to presuppose the very condition of social solidarity they were designed to explain. Therefore Hume and others maintained (if we may use a later terminology to explain their views) that status must have preceded contract, and that the binding force of moral obligation must really be a dim but powerful feeling of the essentials of social solidarity, forcibly sanctioned by public opinion, popular sympathy, and a rude kind of public-spirited vengeance. When evolutionary theories of ethics became fashionable, there were numerous attempts to explain how the seeming authority of conscience might be generated, even if, as on Spencer's view, the awe and reverence men still are disposed to attach to it would, in course of time, be evolved away.

According to Spencer the transitional moral phenomenon called conscience (or the "moral sense") was the outgrowth of three kinds of fear, political, religious, and social, and this minatory origin explained why conscience appears to bind, restrain, and coerce us even if it be true, as Hobbes and Spinoza affirmed, that the discipline makes men stronger and freer than they would otherwise be. These speculations concerning origins, however, plainly admit that a moral obligation *now* is experienced as something that is primarily within us, not some-

D*

thing induced from outside. The question therefore is whether this "feeling within our own minds" is dim, occult, mystical, and for ever inarticulate, or whether it is possible to give an intelligible analysis of it.

Some may think that feelings are none the worse for being mystical and mysterious, and those moralists who agree with Martineau reach the conclusion, rather easily, that ethics must here join hands with religion. Moral obligation, they say, is experienced as something binding and sacred, something to be reverenced as having divine authority in our bosoms and business, and so as neither more nor less occult than divinity itself.

This view can be defended, *ad hominem*, with considerable force against certain alternative moral views. The Hobbists and utilitarians, on the one hand, may be informed that neither self-interest nor the interest of some collection of men could be an adequate basis for the authoritativeness of every moral obligation, and the evolutionists may be told that their plausible sketches of a possible piece of prehistory do not really get over the difficulty. Such theories may tell us what sensible men might discover and how foolish men might be frightened, but they can never tell us what a moral man actually experiences. Ethical rationalists, on the other hand, at any rate if their views are at all similar to Kant's, may be told that they are really worshippers of noumena, idolaters of an ungraven, unimaged superstition that they call Reason. What Kant called "respect" for the moral law is a ghost from Sinai, a crepuscular thing that sins against the natural light. Therefore consistent Kantians must either bring divinity into their ethics, not as a consequence but as part of the analytic of their fundamental conceptions, or else retire to purely terrene ramparts and abandon their view that the moral fact is unique of its kind.

Nevertheless the claim of ethical rationalism is that moral obligation, so far from being mystical, occult, or even merely religious is, on the contrary, an affair of insight. It has the clarity of intellectual vision not the confusion of inarticulate feeling. Can this claim be sustained?

Since there are several different philosophical opinions regarding the nature and the *modus operandi* of "reason," there may be several different types of rationalistic ethics. Thus if it were maintained that "reason" is an affair of "coherence," the foundations of ethical action, if rational, would have to be found in some harmonious totality, perhaps in the spirit of Turgenieff when he said that he believed in civilization and required no other creed. The sort of view I have indicated, however, takes another and more usual view of reason and of its functions, namely, that reason is the intellectual insight into principles and the capacity for inferring correctly from them. In its ethical application this doctrine means that the moral obligations of any given moral situation are the province of a similar piece of rational insight, or of inference from such insight.

I say "similar" and not "identical" because identity cannot be claimed. It is true that some moralists have asserted that some sort of contradiction is involved in all irrational conduct. Thus a man who breaks a promise may be said to deny the promise by his action, that is to say, to make it not a promise, but there is a clear difference between breaking a promise, on the one hand, and, on the other hand, either denying that the promise was made, or trying to show that the alleged promise was void because it was self-contradictory and therefore nonsensical. Again, it has been supposed that the presence of a literal contradiction could be shown indirectly by applying the test: "What if everyone were to act as I propose to act?" Clearly, however, the proposed test is itself unsound in its usual application. It cannot be inferred that nobody ought to be celibate on the ground that universal celibacy would be as great a disaster as could be conceived for mankind. And since wickedness occurs, immorality cannot really be self-contradictory. For nothing self-contradictory can exist.

If we choose to do so we may speak about a "logic of action"

just as we may speak, if we choose, about a "logic of events."
Nevertheless it is clear that the statement, "So and so is my
father," is not identical with the statement, "I ought not to
kill him," and that the second statement cannot be inferred
from the first by any known process of strict logic. Consequently
if the prohibition of parricide is a moral obligation, this obligation of the "practical reason" is only analogous to not identical
with a logic of any ordinary type. What is meant by the theory
therefore must be that, given a certain moral situation, we can
see (intellectually) what ought to be done about it, what is
"fitting" or "appropriate."

Since a large part of the subsequent discussion in the present
essay will be concerned with this theory and with its moral
quasi-logic, it seems best, at the moment, only to indicate what
the theory is. I may remark, however, that the analogy asserted
in it may be pursued pretty far, and in particular may be
shown to include an element of bindingness or coerciveness.
Thus in ordinary logic if the proposition p implies the proposition q (in the sense of implication called "entailment" by
Cambridge logicians), anyone who contemplates these propositions is logically bound (or is coerced by his reason) to
infer that q is true if p is true. He must either draw that inference
or temporarily cease to be a logical being. Similarly (it is held)
a man's fitting moral action is bound or coerced by the moral
situation, unless the man temporarily ceases to be a moral
being.

The coercive or binding element in moral obligation is
sometimes described as a *command*, as in Kant's celebrated
doctrine of the "categorical imperative" of morality.

Here, however, there is a very serious difficulty. The relation
of command-obedience is essentially inter-personal, that is to
say requires at least two persons, one who commands and one
who obeys (if we omit, for simplicity's sake, the case in which
the obedient party is a poodle or a caged lion). Strictly speaking, therefore, a man cannot either obey himself or obey anything abstract such as the moral law.

True, we sometimes speak of "obeying laws" when we mean simply acting conformably to them; but that is a metaphorical sense of obedience, as may be seen from the circumstance that a man can only obey, in the strict sense, when he apprehends his orders, although he can act conformably to a law without knowing anything about the law (as most of us do, in the legal sense, when we are not trained attorneys). Again, when we wittingly obey the laws of the land we are obeying the declared will of men, not anything genuinely abstract. Indeed there are determinate persons who declare and interpret this will.

It cannot therefore be strictly true that a man "obeys" either "reason" or "himself." Reason in the abstract is not a person and cannot command. Reason, in the sense of the rational part of a man, is also not a person but a part or aspect of a person. It seems improbable that such a fragment could literally command. Kant's theory seems illegitimately to incorporate, in the name of "reason," the theological view according to which God really did command His moral laws in a juridical sense.

Nevertheless it may be maintained that moral obligations have an *authority* that is analogous to command, and that an authority of this kind is part of their essential analysis. Thus it may be held that our reason is the highest part of us, essentially fitted to guide our action, and to control our impulses and inclinations.

Regarding this there may be long dispute. It is one thing to claim that thinking and reflection cannot be entirely absent from human consciousness or behaviour in any high-grade activity, quite another to claim for "reason" the sole dignified hegemony. Many would say instead that the human heart, human love of beauty, human reverence for deity are quite as exalted as the capacity for putting two and two together or for apprehending that two straight lines cannot enclose a space. The mere subordination of *such* inclinations is a doctrine very precariously justified. It is not nonsense even to maintain that, on a broad view, the heart should control the head.

Again, while a certain rigour seems to be implicit in moral obligation (in much of it usually and in all of it upon occasion), so that the language of gentle persuasion seems inappropriate and the language of stern prohibition inevitable, moral tyranny, that is to say what looks like tyranny and proclaims itself moral, is also quite possible and even frequent. Again, self-coercion, in some sense, may necessarily be mingled with moral obligation, but it is not, quite simply, the same thing.

The clearest sense of authority is that in which there is a justifiable inter-personal relationship of a hierarchical kind, such that certain definite persons ought to command, in certain matters, and certain other definite persons ought to obey. It is an intricate question, largely moral, what hierarchies can be so justified and how far; but there is no other clear and adequate meaning of authority. The extension of this meaning to the authority of principles, or to some part of personality, is perhaps inevitable, and can rely on analogy. It has, however, all the dangers of metaphor, and so should be employed circumspectly if at all.

A further point remains. Spencer, as we saw, held that the sense of duty was destined to disappear as evolution continued on its blessed way; and other moralists, very different from Spencer, have applied a similar view in a very different way. Thus according to Kant duty and obligation would have no meaning for a *holy* will. These terms imply the possibility at least of moral struggle, of mastering something wicked or at least unruly in a moral conflict. The saints made perfect would have no such struggle, and so, in strictness of language would have no duties and no obligations.

On this view, it would seem that the word "right" would maintain its meaning in a world of moral supermen, although "duty" and "obligation" would not; but these questions seem rather to be curious than instructive. Indeed, the same sort of argument is sometimes employed regarding the whole of ethics, and in that case would have no special application to the particular terms "duty" and "obligation." Thus McTaggart held that virtue itself would have no meaning in an ideal universe. "For virtue," he said, "implies a choice, and choice implies either uncertainty or conflict. In the completed ideal neither of these could exist. . . . There would be no more virtue in obeying the law, for example, of courage, than in obeying the law of gravitation. The use of the word "law" in both cases would no longer be misleading, for all difference between precepts and truths would have ceased when the righteous was *ipso facto* the real" (*Philosophical Studies*, p. 222).

IX

DUTY AND THE WILL

A SALIENT feature of many renowned moral theories is their
contention that duty and obligation are strictly and always
voluntary actions. From this premiss, as will duly appear,
many important consequences are drawn, important, that is,
from the standpoint of moral theory. Indeed, we are frequently
told that the European and relatively modern discovery of an
adequate psychology of willing has enabled present-day
moralists to make a definite and very considerable advance
upon older or upon Eastern speculations on ethics.

In view of these claims, it seems necessary to attempt a
rather stringent examination of this contention, and we may
begin by reconsidering the nature of a voluntary act and,
generally, of voluntary action.

As we have seen, the adjective "voluntary" is intended
to denote that some given action could be performed if it
were willed, or (roughly speaking) could be accomplished by
trying. Thus "voluntary" is wider than willed; for we call
actions voluntary when we could have willed them but neglected
to do so. No doubt this definition raises difficulties. A man,
let us say, could have wound up his watch, but forgot, one
evening, to wind it. Since presumably there were sufficient
causes for his forgetfulness, it may be argued that he could
not have wound it on that particular occasion although he had
the physical capacity for winding it, and although for the
most part he proves that he can wind it by actually winding
it. In substance, however, the distinction between having a
capacity if we choose to exercise it, and having no such power,
is sufficiently important to justify most generous emphasis
upon the difference between voluntary and non-voluntary.

Accepting, then, this account of what is voluntary we have
next to ask what is properly to be called "action."

Here there may seem to be no difficulty. An action is a deed, and everyone knows the difference between deeds and words or, again, between doing something and merely thinking about doing it. There is all the difference in the world, especially to the possible victim, between poisoning a man and talking or thinking about poisoning him.

Yet although words are but breath, the utterance of the words is a deed, as slanderers learn; and even if words are not uttered, thinking is also an activity which may be decidedly strenuous.

If breaking a leg is a deed, so is the process of its repair, and, plainly, men are doing something when they are growing or when they are digesting their food. On the physical side, however, it is relatively easy to explain where we are; for a *voluntary* physical deed must be a muscular movement of some sort, raising an arm, kicking a ball, or the like. Growth and secretion are not deeds of that kind. Nevertheless, thinking may also be a voluntary activity. It may not be so when ideas (as we say) come out of the blue, or when we are the victims of some obsession; but frequently it is voluntary. We can decide to deliberate if we are not pressed for time. We can concentrate our attention or relax it. We can give our minds to close study. Physical movements may assist in such cases, it is true, just as black coffee or a wet towel may; but thinking itself may be voluntary, and it is not simply a muscular movement.

It would seem, therefore, paradoxically enough, that the volition defines the "action." Whenever we decide, we decide to effect something; a voluntary deed is the effecting of what we have decided to effect. It is a moot point whether experience alone has enabled us to discriminate between what we can effect in this way and what we cannot effect, or whether we can also divine a great part of the distinction by some sort of "instinct" in advance of experience. Within ourselves we can voluntarily initiate, inhibit, and control certain muscular movements and some part of what we call "thinking," and it is debatable whether we can voluntarily initiate anything else.

Outside our bodies there is also room for debate. It is not plain to me that a marksman does not control the course of a bullet in much the same way as he controls the sighting of the rifle or his pressure on the trigger. Certainly, the rifle has to be in good working order; but so have his eyes and his fingers. The question, I suggest, is simply what he can effect in the normal way by deciding to bring it about, or, more accurately, what he can probably effect.

However that may be, it seems plain that the restriction, in Mr. Ross's fashion (*R.G.*, p. 5) to what can be performed "at a moment's notice" is, to say very little, decidedly startling, even when accompanied by the explanation that more elaborate moral affairs may be regarded as a series of such voluntary acts. Accordingly, it seems advisable to consider some of the more important distinctions of this order before attempting to indicate any of the implications of our analysis.

The kind of voluntary act Mr. Ross has in mind may be called the "immediate voluntary sequel" of a decision, and may be illustrated by such a voluntary movement as pressing a trigger. Such immediate voluntary sequels, however, are seldom what we design in willing. At the most they are the inception and the instrument of what is really designed, and are chosen because of the design. We should therefore distinguish, in general, between the immediate voluntary sequel of a decision and its "voluntary aim," and this voluntary aim, in its turn, should be distinguished both from the obvious probable consequences of the decision together with its immediate voluntary sequel and from the actual historical consequences. Further distinctions might of course be drawn, for example between the obvious probable consequences and the less obvious or quite recondite probable consequences. I have tried, however, to indicate only the more important distinctions.

To illustrate by a stock example. An anarchist wills to assassinate the Tsar in his carriage by throwing a bomb. At the critical moment, the throwing of the bomb is the immediate voluntary sequel of his decision. The destruction of the Tsar is the voluntary aim of the action, that is, the proximate voluntary aim (for subsequent political changes are doubtless also aimed at). Among the obvious probable consequences are the destruction of coachman, carriage-horses, and bystanders as well as the destruction of the Tsar, whether or not this additional destruction were part of the anarchist's voluntary aim or, in his view, a regrettable incident in his devastation. The actual consequences would be the historical sequel of the assassination in all its details, however remote.

In the ordinary way we regard a man as responsible for the probable obvious consequences of his enacted decisions. In other words, we hold that there is a duty concerning them. Again, we judge the morality of his action principally with respect to what I have called his voluntary aim. Indeed, we do so in all cases (I think) in which the immediate voluntary sequel cannot be regarded as an end in itself.

Each of these common-sense opinions seems inevitable. The first of them, in substance, is simply an expression of the presumption that our decisions are serious practical realities. If the agent does not know what he is doing, that is to say does not know what sort of difference he is likely to make by enacting his decision, he is like a child playing with poisons. He may be lucky or he may be mischievous, but his ideas contain no grasp of fact, and so do not have the efficacy that is reasonably presumed in all serious moral enquiry. The second is a clear implication of the truism that we judge a man in terms of what he means to do. We may judge him indeed by more than that, but not by less; and it is evident that, unless the immediate voluntary sequel is all he means to do, there would be little or no meaning, if more than the said sequel were not taken into account.

Suppose, for instance, that a man decides to make a payment by cheque. The immediate voluntary sequel of this decision is to grasp a pen, and to move wrist and fingers. That, however, would be a vain flourish unless the pen had ink on it and made special marks on a special form. The flourish by itself would be meaningless; the signature would not. Therefore it is the aim that is significant, and, as before, we come back to the view that if the man signs his cheque and posts it, we judge morally, not these immediate voluntary sequels by themselves, but the payment. True, the Post Office, the bank, and the Treasury have something to do with this matter; and nobody by signing a cheque can make himself personally responsible for his bank and for his Government. In all reasonable probability, however, the man can make the critical difference between the retention of certain figures in his own banking account, and the transfer to another banking account. So much, in all probability, he does control voluntarily. So much he means; and so much, precisely, is morally judged in that particular instance.

Even in the case of a very rapid decision, when *pros* and *cons* are scarcely weighed at all, the decision, more often than not, anticipates the immediate voluntary sequel, and looks ahead. When we run for a bus the dominant thought is the act of boarding that vehicle; and similarly in nearly every instance in which we are not actually engaged in learning the initial technique of relevant movement. Certainly, there is some difficulty regarding what may be called the units of voluntary action. A short and rapid pursuit of the bus might be called *one* voluntary action; a longer pursuit, where the pursuer had to dodge a child or two, is single in a general way, and multiple in detail; but the problem of the one and the many is not really more exasperating in the case of volition than elsewhere. In any case, since the relevant movements or other actions, being voluntary, are defined by their possibility of being willed, the scope of the conscious decision determines all such questions of unity or plurality.

Anything that is willed must be consciously willed, and this consciousness includes certain beliefs regarding what we are doing, that is to say regarding both the nature of the process to be performed and the character of its effects. For it is a performance, a doing of something *to* something. Such beliefs,

it is true, need not be explicitly formulated. They may be
only a "taking for granted" and commonly are so in the case
of rapid decisions. But the beliefs are present. They are not
the only conscious antecedents of volition, but they are among
those conscious antecedents. This circumstance has considerable importance for moral theory.

For example, it forbids us to say, without careful examination and qualification, what nearly anyone would be disposed
to say. Nearly anyone would say that duty is duty whatever
the agent happens to think about it; and it is true that an agent's
false opinion regarding the morality, the nature or the effects
of some proposed action on his part cannot of itself turn wrong
into right. To be sure, if the agent, in such instances, has
seriously pondered the question, his conscience, although in
error, does direct him, and his action is morally commendable
in one very important aspect, viz. that it is conscientious. We
may say, indeed, that such fidelity to the personal conscience
is so fundamental in morality, and, in the face of opposition,
so rare, that we should think much worse of a conscientious
objector (assuming his objections to be mistaken) if he did not
follow his erring conscience than if he did follow it; but we
could not say, without qualification, that he did his duty or
fulfilled his obligations. His opinion cannot make these what
they are.

Nevertheless, it is equally impossible to maintain that moral
duty can be independent of all the agent's beliefs. Suppose,
for instance, that some treacherous X, in the belief that he
would discredit Y, tries to spread the rumour that Y is not a
whole-hearted supporter of the dictator. Suppose, further, that
the dictator's power, to X's chagrin, collapses simultaneously,
and so that X does Y an unintended service. It surely could not
be held that X had fulfilled his moral duty of being loyal to Y.
There is no need, however, to search for examples. In so far
as any duty is voluntary, it necessarily presupposes certain
beliefs on the agent's part, viz. those beliefs about what he
means to do without which a volition could not occur.

Obviously, therefore, duty or obligation implies certain *true* beliefs on the agent's part. Since a man may tell the truth, be generous and so forth without thinking about the duty of veracity or generosity, since indeed (as we have seen) he would be a moral prig if he never did his duty without remarking that it was a duty, we cannot (it is true) hold that beliefs concerning the morality of an action are necessarily present in any explicit form. We may think, perhaps, that candour and generosity are all the better for not being calculated. In such instances, however, since the action, although it might be beautiful, could scarcely be moral unless the agent could justify it morally to himself (although not, perhaps, in a very scientific way) if the question of its morality came home to him, we should probably infer the necessity of a certain "taking for granted" in the moral way. None the less, the agent must have true beliefs (or assumptions) regarding what he is doing i.e. that he is conveying correct information, doing what is likely to help a friend, or otherwise performing the kind of action that, if examined from the moral standpoint, would be called dutiful or right.

The relation of beliefs of the latter class to these questions of voluntary duty and obligation raises rather intricate problems for analytical ethics. To these I now proceed.

The maxim that "ought implies can," or, in other words, the principle that no one can have a moral duty that he cannot fulfil is Kantian in the look of it but is none the worse for that, and is accepted without qualification by many considerable moralists, for example by Mr. Ross (*R.G.*, p. 5). From it, these moralists deduce a variety of consequences. The maxim has a strong claim, therefore, to be made the pivot of the present discussion, and I propose to examine its relation to the beliefs that are essential to all volition.

We may ask, in the first place, whether the truth of the maxim may be deduced from the elementary psychology of human volition. Such a deduction would run as follows: The belief in "ought" implies the belief in "can"; for no one can seriously

decide to do what he believes to be a plain impossibility; and
duty and obligation must be voluntary.

It must be admitted that we never will to do what we know
to be absolutely impossible. We do not will to jump over the
moon, or, if we are over twenty, to grow six inches taller,
unless we have views about the efficacy of faith to work
miracles, in which case we do not believe these impossibilities
to *be* impossibilities. On the other hand, the not-impossible
covers a very wide range, and it is frankly absurd to argue that
every male American believes he "can" become president of
the United States simply because it is not absolutely impossible
that he should become president of that country. There is no
psychological impossibility in resolutely pursuing an end, by
voluntary action, when the expectation of achievement is
excessively slight, and I can see no psychological impossibility in the view that men may and should elect to follow a
standard of duty higher than any human being has hitherto
attained, although each of them knows very well that he
individually is very unlikely to succeed where all the others
have failed.

In short, what these psychological arguments really prove is
that where there is will there is hope. Where impossibility is
apparent (or seems to be so) hope dies; and where hope is
dead volition also ceases. Yet hope may live, and does live,
when the reasonable chances of success seem very slender
indeed. Consequently, it is absurd to argue that the viability
of hope is the same thing as a conviction of one's ability to
achieve.

After all, however, the argument was not that all voluntary
action implied the belief in "can," but that a particular species
of voluntary action, viz., moral obligation, implied this belief.
I cannot think, however, that this proviso, regarded as a
piece of psychology, is at all plausible if the wider psychological
argument is admitted to be faulty, and its falsity appears to
be assumed by the more considerable moralists who maintain,
in principle, that ought implies can. For they argue that duty

is always (voluntarily) in a man's power *although the man may not think so*.

Thus Kant endeavoured to prove "from experience" that anyone "can do a certain thing because he is conscious that he ought" (*Analytic of Pure Practical Reason*, § VI, *ad fin.*) in the following way: People say that their lusts are sometimes irresistible; but that is absurd because they could restrain their lusts if there were a gallows before them and if they knew that they would have to expiate their lecheries upon it. The love of life, therefore, is stronger than any lust; but the sense of duty is stronger than the love of life as is shown by all martyrs for conscience' sake.

That was a very weak argument. It would prove (if the motives alleged were correctly assigned) that some men, at a time of exaltation, had found conscience stronger than love of life, but even if the love of life were stronger than it is in fact—one thinks of sea-captains who voluntarily go down with the ship or of the occasions for *hara-kiri*—Kant's argument would not even begin to prove that every man at every time can conquer his fears and obey his conscience. The intention of the argument, however, was to convince doubters, that is to say to convince those who thought they sometimes couldn't do their duty that really they could always do it.

Moreover, Kant's argument calls attention, perhaps unwittingly, to a point so very obvious that the omission of it may have given an air of unreality to the whole discussion. If the belief in "ought" psychologically implies the belief in "can," what happens when the second of these beliefs is false?

Clearly, the case occurs very frequently. We know a good deal about our voluntary powers, that is, about what we can effect by willing; and it is our proper business, both as sensible and as conscientious men, to learn to discriminate between the times when we can rely on our volitional efficacy, and the times when we cannot do so. Even when we have performed this part of our proper business, however (so far, at any rate as is reasonable for a scrupulous person), the fact remains that we are and must remain ignorant, in many respects, of our own capacities. We think we can do what in fact we can't; and we think we can't do what in fact we can. How is a recruit to know in advance what effect the terrors and the horrors of the battlefield will have upon his courage, or how far, if his courage ebbs, he will still be able to acquit himself in a soldierly fashion? How can a veteran know for certain that he will not flinch at the hundredth danger, although he has successfully endured the previous ninety-nine? The imaginative soldier is likely to distrust himself more than he should and the unimaginative to trust himself far too easily. Again, ship-wreck or the battlefield are not the only places from which such examples can be culled. They are strewn over the pages of life. "If youth but knew"; "If age but refused to say 'I can't go on with it.' "

It is a mistake, I think, to attempt to evade the force of these contentions by saying, "Well, at any rate you can always try," or "You can take the first steps voluntarily, and the rest will come." In the first of these statements, if "trying" means "willing," there is, in the first place, a doubt, since the condition of partial aboulia or paralysis of the will may exist; and in the second place there is an irrelevance, since the question refers to the *efficacy* of willing, that is to say to its practical sequel or sequels. In the second statement, the prophecy is clearly precarious. The rest may not "come," and, as we have seen, a voluntary action has to be defined by an *aim* that is seldom confined to the immediate sequel. When the first step counts, it counts either because we have committed ourselves or because it is and is meant to be the first step *of a series*. The first step left to itself would not be what was willed.

Indeed, there is a nest of fallacies in this region. The funda-mental contention of Kantian moralists is that duty is always within the power of the will in the same fundamental sense as raising one's arm or winding one's watch is within that power, except, indeed, for the difference that the arm may be paralysed or the watch broken while duty is unimpaired so long as conscience and will remain. Duty may indeed be enormously difficult to achieve, but (on this view) it is always voluntarily possible. Here, however, among other perplexities, we appear to have the dubious assertion that a man can sustain for an indefinite period an activity of which he is capable by a special effort for a limited period; and nobody would argue in that way regarding the ordinary affairs of life. The best bridge players sometimes revoke, although both they, and players far inferior, would not revoke except by inadvertence, and, in a general way, are obviously capable of the very modest standard of advertence that is required.

Indeed, what this Kantian argument needs is the existence of *true* beliefs (or, perhaps, irrefragable *knowledge*) of our capacities as well as of our moral obligations. Yet certainty (or even a well-grounded conviction) regarding the former is very hard to attain. It is not guaranteed by past experience (for even a veteran may behave as a novice to his own chagrin and to everyone else's astonishment) and it would seem to be unattainable without experience. Nevertheless, according to the theory the rational fact of duty is inextricably allied with the empirical fact of voluntary capacity; for by ordinary logical processes (*contraponendo*) we can infer "if no power then no duty" from "if duty then power."

Indeed, it is difficult to suppose that Kant would have argued as he did if he had not assumed that *any* one's duty is always something that *every* one could perform. In that case the man who believed he could not do what he believed to be his duty would confess himself to be sub-human. In the view of most moralists, however, the difficult questions arise, not regarding moral hysterics and the people who jib at tasks of which anyone retaining the shreds of humanity may be presumed to be capable, but regarding hard duties that call for exceptional resolution or other moral capacity. The question in that case is not whether everybody could do what is held to be so-and-so's duty, but whether so-and-so could do it (or anyone with so-and-so's exceptional powers). It is therefore necessary to ask, and very difficult to know, whether so-and-so *has* these exceptional powers.

Moreover, and even more importantly, the doctrine that "ought" implies "can" is frequently interpreted in a strained and peculiar fashion. From the premiss that a man *can* perform because he *should* perform, the inference is drawn that a man can always do his duty *voluntarily*. Certainly, if duty be necessarily a matter of volition, it may be argued, rather plausibly, that the adjective "voluntary" applies to the "can" in the premiss because it applies to the "ought." Those, however, who dispute the view that duty implies the power to perform, for example, those who, like Luther, assert the contrary maxim, *A debere ad posse non valet consequentia*, might be prepared to deny that our duties must be wholly and inevitably voluntary. We must therefore be ready to discuss this question in a broader spirit than hitherto.

Clearly a man *does* and *is* much that he does not choose to do or to be. His influence upon others and what is called the force of his example includes what he chooses in this kind (if his choice corresponds to the reality), but is not confined to such choice, and, regarding himself, there may be much for which he deeply yearns, such as peace and joy of the spirit, that he would be very foolish to strive for. Such goods are either not expetible at all, or are treated as non-expetible by those who are wise. It is hoped that they will *come*, but although obstacles to their coming may be voluntarily diminished, they cannot be obtained by direct willing.

Nevertheless, it should not be inferred that these things necessarily come as gifts from the outside or from above, and that the man himself cannot win them. All that is true is that he cannot normally win them *by trying*; it is not true that *he* can never win them, unless we fall into the foolish error of supposing that *he* himself is just his "will." Certainly the advice, so often helpful, "Don't try to get better but wait. Nature herself, that is, in the main, *your* nature, will work the miracle," may be said, in a sense to have semi-voluntary implications. If the "will" is to abdicate in favour of "auto-suggestion," it abdicates voluntarily. The meaning of the advice, however, is that if the "will" abdicates, *you* do the rest, and do it well; and that, of itself, is an assertion that what you can do, what is within your power, may be a non-volitional achievement.

It may be true that lawyers have to deal only with matters of volition, although the current legal presumptions in this country regarding legal responsibility are surely not exempt from dubiety in view of the controversies regarding the McNaghten rules, "moral imbeciles," etc., and of the obvious desire of many judges to throw the onus of such decisions upon the jury with very little guidance from the bench. Even if it were true, however, that the threat of punishment is either a voluntary motive or utterly useless, it is not true in fact that persuasion and example do not move us unless they are accompanied by threats or similar inducements. When ideals move us, the initial acceptance and the following of the ideal is actually willed in a part of it only, and although "voluntary" is wider than "actually willed" the greater width is due to the difference between what is and what might be willed.

Indeed, this alleged "modern" discovery of an adequate psychology of the "will" seems to me to embarrass moral theory quite as much as it clarifies it. A decision upon evidence (part of which is moral evidence) is certainly a matter of great importance, and so is the extent to which we are able to control our movements and other activities by taking thought. It is wise and most necessary to call attention to these critically important regions in human practice, but not nearly so wise to treat these special features of, or incidents in, human activity, as if they constituted a distinct entity, the man within the man, a sort of policeman in his box directing the traffic. An analytic being of this sort is not the "power" within us and may not be properly speaking a "being" at all.

I should like to repeat that the apparent lucidity of these

conceptions of the "will" among moralists, lawyers, and the plain man, their humble follower, is apt to induce a complacent and misleading sense of clarity. In particular, when I am asked to distinguish between a man's "gifts" and the man himself, between what he can't help and what he himself originates and controls, I am surprised at the glibness with which this way of speaking proceeds. To me the man is an integrity. If he is accountable at all, he is accountable in his integrity. He did not originate himself. His parents originated him, with some help from Nature and, I daresay, from God; but when parents speak of the "gift" of a son they are speaking more accurately (I submit) than the people who, within a man, distinguish between what is a "gift" and what is not. It is the man that acts, and the man himself, not his "will" or some other part of him, has whatever measure of independence a human being can have. It is of the utmost importance to recognize that the man's internal organization is hierarchical and to distinguish between "higher" and "lower" controls; but the "will" is an incomplete description of what is meant by "higher control," and it cannot describe the whole of a man's power or agency.

Certain debates, largely recent, concerning the relation between moral duty and moral motives seem to aggravate the difficulties of the "modern" theory of the "will." The contention of several modern writers is that, within morality, an absolute distinction should be drawn between the morality of works (or acts) and the morality of the spirit (or motives). A moral deed (on this view) implies a mind, for, being voluntary, it is consciously performed, but it is spiritual only in this attenuated sense, and its rightness or wrongness is wholly independent of motive. The "motive," according to this theory, is of great moral importance, for we base our estimate of the agent's character, virtue, or moral goodness on his "motives"; but it has nothing to do with questions of duty or of obligation.

Such opinions are almost inevitable when moral law is

assumed to be of the same nature as legal, although differently enforced or not at all; and I allow that they might be able to defend themselves against the plausible objection that volition itself implies that very type of motivation which it is the business of the rest of the theory to exclude from moral obligation.

This particular objection might be stated, and met, in dialogue form, as follows, A being the objector and B his opponent:

B. In my view the motive makes no difference to the morality of the act. The man who saves a fellow-creature from drowning is doing his duty, whether on the one hand he simply sees it and does it, or, on the other, expects a medal.

A. When you say so, you are isolating the deed from its intention, and since, by your own admission, the deed must be voluntary if it is a duty at all, you have no business to make your assertion.

B. I am concerned with one particular deed, the voluntary rescue. You are not denying, are you? that the rescue is, or may be, a moral duty. When it is a duty I say the motive is irrelevant.

A. You are forgetting that a volition is defined by its aim. Suppose the rescuer belongs to the Emperor's bodyguard, and is rescuing a miserable captive who prefers death in the Tiber to a spectacular death at the jaws of the Imperial lions. Suppose again that the rescuer's object is subsequently to blackmail the rescued.

B. You are now producing instances in which it is doubtful whether the rescue *is* a duty.

A. Granted: but why does the doubt occur? Surely because the rescue is an incident in a wider aim which is either morally dubious or morally disreputable. You are not entitled to assume that because a short series of physical events, say the rescue, can be treated as a single incident, it can also be treated as a single moral action. The truth is that when two such incidents have different aims they are two distinct moral actions. They are not two instances of the same action performed with different motives.

B. I dispute your analysis. What you are talking about is the distinction between a proximate and an ulterior aim. The proximate aim of rescue is rightly intended in any instance you choose to excogitate. When the man is struggling in the water *any* bystander who can swim or can get hold of a rope ought to help him. That is another way of saying that all special or personal motives are quite irrelevant. If the rescuer has a wicked ulterior aim, the conclusion, quite simply, is that he meditates *two* actions, the first of which is a moral duty, and the second criminal. You can never prove that the first is not a duty by proving that the second is a crime.

A. The example is specially favourable to your theory because the rescue can be treated as a separate incident, and may plausibly be treated as a duty of common humanity, that is to say as appropriate to a universal motive. You could not argue in this way if the proximate and the ulterior aim were not really separate. Suppose I left some sandwiches lying about near a place where I suspected an escaped convict was hiding. Would you then argue that there were two acts, the right one of feeding the hungry, the wrong one of hindering justice?

B. No. In that case there is one action, the feeding of a hungry man who is also an escaped convict. All that the instance shows is a possible conflict of obligations.

A. Similarly it is one action to rescue a drowning man who is also a source of revenue if alive.

B. I have told you that the rescue as such can and should be treated as a single moral obligation, and you, by calling the instance favourable to my case, have admitted as much.

A. Your position is that the motive is always irrelevant to the obligation. You are now saying that it sometimes is. A limping conclusion.

B. If so we are both lame, for you are saying that the motive is never irrelevant. But I seem to walk quite steadily, thank you.

A. I also seem to be pretty firm upon my pins.

In this dialogue, I submit, neither party makes much head-way. Granting that a voluntary deed must be something meant, there may be interminable argument regarding what is one meaning, one deed, and a unity of the two. We may infer, I think, that if the "motive" of an action includes its aim (proximate or ulterior) then (a) voluntary action cannot be entirely independent of motive *in that sense*, but (b) might well be such that the duty of fulfilling a proximate aim was not affected by its relation to ulterior aims.

If by a "motive" we mean that which moves us to action, I do not see that our aims, and the beliefs that go along with them, can be denied to be a part of our motive. It may be true that many such beliefs are in themselves mere pieces of know-ledge, for example the belief that such and such a rope could be attached to a tree and would help a swimmer in difficulties. The question, however, is not whether such a belief would of itself move to action, but whether it may play its part among the relevant antecedents of some particular action; and it seems plain that the belief, "Here's my chance; luckily there's a rope," is one of the relevant antecedents in an unheroic but effective rescue.

Men have a certain voluntary control of their aims as well as of their action in accordance with aims. Again, they them-selves form, mature, and perpend their aims voluntarily, semi-voluntarily, and non-voluntarily. In the main, however, modern deontologists prefer to treat of "motives" in relation to duty not in the sense of "motive" that includes aims, but in a sense that does not directly include them, and so they chiefly consider (a) the sense of duty regarded as a motive, and (b) the motives of emotion and desire.

(a) The "sense of duty" is a vaguish term, but convenient. Regarding it, I take Kant's position to be, broadly speaking, typical of most ethical rationalism, including Stoicism, although opposed to the New Oxford Intuitionism, itself rationalistic. Kant, I should say, held in substance that we did our duty, strictly speaking (if we ever did it), only when we acted wholly from duty, that such action implied that duty *alone* moved us to act, and that since all moral obligation was a behest of our reason, action *from* duty (as opposed to action either against or merely in accordance with duty) meant action of which our "practical reason" was the sole moving cause. Action from other causes (e.g. from human pity) might be commendable, but not morally commendable; and if any part of the motive were a selfish inclination, the action, to that extent, would not be commendable at all even if it were wholly in accordance with duty.

If so, the "sense of duty" (to use ordinary speech) would be simply the rational apprehension of moral obligation; and moral action would be (pure) reason in action. Kant held, it is true, that this exercise of our reason induced certain emotions of "respect," that is to say, of awe and reverence, for the moral law. Such emotional results were, however, consequential (in his view) and did not affect the truth that reason itself moved us when we acted from duty. He held further that this exercise of reason was precisely what was meant by the *will* of a rational being. Consequently there could be no doubt whatsoever that action from duty (in the sense explained) was (voluntarily) "within our power." We possessed the power whenever we were in our right minds.

It is reasonable to object to Kant as Mr. Ross does (*R.G.*, p. 158) that if the sense of duty were strong enough to cause a man to act morally, there would be no moral objection to the co-operation of other motives, or any indication of a deficiency of morality. For the action might be over-determined from various concurrent causes, and would be morally defective only if the moral motive were of itself insufficient to bring it about (although capable of being a contributory part-cause). Plainly we could not infer that a man would not have acted honourably without reward on the mere ground that he might have expected his honourable action to be rewarded. We should require other evidence to justify such suspicions. This criticism of Kant, however, does not affect the main question

E

now in dispute, viz. whether the "sense of duty" may move us to voluntary action.

Here the New Oxford Intuitionists differ sharply from Kant. The sense of duty, they say, is a motive; and motives are always entirely distinct from obligations. Obligations are voluntary acts and within our power. Motives are never within our power, and therefore it can never be a duty to have them. Kant, indeed, according to these authors, was wrong in two ways. He held that the sense of duty was voluntary; and it is not. He also held that commendable non-voluntary motives are not morally commendable; and they are (for they may pertain to virtue and excellence in moral character).

This clean-cut division of ethics into the two mutually untouchable regions of duty and of moral goodness is further defended by an argument to the effect that the sense of duty could be roused (without plain error) only if there *were* a duty to be sensed (Ross, *R.G.*, p. 5). This seems plain; but Kant's argument (I submit) was simply that the apprehension of an obligation is a rational act, and that this rational apprehension (of the practical reason) is the sole motive to moral duty. If so, the sense of duty is just the recognition of duty, not an additional obligation of a higher order having obligations of lower order for its logical field, and, although Kant might not have said so, the sense of duty, in its natural interpretation, would be entirely consistent with indefinitely little reflection about duty in general. We are accustomed to speak of men whose sense of duty is punctilious in some directions and lax in others. So-and-so, we say, may be trusted to keep his word, but is as slippery as an eel if he has not actually promised. Nevertheless, such a man might very well act from duty when he had given his word, even if he seemed otherwise to be conscienceless and to have only the vaguest ideas about moral principle in general.

I submit therefore that duty need not be counted more than once when the sense of duty is in question, and consequently that this particular argument manufactures the infinite regress against which it inveighs. We have to return, therefore, to the other argument.

(*b*) In what sense, if any, must all motives be non-voluntary? And if they must be non-voluntary, must they consequently belong to a sphere altogether separate from the province of duty?

The writers I have called "separatists," so far as I can observe, assume that all motives are emotional motives, at any rate if our wants, our desires, and the broad emotional patterns that are sometimes called "sentiments" are included in this designation.

It must be allowed, as we saw in earlier discussions, that direct action is less effective in the case of our emotions than in the case of many of our movements and of some of our thoughts. We cannot summon love and hate with the same celerity as we can post a letter, or think upon a number and double it; and in general it is easier to control the usual expression of some emotion than to control the emotion itself, easier to say one is sorry than to *be* sorry, easier to stop a blow than to check one's indignation. On the other hand, it is quite absurd to say that we have *no* control over our emotions themselves, that we cannot nurse them when they are commendable or diminish them when they are not commendable; and if such processes are usually gradual, and often indirect, the absence of all control does not follow from the existence of a prolonged refractory phase or of some need for sapping and mining. It might be argued, indeed, that just as, in physiology, there may be control by the autonomic as well as by the central nervous system, so, in moral matters, there may be at least two higher controls, only one of which is the control of volition. If so, we might control, nourish, or check our emotions; but not voluntarily. I cannot see, however, that such emotional control is less of an *action* than the voluntary control of our thoughts; and I do not see that it is less a matter of duty.

Certain plausible arguments in this field, we may note, are

quite inconclusive and should be avoided. If we held, like Kant, that any sympathetic feeling or emotional love for our neighbour could not be a matter of duty, although the Scriptures were right in commanding us to act as if we loved that neighbour, we might find the consequences acutely disturbing. It would not be a husband's duty to love his wife, but only to act as if he loved her: not a father's duty to love his children, but only to act as if he did; not a Christian's duty to oppose his enemies without rancour, but, instead, to fraternize with them although the hatred continued. Since deceitful practices are also morally reprehensible, it is surely apparent that Kant's exegesis of the second great Commandment floundered in a slough of contradictions, and so was intolerable as well as unscriptural.

If, however, we further held, with the New Oxford Intuitionists, that what was denied to duty was simply transferred to virtue, so that love of one's wife or sympathy with one's fellows were morally good but not affairs of duty, we might perhaps infer that duty was a very impoverished department of ethics, but could not infer that morality (which includes moral goodness) had suffered any loss. (And, no doubt, the wife might not care very much whether her husband's affection sprang from duty or not. What she wants is the affection itself; and she would appeal to the husband's conscience only when all else failed.)

In a general way, however, it seems reasonable to conclude, not only that the denial of voluntary control of emotional motives is itself very questionable, but also that if the denial were justified there would be no sufficient reason for holding that we may not have non-voluntary obligations directly affecting our emotional motives.

According to all intuitionists, we have rational insight into the truth that certain moral situations entail certain moral obligations. The moral obligation can be seen (with the mind's eye) to be "fitting" or "appropriate" to the moral situation. Why, then, should this insight be restricted to volition? If voluntary action can be seen to have this kind of "fittingness," why should not states of mind and character, an emotional pattern, or the like, be similarly fitting? If philanthropy be a virtuous emotion, is it not for that very reason moral and appropriate? If there is any moral insight, is not *that* a piece of moral insight?

If so, what have the separatists to allege in their own favour, except, perhaps, certain verbal advantages of terminology, advantages, moreover, which their opponents either cheerfully deny or joyfully renounce? If, by a sort of ethical logic we had rational insight into the fittingness of certain voluntary actions to certain particular situations, and had no other rational insight into any sort of moral appropriateness, then voluntary obligation would have a rational basis and the rest of ethics would not. Such a difference would be of the first importance to all moralists: but does it exist? On the other hand, if the moral goodness that the separatists dissever from duty yet willingly include in morality, has the same sort of rational basis as duty has, i.e. if it also is known by rational insight into what is morally appropriate to a situation, the difference between the things separated seems of minor significance. Differences, where they exist, should, of course, be acknowledged and should not be blurred by a lax use of words; but they need not justify a bill of divorcement.

It seems advisable, at the end of this discussion, to revert to a question previously raised.

From the premiss that "ought" implies "can" (whether or not that premiss is interpreted voluntaristically), it certainly cannot be inferred that one's duty is *easily* performed, but there is no special reason for holding that duty is always very difficult. Yet, as we saw, many worthy men and many earnest moralists find inspiration in the thought that their duty is always too high for them. They are humbled in a salutary way by the scrupulous remembrance that it is not theirs to hope for complete moral victory at any time.

Many duties, however, seem to be quite simple to perform, although others are not. It may be hard to bear true witness on a proper occasion, e.g. on oath in the law courts; for accuracy is hard to attain, the truth may damage the accused and cause despair to many others, and so forth. Frequently, however, there are no special difficulties of that kind, and it would take a very ingenious moralist to explain the height and the difficulty of the duty of giving one's correct name and address on most lawful occasions. In short, certain duties (not necessarily as a class, but on this or the other proper occasion for them) would seem to be easy and low, others to be hard and high.

If this be denied, the reason for the denial (it would seem) must lie in some theory of motive. For Kant the difficulty lay in excluding all motives except duty in its purity. There might always (he thought) be something fleshly or selfish in what seemed to be the simple execution of a plain moral duty. Others, I suppose, would hold, if some scorner took his stand upon meticulous logic, that a saint could not even give his name and address in the same spirit as another man. The saint's motives would always be interfused with an absolute devotion to some great and all-pervasive cause.

Any such view may appear exaggerated in the case of giving one's name and address, or of paying one's grocer's bill; but there may be comparatively few instances of precisely that kind. Many, for instance, might be disposed to think that a man who pays his civic rates simply to avoid trouble and without any regard to the obligations of citizenship would only have done his legal, not his moral duty; or again, that if he believed the city's expenditure to be morally unjustifiable in any given respect, it would be his moral duty to refuse to fulfil his legal obligation in that particular regard, and to suffer accordingly.

In other words, our usual moral opinion is that motive is not entirely distinct from the great majority of moral obligations.

X

CLASSIFICATION OF VOLUNTARY OBLIGATIONS

An ideal classification should follow a single principle, and should have a place, but never two or more places, for each of the items to be classified. This counsel of perfection is seldom observed, and may not be feasible in the present instance. We should probably be lucky if, instead of a single principle of division, we were able to operate with a few such principles, and the rule that classification should (*a*) be exclusive and (*b*) exhaustive may be impossible to follow quite faithfully. As regards the first part of it, obligations have a way of intertwining. Is adultery simply a form of promise-breaking, or is it a separate obligation? Is a parent's duty to cherish his children simply an instance of benevolence, or is it a distinct commandment? To such questions there is no end. As regards the second part of the rule, there is a moral aspect in most human behaviour, and there is some justification for regarding all the departments of any code of behaviour as a moralist's undoubted province. It is part of medical ethics whether a doctor should advertise, of business ethics whether a director should be able to get rid of his stock before the general public, of diplomatic ethics whether instructions should be followed scrupulously when their failure is inevitable and yet precisely what the individual diplomatist wants. It would also be a moralist's business to examine all the prohibited degrees of marriage.

A certain degree of overlapping, therefore, seems inevitable in this affair, and also an attempt, frequently rather arbitrary in its applications, to avoid questions of detail and to stick to general principles. Nevertheless, moral map-drawing is a highly instructive enterprise.

As we saw, certain distinguished moralists affirm that every voluntary obligation is an act of will that can be seen, by rational insight, to be appropriate to a given "situation," and indeed to be a moral implication of the situation in a way analogous to a logical implication. For convenience sake, I propose to confine this discussion to obligations that can plausibly be represented as voluntary, and have now to ask whether we can say anything in general about the type of situation that, in some sense, may be said to entail a voluntary obligation.

It is generally affirmed that such a situation is relational. This may perhaps be doubted if the meaning be that the morality of the action depends upon some specific relation *inside* the situation. Obviously, however, there must be a relation between the agent and his situation; and there may be other relations in addition.

Obviously, again, the relation between the agent and his situation must be one that justifies him in attempting to bring about some change, either by preventing a change in the situation (such prevention requiring the agent's intervention) or by altering the situation (or its development). That, however, is only another way of saying that the situation calls for action, and the really interesting question is whether we can say anything in general about situations that call for action.

Most people would hold, I think, that what justifies intervention in a situation is the improvement, or perhaps the probable improvement of the situation, and that the agent should intervene voluntarily when he has reason to believe that he can effect such improvement by voluntary action. Indeed, it seems evident that such improvement would be *a* reason that justified voluntary intervention, and that, in its absence, intervention could scarcely be justified. On the other hand, it might reasonably be maintained that not all voluntary actions designed to effect an improvement are moral (e.g. putting fresh coal on a feeble fire), and that there may be interminable debate concerning what is or is not an improvement. In particular we might "improve" a situation, if commendable, by completing it, as well as by introducing some new additional good, and we might effect an improvement by altering the external relations of the situation, even if such action did not improve but actually injured the situation internally. In view of these complications we cannot simple-mindedly classify all moral duties as forms of beneficence.

Another thing we might try to do would be to see if we could deduce any consequences of importance from the fact that at least one moral agent must participate in any moral situation.

So long as the analysis depended simply upon the possibility of voluntary intervention in a situation, a moral agent would simply mean a voluntary agent. Among such agents ordinary men and women would be included, but also supermen (if any), children, and some higher animals (unless, indeed, we defined volition in such a way that children and the higher animals were incapable of it). In the main, however, we suppose that a certain persistent level of volition is requisite in a moral agent, and exclude all sub-human creatures as being incapable of volition at this level. I shall assume then, without further discussion, that we are engaged in classifying obligations with which some man or woman is concerned. I shall not separately discuss the obligations of bodies of men, for these, I think, are, in the end, highly complicated obligations of the men who compose such bodies, and I do not know enough about the obligations of beings higher than men to begin to talk about them.

We cannot hold, however, that a man's obligations are always obligations to other men, for men have obligations towards children and towards other animals as well as (it may be) towards superhuman beings. Moral relationships, therefore, cannot always be those of some kind of human partnership, but there may, nevertheless, be necessarily something companionable in all of them. In general, we believe (although not perhaps on wholly impeccable grounds) that men have no moral duties whatsoever regarding inanimate things. If they have a duty, say, to preserve the beauties of nature, they have it (we are told) for the sake of themselves and other men, and not for the sake of inanimate beauty itself. If this be assumed, the lower limits of a possible moral relationship are defined by the possibility of suffering. It is a moral duty (I assert categorically) to prevent all unnecessary animal suffering, so far as men can prevent it. Consequently we can infer that all terrene moral obligations hold between a man and either himself or some companion, if only a companion in suffering.

Accordingly the conclusion emerges that moral obligations are entailed by a companionable or neighbourly relationship, and would seem to be designed to improve some companionable situation, provided that, under "improvement" we include the external as well as the internal companionable relationships, and leave a place for what I have called the "completion" of the situation as well as for the addition of benefit. Among companionable obligations we should, I think, distinguish between those that hold for all men as such (that is to say, for the agent himself and for *all* his fellows) and those that are more specialized, and hold for particular men in particular types of situation only. If this distinction be combined with the different types of "improvement" of a neighbourly situation, it should be possible to divide the major moral obligations, in terms of principle, on an intelligible plan; and I shall try to follow this six-fold method of subdivision. In the course of the attempt I shall restrict myself to those moral obligations that hold between men, that is to say between moral beings assumed to be morally responsible in the full sense, admitting that certain modifications, not necessarily easy, would be required if one of the companions were a child, an adolescent, a moron, an imbecile, or a mere animal.

(1) In a justly celebrated part of his moral theory, Kant (remembering his Pufendorf and his Rousseau) said that the supreme rule of all morality was to treat humanity, including oneself, always as an end, never as a mere means, and he explained in the course of his commentary that what was inculcated by this principle was universal respect for the dignity of man, oneself, or some other.

Here the first formulation seems defective. True, it does not assert the absurdity that we should never treat others as means, or ourselves as means to others. Anyone who is of service to another is, so far, a means; and plainly we do make use of the services of postmen, engine-drivers, and letter sorters. The business end of Kant's maxim, therefore, is the little word "merely." We should not use the postman *merely* as a means, or allow ourselves so to be used if we happen to be postmen. On the other hand, the little word "merely" is too feeble for its ethical office. We should not treat the postman *merely* as a means if we ever nodded to him at a football match; and one might nod to a slave. Bishop Berkeley, when in America, had his slaves baptized, and doubtless treated them with consideration; but the legal institution of slavery comes as near to treating humanity merely as a means as anything that can readily be imagined.

The vaguer formula of "treating humanity with respect" seems more satisfactory because, instead of attempting to define the minimum of proper respect, it is content merely to suggest the maximum. Hence it could not easily be reconciled with the doctrine that a slave's soul should be respected, although his posterior might be kicked with impunity. Certainly, it does not of itself inform us what indignities (if any) are licit and what illicit, why corporal punishment should be an indignity for a grown man but not for a schoolboy; and so forth. It formulates a standard, however, in terms of which such questions may be rationally discussed with some hope for their solution.

Some would say, no doubt, that certain men are entitled to no respect whatsoever. They are mere trash, white, black, or yellow, and are dangerous trash, in part, because they arouse vapid sentiment in others. Let them be hanged and buried in quick-lime. Let the memory of them be blotted out.

Even if there were such moral outlaws, however—and there are few among our fellows of whom we should say so much, although we may sometimes fear that, but for luck, the same might be said of ourselves—the conclusion would only be that we should respect all our fellows, except those who have completely forfeited neighbourly status. The obligation would still be a reasonable service among human companions, and is largely independent of the follies, the weakness, and the actual offences of any individual partner. The fool, the weakling, or the culprit is still one of us. He should not be treated like a dog, still less like a maggot, a weed, or a stench.

These Kantian maxims may be regarded as attempts to state the general basis of men's natural rights or to describe the foundations of natural justice. The former of these doctrines, it is true, seems to have passed the heyday of its plausibility, and the latter (as formerly observed) is apt not to be very precise. Nevertheless, they are important moral principles. The doctrine of natural rights has suffered from the friends who exaggerated it into a doctrine of inalienable, indefeasible rights antecedent to if not altogether independent of society, and consequently were easily outmanœuvred in debate. If, however, we state it in the form that every man has a moral claim upon his fellows for life, liberty, fraternity, and the absence of arbitrary inequality, we are stating a truism of some profundity which is applicable in principle to every human companionship. Indeed, a certain security for life and limb, so far as human watchfulness can attain such security, and the definite absence of arbitrary inequality may be regarded as obvious deductions from human fraternity, that is to say, from the companionable status of mankind. It may be doubtful, perhaps, whether the right to work, to marry, to be a parent, to be educated, to enjoy artistic treasures, can similarly be deduced, but there would not be much comradeship or much respect for humanity in any social system that sterilized any appreciable proportion of its members or refused a reasonable opportunity for self-development and social service to many or to the bulk of the alleged comrades.

Justice itself is too wide a term to be discussed very profitably.

According to some it comprises all moral obligations, and certainly we sometimes use the term to mean little more than the scrupulous pursuit of moral accuracy. Thus we condemn the tragic error of treating an innocent man as if he were guilty, and subjecting him to the detestation commonly meted out to malefactors in addition to any legal penalty, and we perceive that the attempt rigorously to avoid all moral irrelevance and decide strictly "on the merits" may be among the most difficult of human enterprises. According to others, justice is primarily equity or fairness between man and man. This duty, however, might itself be regarded as a corollary of moral accuracy, since if A and B are both treated "on their merits" there is bound to be fairness between them, while there is injustice, not equity, if they are treated equally but wrongfully; for example, if both are boiled in oil when neither should be. According to a third party, justice is essentially an affair of distribution—of penalties and rewards, of the means of consumption and of opportunities for production.

Argument should not be necessary when all that is to be proved is that every moral being is morally entitled to justice on the part of other moral beings, and should respect himself as one so entitled. The lessons to be drawn from this important truth, however, are much less apparent. Thus (regarding justice in the third of the above senses) some have argued that the distribution should be according to need, like rationing in wartime; others that food should be the reward of useful labour, so that a man should not eat if he does not work, and work profitably; others again that the distribution should be largely in terms of capacity to enjoy, so that we should not have to deplore the injustice to London clubmen when officers on leave drank their best port in a tumbler like so much beer. None of these deductions is wholly unreasonable; but they lead different ways and are not very easy to combine.

Nevertheless, the obligation to universal justice may lie at the roots of all human morality; for an obligation may be primary without being fitted to tell us the whole of our duty.

We are entitled, therefore, to include universal justice as one of the greatest of moral principles.

(2) The obligations which may be said to be obligations of completion seem for the most part to be circumscribed in their application to persons, and in so far as they deal with some particular person or group of persons, rather than with any other person or group, will be considered later. Here, however, it is convenient to pay further attention to the general thesis that all dereliction of duty is a kind of logical incoherence or formlessness so that what is morally wrong is really what is self-contradictory in moral action.

Such arguments are very familiar in moralistic literature. Suicide, we are told, is an act in which life contradicts itself, since the principle of life becomes the principle of death. Deliberate drunkenness is an abdication or contradiction of our critical faculties. Unnatural vice denies the natural boundaries of certain valuable functions. To break a promise is to make the alleged promise not a promise. To punish an innocent man is to deny his innocence, and at the same time to affirm it, since only the guilty can be punished.

I do not suppose that these, or other similar arguments, are at all convincing in detail. The particular argument against suicide would apply with equal logic to all self-sacrifice. The particular argument against drunkenness would apply to going to sleep. The particular argument against promise-breaking would also apply to every release from a promise. It is unnecessary, however, to examine such arguments *seriatim*, since there is plainly something wrong about the general principle upon which all of them are said to depend. What is self-contradictory cannot exist. It is nonsensical, and therefore impossible. But suicides, broken promises, drunkenness, and the like do undoubtedly occur.

It may be replied, no doubt, that nonsense may occur—in some confused human mind—and consequently (since volitions are defined by their aims) that nonsensical voluntary action is equally possible. That is true. Indeed, as we have seen, moral obligation presupposes *true* beliefs both about fact and about the morality of the fact; and true beliefs must always be consistent *inter se*. There cannot, however, be self-contradictory events, and what these arguments attempt to show is that "annulment," "abdication," and the like are instances of contradiction, and therefore wrong. No such conclusion is justified. There may be an obligation to rule, and later an obligation to abdicate; to condemn, and later to pardon. Inconsistency is quite another thing; and consistent evil-doing is perfectly possible.

Examining other general matters of completion, one might say that if any vows were made to humanity at large, in the way in which a doctor's Hippocratean oath may refer to suffering humanity wherever the doctor may chance to encounter it, the keeping of such vows would be an obligation of completion, and would be quite general. The completion, in this case, would be an obligation entailed by the temporal continuity necessary in all human action, and this general point will be discussed later in its connection with more specialized obligations.

Veracity is sometimes inculcated as a mere completion. The very meaning of speech, it is said, is to convey information. Therefore deceitful speech belies itself. Since, however, there may be legitimate occasions for deceit—even, perhaps for mere amusement, and, pretty obviously, where it is wrong to demand a truthful answer (as in matters properly secret like the ballot) this argument is inconclusive. On the other hand, it might reasonably be claimed that all companionship implies certain highly general fiduciary obligations without respect of persons.

We may suspect, I think, that many of the alleged duties of completion are rather a *definition* of a certain type of obligation than any proper justification of the obligation. Thus punishment may be by definition penal, that is to say inflicted upon an offender for an offence committed. If any action is to be called punishment it must have these characteristics; but the possession of such characteristics does not necessarily justify the action.

(3) When we think of universal duties, the duty of doing good to mankind occurs to all of us as one of the first and chief. The traditional name for this duty (in British ethics) was benevolence; but good works should be included as well as good will, and some moralists would therefore prefer to speak of beneficence. We should also include, on the negative side, non-malevolence and non-maleficence. For all this, the term philanthropy is also commonly used, and with reason.

It is sometimes supposed that a general indiscriminating benevolence as opposed to a "limited generosity" or to a "confined affection" is only a watery kindness—in brief, that philanthropy begins at home and seldom survives foreign travel. Such views have a certain plausibility. The very closeness of social cohesion in family, clan, township, or nation is apt to contract any wider affection, and men have been slow to learn, or have still refused to learn that a barbarian and a Scythian are a Semite's comrades, and the Semite a comrade of the Nordics.

Few can doubt, however, that the general moral obligation exists. Purposeless injury to any man, that is to say an injury not necessitated by some other and governing moral obligation is, morally speaking, a prohibited act among all human beings (to say nothing of other beings). The rule *Neminem laede*, in this sense, is quite universal, and does not depend upon any special relationship between particular men. Consider the major injuries one man can inflict upon another. He may kill him, weaken his health and strength, cause him suffering, slander him, cheat him, starve him of spiritual food. Can it be denied that every man, as such, has a certain definite claim upon his fellows for protection against all such injuries? I do not say we can straightway deduce the degree of effort, if any, that British subjects should devote towards the introduction of higher-class cinemas into Canton, towards improving the sanitation of villages in the Congo, or towards reducing the proportion of illiteracy in the Abyssinian army; but there are pretty obvious deductions regarding the opium and slave traffics.

Again, the negative marches with the positive. There is a positive duty of succour as well as a negative duty of abstention from injury. If it is wrong for any private man to put another private man's head in a gas oven (however useless the head), there is also a general moral duty, even officiously, to keep alive. There might, it is true, be merciful homicide, morally justifiable, and it is possible that certain communities are justified in practising a species of death-control in a humane fashion and in a regular, legal way; but we are not talking about obligations that can *never* be overridden upon sufficient moral grounds. The general moral duty of relieving human suffering, wherever encountered, of helping every man to stand on his own feet and to walk with his own legs, is a duty of philanthropy as well as of justice, and seems more fruitful in its obvious moral consequences on the latter ground than on the former.

(4) In discussing the obligations of universal justice I tried to show that the companionable relationship of human beings in itself implied a certain status of all the members, and a consequent moral obligation of each member towards every other. Clearly, however, this general relationship between all the members (who are sisters and brothers under their skins) is consistent with the existence of special companionable relationships and of moral obligations appropriate to these special relationships. A man may have obligations towards himself, towards his closer associates, towards benefactors, towards his social leaders, that he does not have towards any other human being indiscriminately. Such special moral obligations, however, are subordinate to universal justice in the sense that they should not directly or indirectly deny the companionable status of any other man.

If, for example, to borrow a Socratic phrase, each man has better (indeed unique) opportunities for tending his own soul, the duty of paying special heed to one's own moral development is a special duty of each towards himself in special; and there is no general injustice in the circumstance. Indeed, where there is any relevant moral inequality, it is an implication of bare justice that such inequality should be appropriately recognized in moral conduct. Many human differences, it is true, are morally irrelevant. Blondes and brunettes should both be truthful, and so should spinsters and married women, but it could not be inferred that married women have no special duties, in justice, towards their husbands or towards posterity that spinsters do not have. If what is morally equal should be treated equally, what is morally unequal by the same logic should be treated unequally.

The existence of moral duties towards oneself has been a subject of moral debate. A man, of course, is not his own companion, but he is a member of the company in the same sense as any other man, and should so regard himself in his moral action. He may, indeed, willingly submit to something he would not ask of another, but not to anything that any other, similarly situated, ought not to suffer willingly. To discriminate arbitrarily against oneself is quite as unjust as to discriminate arbitrarily against a companion. Among companions each companion counts independently, and therefore each should count himself.

It follows that the self-regarding aspect of every moral obligation is always morally relevant; and every obligation has a self-regarding aspect, sometimes secondary, and, so to say, retroactive in the agent's normal aims (as when he is trying to benefit some other without reflecting upon the effects of his generosity upon his own character), and sometimes primary (as when he is thinking about his own personal honour). As we shall see, special questions may arise, when the moral question is how far one should become one's own prudent beneficiary, but there is no general difficulty of a formal sort. Identity, it is true, is not a relation. Therefore nothing can be related to itself. The question, however, is not whether an obligation can be related to itself, but whether there may be an obligation towards oneself, and every human action *is* related to the agent, that is to something in the agent, say his future, which is not the particular action under dispute.

Let us turn, however, to special moral duties of an interpersonal sort.

Here it is clear that if any companionship is organized or even differentiated there will be special relationships between special sets of people as well as general relationships holding between all the companions as such. I do not say that all such relationships are exclusively moral. Division of labour, for example, may in the main be an economist's rather than a moralist's question. Nor do I say that in morality we have simply to accept our station, and deduce our moral duties (or many of them) from a completely docile acceptance of that station. On the contrary, questions of government and of other social organizations are themselves debatable territory in the moral field. It is evident, however, that whether the settled personal interrelations in any complicated companionship are natural or artificial, overorganized or underorganized, cast-iron or fluid, they are bound to involve special relationships between special persons. Such special relationships commonly imply special moral duties, and their validity could be denied only if it were conceivable that the specialized interpersonal relationships among human companions had no specialized bearing whatsoever upon men's moral obligations.

Property is not a purely moral question, but a certain exclusiveness for personal use is requisite with regard to food, clothing, and shelter. Therefore, even if friends should in some sense have all things in common they could not have an indiscriminate claim to everything, and the discrimination would involve moral questions. The sex difference among good companions affects human conduct in the important matters of decency, cohabitation, and the continuance of the species, and it would be an odd system of ethics that did not recognize that quite special moral obligations arose in consequence. Again, wherever leadership is justified, or even accepted in a way that is not wholly spineless and wrong, special duties of allegiance arise.

In general, wherever there are hierarchical interpersonal relationships and wherever, without sub- or super-ordination, the principle of specialized social solidarity prevails (local, regional, professional, or whatever it may be), there moral obligations arise of a special kind and the justification of such principles themselves, as well as the duties implied in the principles is, in part (and frequently in its principal part) a moral question. In certain cases, it is true, there may be no appreciable moral difference. It may be just as reprehensible to poison a tramp as to poison a husband or a mayor. In other cases, the difference may be of degree. A certain fidelity is incumbent upon all towards all, or at any rate towards all who have not proved themselves utterly faithless. So is a certain readiness to forgive; but among close companions a stronger loyalty is reasonable and just. It would not, however, be true to say that all marital or filial duties belong to either of the above classes.

(5) Obligations of completion for the most part specify particular persons rather than others. Thus only offenders of a given type should be punished in a given appropriate way, and then by the proper punitive body, not by anyone indiscriminately. Gratitude is not a duty that everybody owes to everybody, but a special obligation of M or N towards X or Y. And so forth. As we have seen, specification towards particular persons is not logically inevitable in all duties of completion, but it occurs so frequently that the present subdivision is the natural place for examining such obligations. Most of these obligations, again, are strictly inter-personal, although not quite all of them. Thus one cannot either be grateful to oneself or make a promise to oneself; but although one cannot, strictly speaking, make a promise to a dog or to a horse, one can very well be grateful to these animals.

In so far as moral completion is not determined simply by avoidance of ethical nullity through internal self-contradiction

—a case already examined—it is largely a matter of time. Thus promise-keeping, in the Scots phrase, *implements* at a later date the promise given at an earlier date. Similarly gratitude, and, in general, all obligations of requital are, in an essential part of them, retrospective.

Clearly, the relative permanence of human life, brief as it is, involves some such obligations. There are very few moral situations in which the agent makes a completely fresh start; for moral aims are seldom restricted to the present or to the proximate future, and they count upon a certain stability and calculable regularity, not in Nature only, but also in ourselves and in our fellows. Mutual confidence over a relatively prolonged period is necessary for moral companionship. Therefore, quite apart from any explicit promise, M or N should take account of the reasonable expectations of X or Y, especially when their partnership is close. M need not take account of X's unreasonable expectations, although he should usually take some account even of these if he is really a loyal and considerate companion; and certainly he may change his mind. If, however, he changes his mind he ought, at the very least, to explain the matter to X.

The special moral obligation of a promise is much more detailed. When M gives his promise to X, he does not merely arouse reasonable expectations in X, thus affecting X's response to his environment, or merely state his intentions. He pledges himself to a particular future action on which X may count, and such a pledge is a very special kind of moral act, whether or not it has the force of a legal covenant enforceable by penalties.

This obligation has two parts, its giving and its keeping. As regards the first part, certain promises should never be given; for they are foolish or worse. Even in such cases, however, it seems plain that M is not morally at liberty to ignore his former promise altogether, although he would be a scoundrel if he kept it; and if the giving of the promise is not unjustifiable, the keeping of it is an obligation of completion. The fulfilment of this obligation, no doubt, is not always M's duty. The situation may change in a relevant and wholly unexpected way, as when M, having promised to marry X, finds to his dismay that he is suffering from tuberculosis; and a morally perplexing situation arises when X offers to release M, or when it is clear that X's part of the bargain is not going to be kept. Nevertheless, literal completion of a promise justly given is usually M's duty, and M's subsequent actions, if he acts morally in the relevant situation, are always affected by the circumstance that he has given his word.

Another very important class of obligations of completion that apply in special to particular persons rather than to others may be generally described as obligations of requital. Here the obvious instances are, on the positive side, gratitude and reward, on the negative side, resentment and punishment.

If it be insisted that all moral obligations are voluntary, difficulties arise regarding the first member of each of these pairs; but there are graver ethical difficulties regarding all of them.

As regards the first pair, there is, of course, no moral difficulty about doing good to anyone, but it is not quite so clear that the *returning* of good for good is a special duty, and we may perhaps suspect that the basis of the obligation is the employment of the natural and pleasing but highly selective impulse of gratitude to supplement wider benevolent tendencies. Both gratitude in general, and the particular species of it called reward, are frequently held to be dangerous to the recipient, on the ground that duty should be disinterested and is therefore imperilled by the prospect of recompense; and many prefer an ethically neutral physical universe to an ethically partial one, because they believe it is better that the rain should not discriminate between just and unjust than that righteousness should help the crops and bring immunity from disease.

It does not follow, however, that an ethically neutral *society* is commendable. Gratitude, unless smirched by the too lively expectation of favours to come, is a joy to the giver if a peril to the receiver, and it is plausible to argue that, in an imperfect world, a society that honours righteousness even with ribbons and with gold is expressing a state of soul far superior in mankind to any ethical neutrality, however childish and primitive its utterance may sometimes be.

Resentment and punishment, however, are even more perplexing. Even if a society that is resentful of wrong-doing and interposes artificial obstacles in the way of the prosperity of the wicked earns in consequence a certain moral commendation, it is not at all obvious, in the abstract, that evil should be requited with evil, or that the returning of good for evil, without any side-glances at the coals of hell, is not invariably a higher moral obligation. If, however, we hold that evil should be requited with good (although not in the way of honouring evil) except in the case of legitimate punishment, we obviously cannot justify punishment *on the ground of requital*, and would have to justify it as a necessity, or as a warning, or as a compulsory prelude to expiation, or as a combination of these.

In short, the special obligation of requital as such seems precariously based, although few would argue that there is a moral obligation to treat evil-doers in all respects precisely as others should be treated. It should also go without the saying that the particular form of appropriate requital can hardly be determined on any plausible abstract principle. A few would argue that capital punishment is peculiarly appropriate to the crime of murder, for death, they think, is incommensurably the greatest of all evils; therefore (they say) nothing less than a life should be exacted for a life. The very idea of a tooth for a tooth, however, is fitted only to provide patter for a Victorian librettist, although the vague proposition that a trivial offence should not receive severe requital may be sensible enough.

Nevertheless, if penal action is justified, punishment for wrong-doing is an obligation of completion once the wrong is known to be done, and, *if* it is justified, it is not clear how

mercy and pardon could be an overriding obligation. Even
Hobbes saw a difficulty here. "As having only humane ideas,"
Hobbes, in advance of his age, declared that punishment was
only a hostile act unless it was designed for future security
or other benefit. He admitted, however, that at the Last Judgment, when nobody could sin any more, it might be inevitable that the high Gods should exact the penalty they had
ordained.

It seems sometimes to be held that all moral obligations are
obligations of requital, on the ground that to treat a man morally
is just to treat him according to his deserts. The notion of
desert, however, is wholly retrospective and therefore could
not exhaust the future-regarding possibilities of moral obligation. All that the proposition could come to would be that
so far as moral obligations are properly retrospective, they
should be retrospectively just.

(6) Certain obligations of benevolence might be regarded
as obligations of completion, for many actions once begun
are such that they convey no benefit until they are fully accomplished. Again, it should not be held that any obligation of
benevolence in special is independent of the general duties
of justice, logical intelligibility, or universal philanthropy
already discussed, or of the special duties of particularized
justice or of particularized completion. This notwithstanding,
there remains an important place for special or non-universal
obligations of benevolence.

Philanthropy and benevolence are usually defined as well-
wishing and well-doing to *others*, and therefore as quite distinct
from prudence and self-help. Beneficence, however, need
contain no such restriction, and when we are dealing, as at
present, with moral obligations whose basis is the doing of
good to some particular man or class of men in particular
rather to any man indiscriminately, it seems clear that the
doing of good to oneself belongs to this category.

Thus self-preservation, self-help, self-development, and self-
culture are commonly regarded as possible moral obligations,

although not in the sense that they must override moral obligations to others. Certainly it might be argued that such obligations, although valid, are wholly subordinate. On this view a man should take care of his own life, health, liberty, and education, not for their own sakes, but simply for the ulterior purpose of benefiting his clan, nation, or species. This extreme view, however, is self-contradictory. To act for the benefit of a group of which the agent himself is a member, is to act, in part, for the agent's own sake, unless (which is impossible) the group counts for everything and its members for nothing. Moreover, as we have seen, if self-help on the part of each is the most efficient means of attaining the welfare of all, self-help is a very definite obligation for the public-spirited.

Thus it might quite consistently be argued that if A is qualified for a certain post, he ought to apply for it even if he knows that another candidate B is a better man for the job. It is not A's business to make the appointment, but it is A's business to take advantage of all legitimate opportunities to serve others and also to serve himself. Again, it is at least a tenable view that although a man who wraps himself up in self-culture so completely as to hide all other human obligations is a sort of moral monster, a man who will not read or write or paint except in so far as he believes himself to be doing a public service is a moral fool.

It is sometimes held that because there is no need of moral incentives towards self-help, self-help cannot be a moral duty. It is meritorious to do one's duty, but where is the merit in abstaining from suicide when at least nine men out of ten cling to life with the most desperate assiduity?

This view elicits the obvious reply that what, under normal circumstances, is not a duty becomes a duty when our inclinations lead the other way. When it takes more pluck to live than to die there may be a moral duty to try to live. Again, it is held that prudence is a moral duty, not because it is a moral duty to look after "number one," but because it is a moral duty to do so with vigilant foresight, taking heed against rashness and impulsive folly.

This reply, although not wholly indisputable, may be admitted to meet the premisses of the argument, but these premisses themselves are false. It is impossible to prove that a moral obligation does not exist, simply because the obligatory action might readily be performed upon non-moral grounds. If strong natural impulses on the whole coincided with morality, where is the moral or any other objection?

Obligations to self-benefit, therefore, may very well be moral, and so may obligations to give priority of benefit to certain types of people, or otherwise for the philanthropist to discriminate between his beneficiaries. One such ground is the amount of probable benefit, another the kind of benefit. Hence the sick have claims that the hale do not have, and the hungry have special claims upon their well-fed neighbours. Again, the capacities of the agent are relevant to the amount of benefit he can bestow. If his beneficial actions have a greater effect upon near neighbours than upon persons more remotely situated, his fruitful beneficence is specialized in consequence.

In general it is not unreasonable to argue on these grounds that near companions have greater claims upon a man's beneficence than others have. If we should be slow to think evil of any man, we should be slower still to think it of a friend. If we should let no one down, we should be specially careful not to let down a pal. Such narrower loyalties may be corrupted into an anti-social code, more dangerous even than naked selfishness; but *corruptio optimi pessima*. The abuse of a good thing is no proof of its universal badness.

We should beware, however, of treating as necessarily unique what need not be treated so. Thus, on the official family system in most reputedly Christian countries, the special duties of parents towards their children, or of children towards their parents, may well seem unique in their kind; and so they are, in so far as the family system is unique. Clearly, however, other systems are possible. Plato, in his

Republic, would have entrusted the education and care of children to the *polis*, and would have taken elaborate precautions to prevent parents from knowing who their own children were. The care and upbringing of children would therefore be somebody's business and would imply special duties, but it would not be true that paternity as such implied any special duties of parents towards their own children rather than towards the children of others, or that children have the duty of honouring or obeying their parents in any special sense. Even within the family system the particular moral duties of the parties remain *sub judice* from age to age, although the boldest innovators would not maintain that there are no special obligations in this affair; and the search for wider ethical principles in all such matters is itself a convincing proof of the vitality of moral theory.

XI

SOME PROBLEMS ABOUT OBLIGATION

In this section I mean to discuss three problems that have a certain although not a very close mutual connection. These problems are (1) whether all moral obligations are matters of principle or whether even the most Lesbian rule of morality must often be too inflexible for many particular cases, (2) the extent to which moral principles should yield determinate guidance, and (3) more generally, the boundary between moral obligation and other human actions (principally voluntary) that are commendable in some regards, but are beyond the province of ethics. (The third problem is an old friend; but he may now have a new dress.)

(1) It would be generally agreed that if some particular moral obligation is our duty, that is, is the decisive moral obligation in some particular case, and if that duty is also completely determinate (like debt-paying, the keeping of a clear promise, or the telling of the simple truth), then the moral agent has only to apply his general rule and he will know, in detail, how to act. It is also argued, however, that much of our duty is far more intricate, and that the niceties of the particular case must very often be decided by trained moral perception and not by the juridical application, *in foro conscientiae*, of general rules. As in the natural world so in the moral. Perception acquaints us with what is individual, or else individuality escapes us. Logic and general rules are too abstract for this office. But moral problems are problems of life itself, and moral principles also are too abstract to insinuate themselves into the particularity of life and change.

It is safest to express this view in Greek, ἐν τῇ αἰσθήσει ἡ κρίσις. The English of it, "the decision rests with perception," is far too ambiguous and far too disputable to be comforting;

but we might perhaps admit that most decisions, moral or non-moral, require gumption.

(a) We need perception to inform us that there *is* a particular case, i.e. that the instance exists and that its actual nature is such and such. This inevitable circumstance, however, tells us only that we have to deal with actual situations, and not that the things we ought to do about them, our moral obligations regarding them, are themselves perceptual.

Moral situations deal with human factors, and very largely with the minds of men. Much of the relevant "perception," indeed, includes the sympathetic understanding of our fellows and, some would boldly add, a sort of "sympathy" with ourselves. Such sympathy may reasonably be classed with perception, although, as the phrase "sympathetic understanding" shows, thinking has something to do with it also. M. Bergson would say that although "intuition" (i.e. perception) and intelligence commingle in nearly all human activities they are utterly distinct in their nature, and he would add that "intuition" must preponderate in all the affairs of life. He and his followers prefer to speak of *two* moralities, the one of rule, conservatism, and intellectual principle, the other of romance, of aspiration, and of sympathy with the imponderables in all human doings.

The interest and importance of such contentions should be beyond dispute. I submit, however, that what they prove is the delicacy of our acquaintance with psychical matter of fact, and not the impotence of moral principles arising out of these delicate facts.

(b) Everyone agrees that the art of expressing principles in their full generality and without irrelevance is an expert's business requiring special training. Most competent people argue logically about the matters in which they are competent, but they would be very unwise if they attempted to formulate their views in correct logical dress without a logician's special training. Consequently there is only the appearance of paradox in Lord Mansfield's advice to the colonial governor who had gumption but had had no legal training, namely, to give his decisions boldly because they were almost sure to be right, but not to give his reasons since he would then become the experts' prey. The expression of moral principles is the business of moralists, not of honest men; but an honest man grasps and follows moral principles whether or not he has had practice in moral conveyancing.

(c) Another suggestion sometimes made is that although morality is not simply a type of skill, it is always a sort of practical efficiency. Practical efficiency, however, can never afford to proceed merely by rule, and we are reminded of the difference (in old-fashioned warfare) between the type of general who directed his troops by trained perception on the battlefield, and the type of general who relied upon his recollection of manuals of the military art. The former type of general, it is suggested, always won.

What this argument really proves, however, is the importance of *quick* thinking on the battlefield. If perception is contrasted with thinking, it is likewise contrasted with quick thinking. The quick-thinking general's decisions become the delight of subsequent military critics, who find no difficulty in naming the eternal principles of warfare he employed.

(d) The suggestions may be made that perception should supplement the indeterminateness of many moral obligations, and again that although all moral obligations are matters of general principle, there may be no sufficient principle to decide the *conflicts* between obligations, so that, where such a conflict exists, the decision should be left to perception. Both these matters will be discussed more fully later. For the present it may be sufficient to deal with them summarily. Regarding the first it would have to be proved that whatever is left indeterminate in the obligation is moral at all. If the obligation, for example, is to give an adequate subscription to the local hospital, it may be morally indifferent whether the actual subscription is ten pounds or ten guineas. Regarding the second it seems preposterous to argue that any mysterious faculty of divination is competent to reconcile or to override warring principles, and it is entirely arbitrary to call such a faculty "perception."

The point of substance regarding all such arguments is surely that any moral decision, if valid, is implicitly general. If a given moral being has a certain obligation in a certain situation, *every* moral being would have the same obligation unless his situation differed in some morally relevant way. This statement may be a truism; but even truisms cannot be neglected without serious risk. The penalty for neglecting this particular truism is the necessity for a prolonged debate that has no justification except the neglect of the truism.

(2) Moral obligations, therefore, are general in their very nature. An unprincipled moral obligation is a contradiction in terms. This truism, however, does not settle the debatable ethical question concerning the extent to which such obligations give specific practical guidance.

Our obligations are practical, that is to say deal with men's rightful practice, and practice consists of particular, completely determinate actions. Again, morality should not compete with anything else. We may indeed admire and in certain ways commend wicked conduct. "A villain, but with something great about him," "A scamp, but a pleasing scamp," are quite defensible statements; but if an action is definitely wrong in the moral way, it is definitely unjustifiable whether or not certain of its features evoke admiration.

Hence it is sometimes inferred that "casuistry" in the sense of determinate application to particular cases is the goal of ethics, and that moral principles are woolly or negligible if they do not determine our particular actions in detail. This consequence, however, is peculiarly disputable. To apply to particular cases is one thing, to determine such cases in all their detail is quite another thing, and the alleged consequence would not follow even on a thoroughly legalistic view of ethics. Scottish lawyers, for instance, distinguish between ordinances, regulations, and cases. Regulations must conform to their governing ordinances, but are seldom simple deductions from the ordinances. The ordinances apply to but do not exhaust the regulations. The particular cases, again, must conform to the regulations, but few regulations exhaust the actual complexity of their instances.

Accordingly, if objections to such "casuistry" are well founded, they should not be based on the view that casuistry is all too legal to be ethically sound. Case-morality may indeed be a poor sort of ethical method, and good moral laws may be extracted with difficulty from hard moral cases. It may further be true that no official of any ecclesiastical or other such body is a good judge of other men's morals, and that there should be no such thing as an extra-legal judiciary with powers of absolution and of penance. Such attempts at moral administration, again, may be abused in the way that is incident to positive law. There are few rules that can never be used for purposes of obstruction or of evasion, and tutiorism, probabilism, and probabiliorism—that is to say clinging to rules for safety's sake, relying on one favourable authority, or upon a bare majority of authorities—may deserve some of the hard things that are said of them by persons who do not realize the difficulties of any honest priest whose professional office involves the giving of spiritual advice.

Nevertheless, *abusus non tollit usum*. Casuistry, in the general sense of the application of ethical principles to particular cases is surely quite unexceptionable, and hard cases should at least put moralists upon their mettle. A general charge of over-minuteness, again, is entirely worthless unless it is possible to explain with clarity where and why over-minuteness occurs. If the wrangles of Catholic doctors regarding what is or is not "water" for baptism, or the disputes of Jews and Scotch Presbyterians regarding sabbatarianism have a ludicrous appearance, it is necessary to give a reason why such squabbles have nothing to do with principles and are not the inevitable consequence of taking principles seriously and attempting to live seriously by them.

In general, it seems clear that moral obligations do apply to practice and that such application is a matter of ordinary logical deduction. If, however (to follow the legal analogy already suggested), all moral principles are of the nature of general ordinances rather than of specific regulations, they may well give decisive but incomplete guidance in practice, and the degree of specific guidance they afford may very well differ in different instances and classes of instances.

Some such distinction seems inevitable. Thus industry may be a moral obligation (and commonly is so unless the cause is bad). And negligence may be culpable. Neither industry nor any other moral quality, however, will, for example, tell a doctor what to do, that is to say, make a correct diagnosis and prescribe with skill. In short, medicine or any other useful art is *not* a kind of applied ethics, and in so far as it should be morally governed, the government permits great local autonomy. The separation of hygiene, medicine, eugenics, economics, civics, and politics from ethics is indeed one of the principal lessons modern man has learned. He should not model his moral code upon the Book of Leviticus. Yet if these discoveries (as we believe) enfranchize ethics instead of banishing it, the charter of emancipation should be able to state its reasons. Again, since few (if any) actions have no moral bearing (at least remote), and since so many of them have a bearing upon health, economics, and the like, it seems inevitable that the general line of division between moral and extra-moral specification of conduct should be of the type we have described.

Moral principles, then, are general, applicable to practice, and (we hold) superior to all others in the sense that *de jure* they do not compete with any others, although they frankly admit that other principles are and should be practical guides, If moral principles, besides being clear and clearly applicable. fully determine the essentials of any given action there is nothing more to be said. The truthful witness of our former illustration may have but to answer "Yes." In that case his duty is completely determinate. His duty, however, may be to give an elaborate narrative, and there may be many alternative ways of conveying a true impression regarding the subject of his examination. On the whole, however, the obligation of veracity is a clear instance of a determinate obligation.

On the other hand, many moral obligations are much less determinate. Generosity, for example, is such an obligation, but there is considerable latitude regarding the time, the type, the subject, and other relevant particulars of the generous act. It would be a complete mistake, however, to infer that generosity is less of a duty than veracity because it is, in these ways, less determinate. The "latitude" in question is not a sign of weakness in the obligation. Instead it indicates a certain width of range in place of a narrow restriction; and the same type of difference might occur within a single class of obligations. For example, the promise, "I shall visit you one of these days in your nursing home," is not less of a promise, or less binding than the promise, "I shall visit you next Thursday at 2.45 in your nursing home"; but it is much less determinate.

(3) According to the doctrine of absolute legal sovereignty all the actions of every legal citizen are *subject* to the law, but nobody infers in consequence that the law directs every detail of every citizen's action, or indeed that it explicitly directs very many actions. Similarly, the fact that all human actions are subject to morality does not tell us much about the degree of specific guidance that morality can afford. On the other hand, law and morality, among their other differences, include the very important difference that, in theory at least, an absolute legal sovereign may decree the legality or illegality of any human action whatsoever, while morality, in theory or otherwise, has no such powers. In law, the will of the legislator has no superior, and is not *legally* bound to distinguish between *mala in se* and *mala prohibita* or even to refrain from enjoining the commission of *mala in se*. (The boundaries of politic, or feasible, or decent, or commendable legislation are, of course, quite another matter.)

In morality there is no such omnicompetence, official or otherwise. An act of will—a promise, say—may create a situation that has moral implications, and so, consequentially, may create obligations that would not have existed otherwise; but no act of will can make moral obligations to be other than they are, can declare the morally relevant to be irrelevant, the good to be indifferent, or the indifferent to be evil.

Hence, in a rather special sense, we have to distinguish between considerations that in their own nature are moral, and considerations that, in their own nature, are extra-moral, and we have already seen that if this question is approached from the side of virtue the answer to it does not readily emerge. We approve, admire, esteem, and respond sympathetically to virtue and moral character, but we also admire and esteem other personal qualities; for virtue does not have a monopoly of what we call noble or splendid or fine, and neither Aristotle nor Hume was able effectively to distinguish between what was morally admirable and what was admirable in some other way. (Indeed, Aristotle did not try, and Hume in effect abandoned the problem with a shrug of his massive shoulders.) We can say indeed that moral nobility is shown in moral matters; but that is scarcely an instructive statement unless we can tell, independently, what moral matters are. And the usual answer would be, "Matters of duty."

It would be difficult, again, to find a satisfactory standard of distinguishing by reference to the magnitude of the issues involved. It may be plausible to suggest that morality deals with great manners, not with small, with the chief aims of life and not with lesser aims, but the plausibility disappears on closer examination. After all, morality may deal with small matters. *Parva moralia* are still *parva moralia*; and beauty, science, and historical greatness cannot be accounted small yet do not seem to imply indisputable moral standards. They also appear to be the chief ends of many human lives, although this circumstance does not transform them into moral ends.

An ethics of benefit and well-being is confronted with the same problem. Obviously, beneficial action cannot forthwith be identified with moral action, since merely natural agencies like sunshine and shower may well be beneficial to humanity. At this point, however, it is usual to explain that morality applies only to voluntary action at a human and high-grade level. This view, as we have seen, contains its own special difficulties; but it is at least a plausible hypothesis.

Assume, then, that morality deals either with willed benefits, or with the omission to will benefits that might be willed. Could we then say that anything relevant to voluntary human action is *ipso facto* a part of morality?

Certainly, it is reasonable to hold that every voluntary action is subject to morality, that is to say should conform to morality and might raise or perhaps always does raise some moral question. On the other hand, aesthetic, economic, political, and other such actions may also be voluntary. Consequently, the mere fact that an action is voluntary does not of itself enable us to distinguish between what is and is not morality's special business.

At this point several additional explanations are commonly offered. It may be said (*a*) that a voluntary act is moralized when it is beneficial to others, (*b*) when it is beneficial to society, (*c*) when it conveys the maximum possible benefit, (*d*) when it conveys the maximum probable benefit.

None of these additional explanations is acceptable as it stands, for no action could properly be said to be moralized if the benefit were (as we say) an *accidental* consequence of the volition. Judas Iscariot, by a voluntary act of treachery, may have conveyed the greatest possible benefit to the human race; but his treachery is not morally commendable on that account. If, however, instead of saying that a moral action is voluntary and is beneficial in some particular way, we said that this particular species of benefit was the *aim* of the voluntary action, we should avoid the objection from accidental consequence and should also have specified something in the

nature of the volition that made the volitional character of
morality intelligible.

An interesting point in this analysis is that, according to it,
a certain *motive* is the sole and the sufficient moralizing circumstance, although both the utilitarians and the new intuitionists maintain that motive has nothing to do with the morality
of voluntary actions. These domestic disputes, however, need
not concern us here, and I think there is substance as well as
prima facie plausibility in the contention that a voluntary action
is moralized if and so far as it aims at any benefit other than a
benefit merely selfish.

Such a proposition, it is true, could be only the beginning,
not the completion, of moral enquiry, but it is the rudiments
of the subject that are now in question. We are asking what
makes an action moral and not, at the moment, what makes it
morally better or worse, decisively right or decisively wrong.
In order to examine the latter questions we should have to
consider whose benefit should be aimed at much more fully
than the proviso against utter selfishness insures. We should
also have to consider how much benefit is aimed at, and of
what sort, as well as other questions of the same kind. We
should have to examine vexed questions regarding the efficiency
and scope of our voluntary aims. The legitimacy of these
questions, however, and the necessity for examining them
are not at all contradictory to the opinion that the rudiments
of the distinction between moral and non-moral are contained
in the very simple proposition mentioned above.

More in detail, it does not seem difficult to meet objections
based on the fact that voluntary actions of an economic,
political, therapeutic, or aesthetic kind may well be beneficial.
The contention is simply that if and so far as anyone aims at
a benefit not merely selfish, his action contains the rudiments
at least of morality, and that if and so far as he does not do
so when he might his action is immoral, not merely non-
moral. The presence of the aim is the moralizing circumstance,
however true it may be that the development and execution

of the aim is extra-moral in the sense that it does not spring from morality alone.

It would seem that if and so far as morality is a high-grade voluntary affair an ethic of benefit may be able to distinguish between moral and non-moral in an intelligible way. Even so, however, it has to be noted that if the simplest description of this difference in these terms is at all similar to the formula I have suggested, certain components of any such simple formula are not themselves matter of mere benefit. The benevolent motive involved is not itself another benefit among others, and since selfish benefits are genuine benefits, the proviso against mere selfishness is itself extra-beneficial.

Indeed, the formula amalgamates considerations of justice and of a morally virtuous motive with benefit. Exponents of any such formula, therefore, have to meet the objection that there may be virtuous motives other than philanthropy, extra-beneficial moral considerations other than those of justice, and that all such motives and standards are *ex hypothesi* moral. Even if everything was moral that the formula included, it need not include *all* that is morally relevant. Therefore it may be held that if virtue has to fall back upon its reserves, duty and benefit, for an adequate definition, and if benefit has to rely in the end both upon virtue and upon duty, it would seem that duty is the final arbiter in all such attempts at definition.

If we ask, however, whether there are any clear boundaries between moral obligations, on the one hand, and, on the other hand, extra-moral considerations that may reasonably determine human action, I do not see that we are in a better condition than formerly to expect any final and completely satisfactory answer. Non-contradiction and the principle, "if everybody were to do this," pretty certainly would not suffice, and I need not discuss these questions all over again. If there were any general formula for duty as such, it would probably be an implication of companionable relationship; but it does not seem to me to be at all likely that anyone could distinguish the moral from the extra-moral parts of the companionable relationship from one another upon grounds that were themselves derived from that relationship.

If moral obligation were something entirely unique, and if this unique thing could also be readily identified, it should be feasible, although perhaps tedious, to discover, by patient inspection, what relationships were attended by moral obligation and what were not. From the list of moral obligations so obtained it might subsequently be possible to employ a sort of summary induction, and obtain an adequate shortish formula for them all. The mixed formula regarding intended and unselfish benefit is the best in this kind I can think of; but I do not think it is adequate. If anyone knows he can always distinguish between what is and is not a matter of conscience, I can only say that he is more fortunate than I am, or (what is much more likely) that he is morally a better man. I do not suggest that my own moral experience does not seem to indicate something unique and (I dare say) uniquely authoritative in the obligatoriness of many clear matters of conscience. The fact, however, that some unique attribute frequently manifests itself with the utmost clearness is no sort of proof that it is always manifest if it is genuine at all.

XII

DUTY AND BENEFIT: A RESTRICTED DISCUSSION

MANY attempts have been made to show that morality, in the last analysis, is based entirely upon benefit on the general ground that enlightened philanthropy is the only intelligible moral principle, and that philanthropy is always the doing of good to mankind. On this view, virtue would be a philanthropic disposition, nothing more and nothing less, and duty would consist of philanthropic acts, or, more precisely, of acts that were more philanthropic than any others.

Some utilitarians and a few others explained in detail that philozoism or philopsychism would be a more accurate term than philanthropy, since human morality extended beyond mankind to all suffering fellow-creatures. This extension of the area of human morality, however, would not affect the general principle that moral distinctions depended entirely upon the beneficence of human character and human action.

An examination of the contention that virtue and duty depend exclusively upon potential benefit may appropriately be deferred to the third part of the present enquiry when the general subject of an ethic of benefit will be discussed. In the present place, however, it is convenient to consider the less intransigent doctrine that the prospect of benefit is *one* of the essentials of anything moral. To say this is of course to say a great deal more than simply to affirm that there *are* moral duties of beneficence. It is to assert that *nothing* unbenevolent could be moral whether or not beneficence is the primary object of some given obligation (say, of justice) or of some given feature of moral character (say, chastity). It will further be convenient to restrict the discussion to our moral obligations (principally voluntary) since these obligations, after all, are our present theme.

This restricted question may, for all I know to the contrary, be a very small thing and perhaps theoretically innocuous. At any rate, an affirmative answer would not disturb many who are most anxious to dispute the general view that ethics might be based upon benefit alone.

For example, John Grote and Mr. Ross are among the most strenuous opponents of mere agathopoeics in ethics that one could possibly select. According to Grote, utilitarianism, being a "partial system of morality," was "unable to face the real difficulties of ethics" (*Examination of the Utilitarian Philosophy*, p. 123). Since it was preoccupied with benefit and with philanthropy, to the exclusion of all else, it was unable, Grote held, to give any tenable account either of virtue or of duty, and so he thought that "the man without moral philosophy" (*ibid.*) was very often a better moralist than many of his would-be teachers. Yet Grote admitted (and indeed strongly asserted) that "the action of the Creator [and of all other moral beings] would not have been reasonable had it not been with a view to good and happiness" (*op. cit.*, p. 82). Mr. Ross, again, attempts to prove that the right act need not be the best, or, in his language, that duty need not be "optimific"; but he claims to be "perhaps certain" that duty is "bonific" (*R.G.*, p. 36). In other words, he holds that although the better part may be wrong, a bad part "perhaps certainly" cannot be right. Since the lesser of two evils (when there is no third possibility) is presumably to be accounted a "good," the last clause in this statement is less startling than it may seem.

Assuming, then, that "benefit" may be only the diminution of evil (in cases in which a preponderance of evil is unavoidable), we have to ask whether benefit is a *sine qua non* of every moral action, and I shall begin by considering a pair of troublesome preliminaries, viz. the time-factor in these matters (in one of its aspects), and the question whether we should talk about actual or about intended benefit. As I have said, however, I am restricting the discussion, in the main, to voluntary moral obligations, and that restriction may ease the burden of theory in the present place, although it may increase the burden elsewhere.

Every act of will is future-regarding; for only the future is alterable. It does not follow, however, that all the benefits a man may seek are wholly in the future, in the sense that they are entirely independent, as benefits, of what has gone before. Thus it might be argued that if a volition is directed towards the completion of a process already begun, and if the entire completed process is the genuine benefit at stake, the retrospective aim of the volition is just as important as the prospective. Again, it seems plain that if we ask what good is done, or is likely to be done, by such and such an action, the good *in* the action should be included as well as the (future) good that comes *from* the action. The utilitarians made a mistake when they treated moral action as a mere means to a good beyond itself. On their own theory there is pleasure in philanthropic action as well as in the subsequent reception of pleasant benefits, and all these pleasures should have been included in sound utilitarian book-keeping.

The other troublesome preliminary is our old friend the relation of actual to intended benefit. Clearly, there may be a very great difference indeed between the results that are actually attained and the results that are aimed at, even on the part of sensible people who know what they are about; and it is quite reasonable to hold, for instance, that, in the main, those who try to do their duty attain more unintended good and less unintended evil than those who are either careless about their duty or deliberately hostile to morality.

As we have seen, however, it is quite impossible morally to commend the unintended good that may spring from intended evil. Consequently, unless the intention to achieve benefit is present it would seem impossible to defend the view that benefit is a *sine qua non* of every commendable moral action. The intention may not be sufficient, and frequently is not, but the point is that its presence is necessary in anything that can properly be called a (voluntary) moral obligation.

Since we never know for certain what results will actually occur, such intended benefit can only be probable; and certainly it may be argued that a man who does good is a better person than one who tries to do it and fails. If he is not *morally* better, we are inclined to say, so much the worse for morality. It is very unplausible to allege that trying to do good is itself the greatest good of all. For the time being, however, we are only concerned with the proposition that the attempt to do good is essential to any morally commendable action, and are not considering what else may be requisite.

Many philosophers claim not merely (what few, if any dispute) that there *are* moral obligations to do good, but that the doing of good is self-evidently essential to any moral obligation. The latter proposition, however, is disputed on various grounds. One such ground would be the assertion that there is no such thing as self-evidence. What is called "self-evident" (it may be thought) is not really evident in itself, irrespective of anything outside itself, but is a brief expression of the consilience and as Dr. Johnson would say of the conglobulation of *all* the relevant evidence in all attested human experience. Another ground would be the view that the thing is not evident at all, and that it would not even appear to be evident to any competent person unless he marled the pitch for his own benefit by assuming that the performance of a moral obligation is itself a great moral good. What is more, this second ground of objection need not be restricted to the obstructionist statement, "I cannot see for the life of me why," but may attempt positively to show that the alleged "evidence" or "self-evidence" must be a delusion, since we may and do accept moral obligations that do not aim at any benefit.

As I have said, I am doubtful how far anyone consistently holds the last of these views; but anyone who says and means what Mr. Ross says when he asserts that it is "self-evident that a promise, simply as such, is something that *prima facie* ought to be kept" (*R.G.*, p. 40), *sometimes* holds them. I propose, then, to examine certain instances in which it may be alleged that there is a moral obligation wholly independent of benefit.

In attempting to classify our moral obligations, I distinguished duties of benevolence from duties of justice and of completion. Our question, when put in these terms, is therefore whether the two latter sets of obligations can be wholly independent of benefit (at least intended); and it seems simplest to begin with duties of completion. It cannot be denied, I think, that among such obligations punishment, promise-keeping, and veracity are instances more favourable than most to the general view that obligations of completion may have nothing to do with benefit. If a negative can be proved in their case, the affirmative is not very likely to flourish in any other instances of obligations of completion, and I shall not, in fact, consider any other obligations of this type.

Take, then, punishment. When Kant argued that, if a society were about to dissolve, "the last murderer lying in prison ought to be executed first" (*Philosophy of Law*, Hastie's translation, p. 198), he was asserting the morality of requital as such in opposition to all theories of the (subsequent) benefit of requital to any society. Even this extreme position, however, might be defended by those who believed that all hangings, if justified at all, are justified by their benefit to society.

One possible argument of this kind, it is true, is not very impressive. It is to the general effect that a wrong that is expiated is in some sort annulled, and consequently that a righted wrong, although not perhaps a positive good, is undeniably better than an unrighted wrong, and therefore is a benefit. The difficulty in this particular explanation, I think, is that the wrong cannot literally be undone (since it is past), and that a tit-for-tat theory of payment for the wrong is not merely crude, but actually immoral. The regeneration of character, in expiation, may indeed be a great good, but the suffering that may cause the regeneration is not a good (to say nothing of the defects of the scaffold regarded as an instrument of expiation). Another line of argument, however, is much more promising. If a doomed society hanged the last murderer before it perished it might do so as a gesture of homage to its settled principles, and argue that although in the particular case no future good was accomplished by the execution, nevertheless punishment, stern but just, was socially beneficial in any society not composed of efficient and very prudent saints. Therefore, in dying they saluted the principle.

Suppose, however, we restrict this problem to the question of *later* benefit. Is it at all plausible to hold that a punishment could ever be justified if it were clear that no good could come of it? I allow that if requital were itself a good this question would have diminished importance, and I also allow that the goodness of requital as such is at least as plausible as the obligation of requital as such. (Even when evil is requited by evil it would be possible for the one to be the antidote of the other and for the two jointly to yield a healthy condition.) Let us, however, ignore the possible benefit of requital as such, and consider instead the proposition that requitals are justified when they are likely to yield beneficial results, and that they are not justified if from the standpoint of probable subsequent results they are futile or actually injurious. (This proposition would hold of reward as well as of punishment, but at present we are considering the latter only.)

If offences as such should be requited, does it not follow that all offences should be punished? and what judge, or schoolmaster, or other such person in authority accepts such an obligation in practice? The reply, presumably, would be that while there is an obligation to punish all offences as such there are stronger contrary obligations against punishment in the majority of cases. But what are these contrary obligations? We can scarcely say that only grave moral offences should be punished, for that is not a reasonable inference from the proposition that offences as such should be punished, yet nearly anyone would accept the position that the punishment of small offences should occur only when they are exemplary or otherwise are designed to have beneficial results.

What other reason, then, is relevant to grave offences? From a legal point of view an offence is grave when a serious penalty is attached, and the weight of the penalty is seldom defended except on the ground that it is adjusted to the social danger of the offence. No doubt lawyers deal with punishments laid down by statute; but if we consider simply the moral gravity of an offence, then, even if we could assess that moral gravity, we should still have to consider the question of who should punish as well as the question of who should be punished. Is it a moral obligation for every righteous man to punish every serious offence that he knows has been committed, unless that offence is punished by the law of the land? And if the transgressor repents, is there *any* reason for punishment, except the fear that the repentance will not last?

In short, the view that every offence deserves punishment would impose an intolerable burden if it were humanity's duty to fulfil this obligation. Setting aside, therefore, all questions regarding the appropriate kind and amount of punishment (which, except for the vague proposition that a trivial offence should not receive severe punishment, are almost invariably approached from the side of benefit, i.e. the reform of the offender, the protection of others, and the utility of examples *ad terrorem*), it would seem that the limitation of the alleged general obligation to requite an offence with some artificial evil is one of its most prominent features.

What principle of limitation, therefore, other than benefit, is at all plausible? If the contention be that people must show they are serious, and therefore must fulfil the threats of punishment they have made, the obligation is a form of promise-keeping, and so falls to be considered later. That could not, however, be the end of the story, for we should at once have to ask *when* it is legitimate (or a moral obligation) to threaten in this way; and if there should not be such threats for all offences, it is almost inevitable to say that the threats should be made and fulfilled only when some special good purpose is served, other than the formal purpose of requital as such. If the contention be that it is unjust, if any offender is punished, that any other offender should escape, we return to the impossible view that every offence should be punished if detected. It will not do to say that God will repair all human omissions in this matter; for in that case men might safely neglect to punish at all.

It is sometimes argued that any attempted justification of punishment other than the justification of requital commits the elementary fallacy of being unable to distinguish between the innocent and the guilty. This objection, however (as was noted in earlier places), is itself but a fallacy, being a confusion between punishment and the means of punishment. Nobody denies, for instance, that restriction of liberty by incarceration may be justified when there has been no moral or legal offence. Quarantine is an obvious instance. But where is the difficulty of distinguishing between imprisonment as a punishment and imprisonment for purposes of quarantine? Again, we have all heard of "reprisals" when the true offenders are too elusive to be deterred by the usual criminal procedure; but in that case the innocent people whose homes are destroyed (supposing them to *be* innocent) are not *punished* although they are made to suffer.

Penal deterrence, in short, is not the only kind of deterrence, nor penal protective measures the only sort of self-protection that a community may employ; but there is no difficulty in distinguishing penal measures from others. Penal action is directed upon a (proved) offender for a (proved) offence committed (or possibly, as in "loitering with intent," for a presumed depravity of character regarded as tantamount to an actual offence). That is what penal action means, but its *meaning* cannot justify it. When we ask, not whether punishment means some kind of requital, but whether that kind of requital is ever a moral obligation, we have to discover something more than its meaning. I suggest that this additional consideration must always include some good that is intended by penal action, just as in the case of quarantine or any other evil justifiably enacted by any valid authority.

Take, again, promise-keeping. Mr. Ross, admitting that disaster to others may be a sufficient moral reason for breaking a promise (*R.G.*, p. 18) holds (*ibid.*) that when, as in the usual case, a promise should be kept, the sufficient and the only moral reason is that it was made. "In our normal thought we consider," he says (*op. cit.*, p. 37), "that the fact that we have made a promise is in itself sufficient to create a duty of keeping it, the sense of duty resting on remembrance of the past promise," and (p. 39) he suspects gross ignorance of the very meaning of promise-keeping on the part of anyone who thought that a dying hermit could have any lesser reason for keeping a promise to a dead hermit than ordinary active members of society have for fulfilling their promises. Is any such view tenable?

The statement contains at least one oversight. In considering promises (as we saw) the making as well as the keeping of the promise has to be examined. No reasonable person supposes that a promise wrongly made, e.g. a promise to elope with another man's wife, should be kept just because it has been made, and it may be doubted whether A, if he has made such a promise to B, has any moral obligation whatsoever *towards B* in consequence of the fact that he has promised. The argument, therefore, must be amended in this particular and is transformed into the contention that a promise not wrongly made should be kept just because it is not wrong *and* a promise, that is to say for two reasons, and not for one reason only.

May there not, however, be further neglected conditions in Mr. Ross's statement? To mention no other point, if M makes a (legitimate) promise to N, may not N release M from his promise? If so, the fact that a promise has been made and was not wrongful is *not* a sufficient reason for keeping it, and although, no doubt, it would be possible to avoid this difficulty by holding that every legitimate promise should be of the form, "I promise you this perfectly legitimate thing unless you release me," there seem to me to be important implications in this amended form of the doctrine. Consider, for example, a promise that is also a threat, such as a farmer's promise to give a mischievous boy a sound drubbing when next he catches him in his orchard. The boy would release the farmer from his promise with great alacrity; but what is the truth about the farmer's duty (if any) to keep his word?

We can all think of cases in which a magnanimous, or even what we call a "decent," man would refuse to be released from his promise (although there are always difficulties about one-sided action in a two-sided affair). Such instances, however, do not affect the general question that if N releases M from his promise, M no longer has the *simple* duty of keeping his word. Indeed, despite the existence of suicide pacts and the like, may we not infer, from the natural presumptions regarding release from a promise, that people who speak about the *simple* duty of promise-keeping usually assume that a promise is always to perform a *service*?

When this point is raised, of two things one. Either a promise is, by definition, a pledge to perform a service, or it is not. In the former case it is (intentially) beneficial by definition, and therefore not independent of benefit. In the latter case, do we seriously hold that a promise to perform a *disservice* (or, more widely, to perform something completely futile) entails any moral obligation at all?

Certainly this question (like most moral questions but in a greater degree than some of them) is complicated by the relevance of the distinction between a real and a fancied service together (in this case) with the circumstance that what most people would consider a merely fancied service becomes genuine, in some degree, by the mere fact that it satisfies someone, however unreasonably and absurdly. Let us, then, keep the discussion to opinion of benefit on the part of the interested parties, and neglect the complications that arise from mistakes in these opinions. In this restricted field I affirm that there is no plausibility in the view that a promise should be kept just because it has been made, unless it is correct to assume that (when M and N are the interested parties) M promises N some service, that is to say promises to do something that N regards as a service and that M believes N to regard in that light. The proviso regarding release would be unintelligible except upon the assumption that N might change his mind about what he wanted, or come to regard the fulfilment of the promise as something unreasonably onerous for M. The man who says that the moral obligation to keep a promise results *simply* from the fact that the promise was given would have to argue that if M cordially invited N to his house and promised him poteen under the mistaken belief that N liked poteen, and later discovered both his mistake and N's polite habit of making no objection, M would still have the moral obligation of plying N with the detested fluid.

Another example (adapted from Mr. Pickard-Cambridge in *Mind*, No. 162, pp. 163 *seq*.) may be even more convincing. Suppose that M promises N that he will attend a concert where N is billed to sing, such being the precise terms of his promise, although his only motive is to gratify N by his presence. Suppose also that N falls sick, but forgets about M and does not release him from his promise. If M does not communicate with N, has he *any* moral duty to attend the concert?

I submit, then, that promise-keeping is not at all a happy field in which to look for instances of moral obligations entirely independent of all presumption of benefit. A happier field, however, might be the obligation of veracity.

The obligation of veracity is currently held to be confined to one of the functions of speech, namely the conveying of information. Since information, however, can also be conveyed by nods and winks and other gestures, it is probable that the restriction to speech is an oversight. On the other hand, the uninformatory uses of speech, to excite passion, to rouse pleasing images and the like are not usually supposed to belong to the sphere of veracity.

Accepting, then, the restriction of the obligation to information, nobody would say that the mere fact that A possesses information imposes the duty to convey such information to B or to C or indeed to anyone. Some information is better kept secret; much is not for everybody, and I think it would be difficult if not impossible to conceive of a case in which there was a clear positive duty to convey information, unless the information was of use to somebody, that is to say, a benefit. The use, moreover, would have to be genuine, for there is no duty to convey libellous information, or to pander to prurience, salacious tastes in history and in gossip, or the like.

Apart from clear duty, however, mere sociableness might prompt to the conveying of much information that was not positively useful; and the fruit of this innocuous employment would be a part of the benefit of company. The usual conclusion, therefore, is that if it is not wrong for a man to convey information, he should always convey such information truthfully, and it is hard to see why the wickedness of deceiving in apparently informative speech is not a special case of the wider duty not to deceive at all.

There is not an absolute duty to avoid all deceit (in a conjuring entertainment, for instance, or, more seriously, on many occasions in a good doctor's practice), and most people would admit, if pressed, that in cases in which silence is either impracticable or itself misleading, deceit by means of informative speech is justified when deceit itself is justified. It would probably be added, however, that special care should be taken about verbal deceit.

If so, some reason would have to be given why verbal deceit differs relevantly from other deceit, and I do not see what plausible answer could be given to this question except the obvious one that speech is the usual and much the most explicitly developed means of human communication, and therefore specially important with regard to the *trust* a man may put in his fellows. I do not suggest at the moment that fiduciary duties are based wholly on benefit, but I submit with confidence that they are not independent of benefit—indeed, that on the contrary they contain benefit as an essential constituent. Consequently I do not think that the view that we should tell the truth *just* because it is the truth is more plausible than the doctrine formerly examined that we should keep a promise *just* because it was made.

When we pass from duties of completion to what (rather rashly, perhaps) I have called duties of justice, we have to deal with moral accuracy (from which equity may be a deduction), and with respect for humanity as such, as well as with all claims to priority or privilege that are based upon inequalities morally relevant. Distributive justice, being a generalized obligation of requital, need not be separately discussed.

Equity, moral accuracy, and the like come very near to being a description of the formal requisites of all morality. To discuss them separately, therefore, might easily lead to a double discussion of the same topics. There are aspects of the question, however, that obviously require special discussion. Thus a just man, unfortunately, is rather rare, not because conscience is rare, or, on the whole, treated as something negligible, but because the extreme importance of a scrupulous regard for moral accuracy and of a constant and perpetual will to decide on the fullest moral evidence available is very rare indeed.

Injustice may very easily be combined with philanthropy. It occurs whenever the philanthropist is partial but kindly. Obviously, however, we cannot infer that justice is not always beneficent simply because beneficence is not always just. On the other hand, in so far as justice is to be regarded as an interpersonal relationship (and that is part of it) we may have to think rather carefully when presented with the obvious and apparently reasonable question *whose* good it serves.

It is often said that men prefer justice to happiness, and (with even greater assurance) that they prefer justice to comfort. They would rather tighten their belts if convinced that it was equitable for them, as between one man and another, to undergo such privations than fare sumptuously if the meal were flung at them as a sort of dole to keep them quiet. At any rate they would normally adopt this attitude if starvation did not degrade them to a sub-human level.

These observations, if correct, would tend to show that men have so high a regard for equitable inter-personal relations that avoidable defects in such relations hurt them individually more than anything else. The relations, consequently, affect them as well as lie between them. Nevertheless, in so far as the relations are the concern of justice, the state of mind of the persons who stand in these relationships is not the whole of the affair. Indeed, there is a manifest oversight in most ethical theories based on benefit at precisely this point. Such theories almost always attempt to assess the benefits *within* X and Y and Z as if these were the only possible benefits. They forget that there may be good in the relation between X, Y, and Z.

Thus when we ask whether an essential part of the reason for the moral obligation to be just consists in the fact that a just treatment of mankind *does good*, we should be prepared to admit that a *relational* good may be a great part of the good conveyed. Even if the appropriate relations could be deduced from the moral properties of the persons related it would not follow that the goodness of these relations was simply identical with the goodness of the persons.

It might be argued, no doubt, that such relations are right but not good, and that their rightness, not their goodness, imposes the moral obligation of justice so far as relational. This proposition, I think, would impose an arbitrary (indeed an indefensible) restriction upon the meaning of "good," "benefit," or other such term; but that question is too wide for the present section. It is relevant to notice here, however, that men's beliefs concerning moral inter-relationships (that is to say concerning the justice of the way they are treated in comparison with others) affect their individual well-being in the profoundest fashion. The benefits of justice, therefore, and the evils of injustice may be very considerable, even if benefit is held to be always personal, never inter-personal; and it is not unreasonable to credit the human species with a perspicuity sufficient for the truth of the proposition that the best way of getting men to believe that they are justly treated is to treat them justly.

I submit, then, that (to speak temperately) there is a very strong general presumption in favour of the view that one of the requisites of every moral obligation is that it should aim at some benefit, and I have discussed particular types of obligation, not so much because I thought that there was room for considerable dispute (although room can be made quite easily) as because I believed that a closer enquiry of that kind threw light upon the general subject with which we are now engaged. When all is said, the "strong general presumption" in question is only in favour of the view that there can be no obligation to do what, in itself or in its consequences, is designed either to be mischievous or to be utterly futile. If this modest proposition in theoretical ethics is supposed to require a special ethical proof, the resources of general ethics are quite sufficient to supply one. There is a duty of non-maleficence, and a duty of industry (which latter excludes intended futility). Every voluntary human action is such that it might be futile or worse. Therefore every human agent, in all his voluntary action, is under the moral obligation to try to avoid mischief and futility. The fact does not exhaust his moral responsibility, but is a necessary part of that responsibility.

XIII

THE GREATNESS AND THE CONFLICT OF OBLIGATIONS

THE new intuitionists deny that they are innovators. On the contrary, they hold that they are expressing and clarifying the sound, persistent moral opinions, indeed the moral *knowledge*, of educated common sense. They are *reminding* moralists of features of the subject that the said moralists, in their zeal for system building, have tended (unlike plain people) to forget.

What such moralists forget, according to the new intuitionists, is the specific correspondence of our moral obligations to specific situations. Thus Mr. Prichard holds (*Mind*, No. 81, pp. 27 *seqq.*) that obligations are discerned by *moral* not by non-moral logic, are "absolutely underivative and immediate," and are pieces of insight, i.e. of the intuitions that certain types of situation morally demand a certain kind of response. These situations, he further explains, are *relations* between the moral agent, on the one hand, and, on the other hand, either the agent himself or some other man. Illustrations are gratitude, debt-paying, and honouring one's parents (these being special duties pertaining to special situations), and also certain common duties in which the relevant relation is that of "being men in one and the same world" (p. 29), for example the general duty of veracity or of avoiding (gratuitous) hurt to some other man's feelings. Mr. Ross (*R.G.*, pp. 16 *seqq.*) argues similarly.

It is admitted that certain perplexities have to be disentangled. (1) These immediate flashes of insight, according to Mr. Prichard, are not necessarily easy intuitions, although being self-evident they disdain all evidence outside themselves. On the contrary, they may require much "thoughtfulness" (p. 30 *n.*). (2) The existence of a multiplicity of situations, each with its unique corresponding moral obligation, may seem to be an untidy business. (3) A situation may be morally complex, giving rise to several distinct obligations, and if there be discordance in this complexity it seems necessary to discover a standard for determining which is the *greater* obligation (p. 30) when a conflict occurs.

Let us then examine these matters.

(1) It would be a pity, I think, if this type of moral theory were held to be inevitably burdened with the philosophical disputes that cling to the notion of self-evidence, although Messrs. Prichard and Ross might welcome the circumstance; and I do not see that the theory need shoulder this additional burden. What is essential to it, I submit, is a one-one correspondence between situation and obligation such that whatever is *morally* relevant in the situation determines the moral obligation wholly on moral grounds. It would be a relief, no doubt, if this moral logic required nothing more elaborate than, firstly, a correct understanding of the situation, and, secondly, immediate insight into the corresponding obligation; and it would be more comforting still if every educated person were capable of performing the first part of this task, and if everybody other than a moral imbecile could perform the second part if he had performed the first. To be sure, those who believe that babes and peasants are likely to have the clearest, because they have the least sophisticated, moral vision might resent the view that education, and the special kind of thoughtfulness that education is supposed to engender, are at all necessary in matters of duty, and would not be reassured by the explanation that self-evidence may be hard to reach, and that those who are moral simpletons in some ethical matters need not be moral simpletons in all or in the greater affairs of duty. The attitude of such people, however, may be altogether too naïve.

Nevertheless, literal self-evidence is a thing that worries many philosophers, for it means that *no* outside evidence is required in any sense whatsoever, and to ask for that is to ask for a great deal. I have therefore offered a humbler suggestion, although I know very well that an apparently temperate suggestion in metaphysics is often more difficult to defend than a bolder one.

(2) Both Mr. Prichard and Mr. Ross remark that if objection is made to the multiplicity of moral obligations asserted in their theory, they have at least an admirable *argumentum ad hominem*, since other moral theories are in fact pluralistic even when they pretend not to be. There is no single common denominator for goods and evils, and the unity of the virtues

> O goodly golden chain wherewith yfere
> The virtues linked are in lovely wise

is a pious moralistic aspiration rather than a demonstrable part of aretaics.

Since aretaics and agathopoeics remain in moral theory (according to these authors themselves) this argument is less effective than it looks. If chaos exists already, that is not a sufficient reason for making more of a mess. On the other hand, it is fair to remark that it is absurd to allow the naughty bogey of ethical pluralism to affright us. Besides, the bogey is not so very imp-like, for the multiplicity of moral obligations is not unlimited, and is pervaded by profound analogies. As Mr. Prichard says, there is an obligation not to hurt another man's feelings gratuitously. There is similarly an obligation not to hurt a dog's feelings gratuitously, and generally not to *hurt*, whether or not *feelings* are what is injured. Indeed, as we have seen, beneficence, as well as non-maleficence, is a necessary part of every moral obligation.

When we speak as Mr. Prichard does of general moral obligations that hold for "all men in one and the same world" (p. 29), we are thinking, in fact, of humane companionship among human partners. It is therefore to be expected that mutual fidelity, reciprocal sincerity, and common respect should be general obligations as well as mutual assistance, in short that there should be a pretty wide range of appropriate moral response. The labyrinth of multiplicity need not be wholly disorderly, and if no modern Theseus has laid a *single* thread to cheat its multiplicity, many have reduced the difficulties of wayfarers by employing a few very prominent threads. If these threads sometimes cross, what harm is done? There is no extravagant multiplicity, surely, in the mere circumstance that an agent may have special obligations to special persons, as well as general obligations to all persons, that he may have retrospective as well as prospective obligations; and the like. In short, the apparent multiplicity of moral obligations is not in itself a ground for scientific alarm.

Indeed, as long as we keep to general rules—and, as we have seen, *every* moral obligation is implicitly general—there is no great difficulty in defending the consilience of moral obligations, and their active mutual support, in a complicated but coherent moral system. Truth may be told malevolently, but there is no contradiction between veracity as such and benevolence as such. Similarly there is no contradiction between respect for the human body (in chastity and purity) and respect for the human mind (in "freedom of speech"). And so forth. What is more, confirmation of the consilience of obligations can be found in the notorious circumstance that any sin is commonly the seed of many more. A kindly and truthful adulterer sets himself a most perplexing moral course.

(3) It is not true, however, that one right step makes all the other right steps easy, or that any one who is careful of moral principle need have no fear of finding himself in a difficult moral situation. The general harmony of moral obligations *inter se* is no proof that there may not be conflict between them; for moral conflicts in special types of cases undoubtedly do occur. When they occur, according to Mr. Prichard (p. 30 *n.*), the proper question is, "Which is the greater obligation?" But how can the question be answered?

On this point Mr. Ross has a good deal to say, and I propose to examine his views pretty fully before attempting to go on.

He maintains (a) that the rightness of certain types of action should be said to be *prima facie* self-evident (*R.G.*, pp. 13, 19 *seqq.* and *passim*), (b) that what is evident in this way is the "tendency to be a duty" (p. 28), and (c) that duty is a toti-resultant attribute, tendency to be a duty a parti-resultant attribute (p. 28).

These elaborate explanations are occasioned by Mr. Ross's resolution to define in terms of *duty*, that is to say in terms of the *one* action that ought to be done in some given situation. If, however, as in the present essay, "obligation" were regarded simply as the implicate in action of any morally relevant feature of the situation, it would follow that there are several obligations in a morally complex situation, although there could not be several duties. We should therefore have a simpler, perhaps even a more accurate vocabulary, as the following considerations (I think) strongly suggest.

(a) According to Mr. Ross himself (*R.G.*, p. 20), the phrase "*prima facie* duty" needs some apology, since, among other disadvantages, it suggests either the appearance of evidence where there is none, or the existence of evidence destined to be upset by further evidence. The first of these is not what he means, and the second seems awkwardly designed. When a moral obligation is overborne by a greater conflicting obligation the first obligation, relatively to its evidence, does not cease to be an obligation. It ceases to be decisive evidence of duty, but that is quite another thing.

(b) For the same reason it is quite misleading to say that an obligation merely tends to be a duty. It does not, of course, merely tend to be an obligation (in my sense); for it is one. Yet to say that it tends to be a duty is either to say that it is relevant to duty (which is obvious) or that it tends to be a decisive obligation (which may very well be false). We could say, I think, that *if* a certain moral obligation were *alone* morally relevant in some situation, *then* that particular obligation would be our simple duty. If it be true, however (as I have argued), that benevolence is relevant to every moral situation, there could be no absolutely simple duties in this sense except the duties of benevolence.

(c) Mr. Ross's terms "toti-resultant" and "parti-resultant" may also mislead. Certainly anyone who tries to do his duty has to try to take account of all his moral obligations. The phrase "toti-resultant," however, suggests that duty is a sort of moral compound, the joint product of various obligation-vectors; and that is only one of the cases that may occur.

It occurs, to be brief, where the complexity of the duty matches the complexity of the relevant obligations, for instance when the obligation of veracity combined with the obligation not to hurt a man's feelings bids us tell an unpalatable truth in a gentle and considerate way; and it applies generally where Aristotle's "on the right occasion, in the right fashion," etc., applies (*N.E.*, ii, p. 6). There are, however, other types of instance. One's duty, so to say, may be overdetermined, that is, the several obligations in the same complex situation may all indicate the same appropriate action, as in the easy duty of telling good news, where veracity and benevolence coincide. Here there is no compounding of obligations; and in the case of a conflict of obligations the phrase "toti-resultant" seems to me to be misleading, unless the duty is modified by all the relevant obligations. Suppose, to take the stock illustration, a doctor has to practise deceit in order to prevent his patient from giving up the ghost to his own fears. If the doctor can adroitly evade a direct lie, and yet deceive successfully, he might perhaps be said to be fulfilling a compounded duty (although, more probably, he would only be compounding with his conscience). Nevertheless the doctor, if he is a good doctor and also if he is a good man, may have to lie, and in that case it is his duty to lie *convincingly*. If so, where does veracity enter into the toti-resultant duty?

To proceed. How could we answer Mr. Prichard's question concerning the greater obligation, especially in cases of conflict?

Mr. Ross, *ambulando*, makes various suggestions. He speaks (p. 23) of the "more urgent," of the less "trivial" (p. 18), and of the "more stringent" (p. 41) obligation. He also sets forth a rather elaborate formula (p. 41). The second of these suggestions seems the weightiest, and I shall postpone the discussion of it. The others may be considered more briefly.

The question of "urgency" in any ordinary sense refers to the timing of an obligation rather than to its greatness. If a man is starving there is an urgent obligation to feed him soon. If he needs a new overcoat he may wait till the autumn. An urgent duty may, however, be quite trivial and need not be "stringent." The sending of a Christmas card, for instance, is urgent in December, but is seldom a very serious moral obligation. Again it is not "stringent," since a letter or a small gift might be just as suitable. In short, time is not everything in these matters and it need not even be much.

"Stringency," according to the context of Mr. Ross's discussion, means the determinateness of an obligation. Thus debt-paying is a "stringent," determinate, or, in the old phrase, a "perfect" obligation, since (apart from legal moratoria) it is the obligation to pay just so much money within a certain time. The payment of a small bill, however, may (in many ways) be trivial, and, as we have seen, the relative indeterminateness of an obligation, say of gratitude, does not diminish the obligatory character or the gravity of the obligation. No doubt, if we used the word "stringency" in another sense, and meant that the more stringent obligation was the more *binding* we might be supposed to be talking business at last, but I doubt if anyone could defend the proposition that one obligation was more binding than another except on the ground that it was greater. He would therefore be perambulating a circle if he tried to explain what was meant by the "greater" obligation in this fashion.

Mr. Ross's fuller explanation runs as follows: "the greatest balance of *prima facie* rightness, in those respects in which [actions] are *prima facie* right over their *prima facie* wrongness in those respects in which they are *prima facie* wrong" (p. 41).

It may be doubted, I think, whether this formula has *any*

precise meaning, and we may be disposed to think that whatever good sense lurks in the general phrase, the "balance" or the preponderant "weight" of an obligation is smothered at birth by this particular attempt at precision. For how is the balance to be determined? Are we simply to count the number of respects in which there is *prima facie* rightness, the number of respects in which there is *prima facie* wrongness, and apply simple arithmetic on the assumption that all these items are equal units? Or are we to *weight* the rightness and wrongness by considerations of "urgency," "stringency," and the like, and then apply some process of more complicated mathematics? Or are we to hold, as the language of the formula suggests, that some rightnesses are *righter* than other rightnesses, some wrongnesses *wronger* than other wrongnesses, and attempt to cast the balance on that basis? "Moral arithmetic" is always a puzzling subject, but there is at least an excuse for believing that this particular variety of it is more perplexing than most.

One of Mr. Ross's standards still remains, however, namely the opposition between triviality and seriousness.

Many would hold, I think, that this opposition is quite inappropriate to moral matters. Morality, they would say, is never trivial, even when it is concerned with matters that would be trivial were it not for the moral issues involved. What would we think of a parent who smiled when he found that his boy was inclined to lie about small matters? Is petty pilfering a small moral offence? Is the murder of a wretched, useless creature, or even of an imbecile, a minor crime? In any case, there is surely no simple relation, in "moral logic," between the triviality of a man's purposes, and the offences connected with these purposes; and there is at least a certain plausibility in the contention that triviality or its opposite is an affair of potential benefit. A great matter may seem to be one in which the services or disservices are great; a small matter is one in which the services or disservices are small.

Mr. Ross's example of triviality is a trivial promise, and the illustration promptly arouses criticism. What business has

Mr. Ross, or any other deontologically minded moralist (we may be disposed to ask), to distinguish between trivial and non-trivial promises? Their contention is (is it not?) that promises should be kept just because they are promises, and this view has a certain appeal just because any other view suggests laxity or evasion. Surely, however, a promise to perform a trivial service *is* a promise. It is just as authentic a promise as a promise to do something big. Therefore, in so far as we use the argument "just because it is a promise," we are not entitled to discriminate between promises in respect of the degree of their obligatoriness.

If anyone were to say that a "trivial" promise is less of a promise than a serious one, in the sense that it is less authentically a promise, and only a half-promise or a bit of a promise, he would not, I think, have a plausible case. A "half-promise" or "more or less of a promise," when such phrases are used, means one or other of two things. Either an agent has *not* promised but has very nearly promised, that is to say has not pledged himself but has indicated his intentions in such a way that the other party has some grounds for acting in the way he would act if a promise had been given, or the agent has promised to perform part but not the whole of a piece of conduct commonly regarded as a unity. That, however, has nothing to do with triviality, since it is possible for people to be partially committed in this way regarding the most serious affairs. The authenticity of a promise raises quite different questions, and these, in essentials, are whether the promise was actually given and whether, if given, it was inadvertent, that is to say neglectful of considerations that could and should have been present in the minds of reasonable contracting parties. A promise about a trivial matter, however, need not be inadvertent at all. In general both parties know perfectly well that the matter is trivial.

At this point, however, a distinction emerges that may be of substance. We are accustomed to distinguish between a solemn promise and one that is less solemn, let us say between a solemn and a casual promise, supposing that the word "casual" can be used without implying inadvertence. In terms of this distinction it might be reasonable to employ the well-worn analogy which remarks that quart-pots contain more than pint-pots when both are *full*. A solemn promise is not more of a promise than a casual (but advertent) promise, but there is more *gravity* about it; and it is intelligible to affirm that there is a greater obligation in the case of a solemn than in the case of a casual promise on the ground that there is a graver although not a fuller obligation.

Indeed, I think that some such doctrine is in harmony with, if it does not actually follow from the theory of the new intuitionists. What they claim is that our obligations are determined, through moral logic, by reason of the specific character of some given situation. If so, the gravity of the situation may well be morally relevant, and if it be said that the general nature of the situation is the same in a solemn and in a casual promise it is surely permissible to reply that the gravity of the situation affects the intensity, even when it does not affect the nature, of the obligation.

Again, one might infer a similar conclusion from a more detailed examination of the instance of promise-giving and promise-keeping. A promise itself is a special device for rendering more binding what might be binding without the promise (although the device is such that, if adopted, it may bind when, without the promise, there would be no obligation of the same general kind). It is a special form of fiduciary relation, and frequently there may be no great moral difference whether or not a promise has actually been given. Breach of promise cases take account of conduct as well as of verbal promises, both when there is "something in writing" and when there isn't. Moreover, there are ways of indicating the special importance of certain promises, as, for example, a legal covenant. A man's last will and testament differs from a verbal promise regarding the disposing of his goods, partly, no doubt, because it supplies specially good legal evidence and can be enforced at law, but partly also because it is a more serious and a more solemn promise. Anyone who (to choose another example) can distinguish between perjury and mere fibbing, and does not base the distinction upon superstitions connected with a Bible oath seems logically bound to admit a difference in the gravity of promises. Indeed, we might say (although I daresay with diminished assurance) that a certain casualness is appropriate to promises about small matters. They are not occasions for solemnity; and, if they are forgotten, a slight apology makes amends for them. In graver matters, on the other hand, solemnity is appropriate even if good taste conceals the solemnity. Such promises should not be lightly given. When given, they should not be lightly broken.

Accordingly, despite the difficulties that attach to the idea that one obligation is more binding than another, and despite the truth that a moral obligation (say, of veracity) cannot be accounted trivial simply because it is concerned with matters that, apart from morality, would be trivial, we are bound (I think) to draw these distinctions concerning the gravity of moral obligations and may do so not merely within obligations of the same type (as when we distinguish between a solemn and a casual promise), but also between obligations of different types (as when we distinguish between mere discourtesy and insult or malignant persecution). Moreover, in a general sense, the gravity of an obligation affects its magnitude, and therefore does supply the rudiments of an answer to Mr. Prichard's question, "Which is the *greater* obligation?"

I do not suggest and I do not think that we can measure the gravity of our moral obligations with any pretence at accuracy. Nevertheless, differences of magnitude may exist and be appreciable in many special cases although there is no possibility of devising accurate standards of measurement.

Again, it seems question-begging to argue that all such differences in gravity are beyond the scope of deontological ethics. These differences, according to an ethics of virtue, are simply the difference between mortal and venial sins, or

between the cardinal virtues and minor personal excellences.
The gravity of a situation according to an ethics of benefit
consists wholly of the magnitude of the benefits or injuries
at stake. Such views, and especially the second of them, are
plausible enough. It would be difficult to describe what we
mean by "a really serious matter," except as one that profoundly
affected the lives of men, had an important bearing upon the
very foundations of society, or in some such way. If, however,
moral obligations, although they contain benefit as an essential
constituent, are not wholly matters of benefit—and that is
what the deontologists maintain—if justice, for instance, is
irreducible to mere benefit, however complex the form of
the benefit may be, why should anyone think that the profundity of justice in human life or in society, and generally
the distinction between the weightier and the less weighty
matters of justice, are distinctions of benefit alone?

Assuming, then, that the gravity of our moral obligations
is relevant to their magnitude, we have to ask whether there
are any other relevant considerations of the same order; and,
plainly, we are accustomed to speak of the height and of the
width of obligations as well as of their weight. All these expressions, of course, are metaphorical, and need not be independent
of one another. They may, however, be distinctive, and they
frequently seem so. It is necessary, therefore, to consider them
separately; and I shall examine the characteristic of width, or
breadth, first.

By the width of an obligation we may mean either its logical
or its personal width, that is to say either its logical generality
(i.e. the extensiveness of the range of instances to which it
applies) or the range of persons whom the obligation affects.
Let us now consider "width" in the second of these senses.

In an ethics of benefit this characteristic is very important,
for even if it is disputable whether each should count for one
and no one for more than one, there is likely to be greater
benefit if many share the benefit than if only a few share it.
Hence in agathopoeics stress is rightly laid upon the pursuit

of goods which, like air and sunshine, cannot be regarded as exclusive private possessions. There is no "corner" in them, and it is sometimes held that benefits are moralized when they are socialized and treated as "common" goods.

So far as obligations depend on a beneficial purpose, therefore, it is likely, *ceteris paribus*, that a moral obligation will be greater if it affects a larger number of persons, and it would be difficult, I think, to deny the relevance of this consideration even in cases in which it is denied that benefit is the sole consideration that is morally relevant. Thus if we return to promise-keeping and accept the view that the obligation to keep a promise may properly be affected by factors other than the simple fact that the promise has been given, we should probably admit the relevance of differences in width. Obviously we would not dream of supposing that *any* promise made to two or three was, as such, a greater obligation than *any* promise made to one person only. The most serious promise of all, a promise to marry, is primarily a promise to one person, in monogamous countries. To make the comparison properly we should have to compare what was substantially the same promise made to a smaller or to a larger group of people. In such instances, e.g. the difference between promising to play a game of golf and promising to take part in a golf-match (no substitutes being available in either instance), we should probably express the greater magnitude of the second obligation in terms of the wider annoyance defection would cause, that is in terms of vexatious consequences, but we should also hold, I think, that the greater range of the promise made it more serious and therefore greater.

If that be true, we should be entitled (I think) to hold in general that any given obligation is greater when it is towards many than when it is towards few, provided that substantially the same obligation occurs in both instances. Here the proviso is obviously important. Certain obligations, for example those of a husband or of a father, cannot be obligations towards more than a few. Other obligations, for example all the special duties of close association, cannot be universal. They apply to all close associates, but they do not apply indiscriminately to all men as such. Indeed, for the most part we hold that special obligations have priority over merely general obligations.

The obligations of friendship, for example, are those that are due to our friends in special, that is to say we owe to our friends not merely what we owe to any man as such, but also, and in a way that implies selective priority, what we owe to a *friend*. In arguing so, however, we assume that the more special duty does not conflict with the wider, or, in other words, that the narrower loyalty does not involve injustice to others. And it need not.

On the other hand, it is notorious that narrower loyalties often conflict with wider loyalties. When such conflicts occur, there does not seem to be any simple moral principle for deciding where the balance of obligation lies. It may be difficult "not to let a friend down" without lowering other people as well. It may be difficult to keep him up without employing subterfuges that we should hardly think justifiable in our own case. The width of the obligation has a certain undeniable relevance; but it does not (I think) yield a plain standard.

As we saw, there is another sense of "width," viz. extensiveness of logical range, and this may now be considered. Such logical "width," however, may also be regarded as logical "height." The thinner the generality the more widely it is spread.

In other words, may there not be a hierarchy of obligations in which the superordinate obligations govern and are more general than the subordinate ones? In that case must not the governing and more general obligation be also the greater?

Put in this way, the question seems to assume a good deal. Have we any reason to presume that there is only one such hierarchy? And if there were only one, how would we deal with one of the most obvious sources of perplexity in this matter, viz. that the problem is not simply whether one obligation, as such, is higher than another (as justice, for example, may always be higher than mere courtesy), but whether there may be differences within the same type of obligation such that, in particular cases, the decisive obligation has to be determined, not by its type, but by its gravity within its type (as, to repeat, veracity does not cease to be a duty simply because the truth may hurt, but may very well cease to be a duty if the truth would kill or cause madness and despair).

Despite these perplexities, however, it would still be legitimate to argue that in so far as any hierarchical relationship of obligations can be established, the superordinate, in general, governs the subordinate, and therefore, for the most part, determines the greater obligation.

Here the most instructive analogy (as we formerly noted) is the legal distinction between ordinances and regulations, the principle being that the moral ordinances should govern the moral regulations, or, in other words, that the regulations would be void if they did not conform to the ordinances.

In ethics as well as in law these distinctions are of vast importance. What the plain man means by morality, far too often, is a rather intricate code of personal behaviour, the code itself resembling a set of regulations much more closely than a set of ordinances. Instead of principles there are rules; and doubts about any of the rules in a heterogeneous collection instil further doubts about all the other rules indiscriminately. The moral rebels at any given time—and there are rebels in every age although antinomianism may be more fashionable at some epochs than at others—need not be supposed to be depraved or anti-moral persons. On the contrary, they may well be persons who believe that regulations are mischievous, wrong, and vicious unless they depend upon some intelligible moral principle intelligently applied. These rebels, it is true, may be in error, as their opponents may also be, although in a different way. They may neither observe nor search for a genuine moral principle when there is one, and they may sometimes forget that in certain instances (as in the rule of the road) mere uniformity is indispensable. Nevertheless, on the whole, it is a healthy thing to put regulations on their trial, to challenge over-regulation, and to try to put first things first by attempting to determine the governing principles of every defensible moral regulation. There is no other direction in which genuine advance in morality can be looked for.

A moral regulation, then,

> Oft spills the principle to save the part

and it is legitimate to argue that ordinances govern regulations (when regulations are justified), that regulations should be regarded as attempts to apply ordinances, that such attempts can be carried too far (when there is over-regulation) and may stultify themselves by attempting to determine *each* member of a certain sub-class of actions when, at the best, they are entitled to determine *most* members of that sub-class. In the extreme case the regulations may be mere technicalities, and their observance a moral punctilio instead of a moral obligation.

Such topics are obviously connected with a point already discussed (viz. the extent to which moral principles can be applied to the detail of actions) and are also connected with a point to be examined later (viz. the degree in which there is a moral presumption in favour of stretching a rule beyond the point at which it is quite plainly justified). Accordingly I shall not develop these matters now; but I should like to offer two observations.

In the first place I think we should note that the main contention of the new intuitionists in this matter, the contention, namely, that some specific relation in a "situation" directly determines a corresponding moral obligation, does not even suggest the relevance of the distinction between ordinances and regulations (or its analogue), but is fully compatible with obligations *ad hoc*. Moreover, it would seem that many very serious moral obligations resemble regulations quite as definitely as they resemble ordinances. This is clear, for instance, in the matter of sex, to which a man's "morals," in current slang, are, as nearly as may be, restricted. Something like a table of prohibited degrees and other rules of exogamy, certain determinate regulations regarding the occasions for valid divorce, and so forth, seem inevitable in this matter; and anyone who regards such things as mere minutiae to be disdained by all bold spirits who are guided by the spirit and not by the letter of morality is likely to be rash as well as bold. We should all admit, I suppose, that if an elderly man whose wife is insane, and an elderly widow, decide to live together because they love one another, their conduct should not be judged as if it did not differ appreciably from the sort of adultery that breaks up a happy home; and we may condemn the laws that make marriage illegal under such circumstances. Nevertheless, this matter is not a *mere* technicality; and hard cases could scarcely be avoided if there were any regulations at all.

In the second place we may note that the harmony between ordinances and regulations, where it exists, is frequently secured by making the ordinances pretty vague as well as (inevitably) very general. It would be possible, therefore, for moral principles to owe their superiority largely to their elusiveness, and this circumstance, although it need not diminish the authority of such principles, may well diminish our confidence in particular cases in which we say that the higher principle imposes the greater moral obligation. It may even be suggested that the consilience of moral ordinances is largely due to a certain convenient vagueness in them.

It may be argued, however, that when we speak of a higher obligation we do not usually mean one that is higher in a merely logical, sense that is to say the thinner generality in a logical hierarchy.

That, I think, is true, but it is not easy to determine this other sense of "higher." If questioned about it, we should usually say that the "higher" obligation has a higher source. Yet if this statement be a proposition in theological ethics it has to encounter the objection that *all* morality (on the theological system) comes from above, and consequently that any discrimination between moral obligations in respect of their altitude would require a special theological warrant.

If we attempt to examine these matters in a non-theological way, it must be confessed, I think, that any distinction we may draw between a "higher" and a "lower" obligation is much more readily conformable to aretaics or to agathopoeics than to deontology. Aretaics professes to give a list of its higher and its lower motives; agathopoeics may consistently speak of a more excellent end. But what is "higher" in the moral logic of deontology?

It might be suggested, perhaps, that an obligation was "higher" in proportion as it exercised the nobler parts of a man. The man who has a great thing to pursue has a high obligation. According to many deontologists, however, one's obligations are always determined by "moral logic," that is to say by rational insight. Therefore they are always determined by the same "high" part of a man, that is to say by his reason. It is inappropriate consequently to differentiate on these grounds, and surely we could not say that our rational obligations in low matters are themselves low. The thorn in the *flesh* may not have to do with high matters, but the conquest of lust is not a minor obligation.

Summing up, then, we may say that a deontological ethics is not incapable of dealing with the question, "Which is the greater obligation?" but that its progress along these lines is tentative and impeded. It is hesitant where opposing theories are confident, and can hardly avoid admitting the relevance of "higher" motives, wider purposes, and greater benefits.

The deontologists admit, however, that there is a moral obligation to confer benefit, and the only reason why many of them (in particular certain eminent new intuitionists) deny the relevance of motive to obligation is a highly disputable dogma regarding the voluntariness of every obligation and the non-voluntariness of every motive. If it were admitted, therefore, that the comparative gravity and magnitude of obligations had to be determined largely, or even wholly, by considerations of virtue and of benefit, it would not follow that moral logic does not have the functions that deontologists say it has, that is to say does not determine the *existence* of obligations. Its incapacity (if there were such incapacity) to decide conflicts of obligation would preclude it from being the only moral monitor regarding our duty; but it might be indispensable nevertheless.

PART III

BENEFIT AND WELL-BEING
WHICH IN THE FORM OF WELL-DOING MAY BE CALLED AGATHOPOEICS

XIV

THE TERMS EMPLOYED

WE have now to examine agathopoeics or the ethics of benefit and well-being, that is to say an ethics based upon the principle that, directly or indirectly, there is only one reason for moral commendation, namely, that good is designed or done, and that nothing is morally reprehensible except on account of some badness designed or done.

In most ways the term "benefit" suitably describes such an ethical theory, because it implies action as well as goodness. In English "benefit" is primarily a substantive which, being no longer used in the sense of a deed well done, has come to mean profit, advantage, or good. Derivatively, and as a verb, the meaning is "to do good *to*."

At the same time, a certain caution should be observed. In conformity with the dictionary, we should naturally say that benefit, the substantive, is a passive good, a good that is done to someone and received by him, and that benefit as a verb is the action of conveying or bestowing such a passive good. Hence it would be easy to slip into the fallacious opinion that the conveying of good cannot itself be good, or, in other words, that all goods are passive goods, and many ethical theories, in particular traditional utilitarianism, seem to me to have embraced this very fallacy.

Accordingly, it is advisable to speak of well-being as well as of "benefit," in discussing general ethical theories of this type, and for the most part to consider well-doing. For well-doing may be and frequently is a part of well-being; ill-doing may be and frequently is a part of ill-being. Moreover, moralists may be concerned to a certain extent with welfare, that is to say with well-being that may be a matter of luck and not of anyone's moral action, although the primary concern of all moralists is with deeds and their efficacy.

In essence, every logical moralist who defends an ethics of this sort has to direct his attention, in the first instance, to the *goodness* of benefits; for although, being a moralist, he busies himself with the theory of good (and evil) *deeds* and with qualities of character closely connected with well- and ill-*doing*, the nature of his theory makes it an application of the theory of good and evil to practice and character.

Therefore some theory of the meaning, variety, and application of good and of evil is required by and should dominate his ethical system, at any rate if good and evil are the best terms for describing what is commonly meant by them, or, if not the best, as suitable as any others.

There are, of course, a great many other terms approximately synonymous, such as interest, profit, advantage, value, and worth, but it may be doubted whether any of these is a better term than "good" and some of them seem distinctly inferior. "Interest," for example, strongly suggests a selfish or merely private advantage, and ethical theories based upon it have a sinister reputation that they may or may not deserve. "Profit" to the unwary may suggest a theory of secular or even of pecuniary advantage; and certain moralists of repute maintain that the "term" value in ethics has been imported from economics to the bewilderment and actual damage of ethical philosophy.*

Such objections, it is true, need not be very serious, and the last of them is clearly an error. There is no appreciable difference between the sense in which "value" is used by modern British moralists and the sense in which Hume employed it (and Hume was fond of it). Indeed, the modern sense is as old as Spenser, for we read in *The Faerie Queene*

> "That all the sorrow in the world is less
> Than virtue's might and value's confidence."—III. xi. 14.

Nevertheless, it is well to avoid even the appearance of evil, and therefore it may profit us to use the term "good" almost exclusively in the present connection.

* E.g. W. G. de Burgh, *Aristotelian Society Supplementary*, Vol. x, p. 121.

In a famous sentence at the beginning of his *Nicomachean Ethics*, Aristotle said that "the good has rightly been declared to be that at which all things aim," implying (it would seem) that it is unintelligible to speak of a "good" unless it is or might be sought. Without necessarily accepting this implication (which may very well be false) we may at least admit that a great many discussions of goodness are Aristotelian in spirit, often to an extent that might surprise the disputants. Hence we may make a beginning with this aspect of the question, and consider the meaning of goodness altogether *sub specie finis*, subsequently debating whether there are wider aspects of the matter, and whether (if these wider aspects exist) there are distinctions within them corresponding to the distinctions in goodness *sub specie finis* as well as (it may be) other occasions for theoretical excitement.

So long as we are dealing with the process of expetition, that is to say with the pursuit of ends, and especially when we are treating of the *conscious* pursuit of ends, the obvious and fundamental contrast is between pursuing something as a means and pursuing something as an end. In consequence, we are asked to distinguish trenchantly between instrumental and final goods.

The distinction is important, and seems clearer than most. It is essential, however, to *keep* it clear, and that may not be easy, particularly in view of the fact that much that is commended as a means may also be commended as an end. To keep the distinction clear, indeed, requires us to distinguish between an exclusively instrumental and an exclusively final good.

Here two points seem to be specially noteworthy. Firstly, it is obvious that what is (merely) instrumentally good is (merely) "good-for." It cannot be "good-for" in general, but must be good-for this or good-for that in particular. It is consequently incomplete and really meaningless unless *its* particular end is specified. Indeed, anything that is good-for some particular end *must* be bad-for the opposite end. Secondly, we must distinguish between a (merely) instrumental good and the stages in the fulfilment of a process that cannot be fulfilled in a jiffy. In a dinner, for example, the soup and the fish are not mere means and the coffee the "end." The soup and the fish are part of an end that, fortunately, takes time to be accomplished, although, by the clock, they are not the last stage in it.

It is commonly held that an instrumental good has a sort of reflected or borrowed goodness derived wholly from the (final) good of which it is the instrument. This view would be absurd if "instrumental goodness" meant efficiency only, since efficiency in general need be neither good nor bad. Since, however, we are not talking about efficiency in general, but about efficiency *for some specific end*, and since (final) goodness, in terms of the present contrast, means neither more nor less than the accomplishment of any given end, there is no need to quarrel with these metaphors of reflection and of borrowing. On the other hand, strong exception should be taken to the view, quite frequently maintained, that "good" has *no* meaning except an instrumental meaning. According to this view "good" is always "good-for." If it were not (so the argument runs) it would be good for nothing, that is to say, not good at all. Here the inference is preposterous. Anything instrumentally good is good-for *its* (final) good. That final good cannot be (instrumentally) good for itself (which is nonsense), and if it were good-for *another* end (which *inter alia* it might be) it would not, in that respect, be a final good at all, but would be only an instrumental good. In this way link after link would be added to a chain that itself depended on nothing. There would be no (final) good to borrow from, and consequently there would be a perfect example of philosophical credit without the least vestige of philosophical security.

In short, while instrumentality does not, as such, imply any goodness at all, the goodness *of a means* does imply final goodness, and is complementary to that conception, although distinct from it in the way in which complementary opposites are distinct. Similarly the question, "What's the good of it?" is just the question, "What's the use of it?" and that, in turn, is just the question, "What end or purpose does it serve?"

If it be further asked, "What constitutes an end, or a final good?" the usual answer would be that an end or a final good is the fruition, satisfaction, or completion of some expetitive process; and this answer, taken simply and quite literally, seems to be thoroughly defensible. The answer presupposes, indeed, that there are certain natural units of expetitive process; but we always do assume that our appetites, impulses, and instincts are precisely such units. They arise wherever there is a void to be filled or some disturbance in organic equilibrium to be removed: and wherever the fulfilment, fruition, or satisfaction puts an end to the process of seeking, not in the way in which death or accident or some fresh disturbance puts an end to particular ways of seeking, but in the way in which a mariner reaches port.

These natural units of expetition, it is true, are for the most part only temporary havens. While there is life there is search, and the fugitive completion of our temporary ends is divided by a hair's breadth only from the process of beginning all over again or of beginning something else. Nevertheless, there is a certain finality, in the temporal sense, even about having dined to-day, and although the time-span of certain final goods, their capacity for hierarchical ordering, the possibility of an intermittent pursuit of some of them, and other such circumstances permit the pursuit of a very complicated teleological pattern there is only complexity, not chaos, in the circumstance. In short, these natural units of expetition do palpably exist. "Ich bin satt" has a perfectly intelligible meaning; and if that intelligible meaning be also the meaning of a final good there is no occasion to quarrel with it.

The conclusion, therefore, is that a means is extrinsically good in so far as it serves a final good, and that a final good is *itself* good, that is to say is intrinsically so. Here, however, an obvious difficulty at once presents itself, and proves, or appears to prove, that even if the extrinsic goodness of a mere means to an end, and the final goodness of an end are sometimes what we mean by goodness, there must be at least one other, and quite different, application of the term.

Up to the present we have discussed a sense of goodness in which a final end really is final, that is to say puts a stop to all enquiry concerning its goodness. The extrinsic goodness of a means provokes instead of stopping enquiry, because we have to ask what the means is good *for*. The final goodness of an end, in terms of this contrast, stops the enquiry, for the end, in terms of the contrast, is not good-for anything else, but is presumed to be self-justifying. It is expetible "for its own sake."

Yet if anything is clear it is that the mere satisfaction of an expetitive process, although it *is* a "final good" need not be "good" in one of the most important senses in which we speak of "good." For surely we can ask significantly whether this or the other satisfaction is a worthy, that is to say a *good* satisfaction; and we may condemn certain expetitive processes, together with their completion or satisfaction, as vicious, evil, and depraved. Any such question or condemnation is meaningless in terms of the contrast between what is good as a means and good as an end. To ask whether a thing is good "as a means" is to ask whether it does serve some particular end, and to ask nothing else whatsoever. To ask whether a thing is good "as an end" is simply to ask whether it *is* an end or final good. There is no sense in asking further whether a final good is finally good, whether a completion completes, or whether a satisfaction satisfies, and it is plainly absurd to condemn a final good for *not* being (finally) good when it *is* (finally) good.

We may call this third and very usual sense of goodness *axiological* good, or, if an English term be preferred, we might call it "worth"; and there is surely no difficulty in proving that in any ordinary sense of language "worth" does not mean simply the fulfilment of expetitive process or the extrinsic relation of serving such a process. Thus we say that satisfied hatred, or ugly lusts satisfied, are evil, not because they do not attain their ends (for they do attain them), and not because such attainments should be distinguished from the fulfilment of some natural unit in expetitive process (for the units are genuine enough), but because the fact that their end has been attained is no proof that the end itself is not despicable.

The axiological sense of goodness, therefore, is quite different from the final sense, taken simply, and also from the "goodness" of a serviceable means to some end. It is natural to ask, however, whether final goodness when it is *not* taken simply may not yield the axiological sense, that is to say whether an axiological good is not a species of final good, a final good with a difference that some final goods may not possess.

Obviously, unless it were held that *no* final good is axiologically good, some final goods must possess the "difference" in question whether or not axiological goodness may also pertain to what is *not* axiologically good. The essential point, however, in any theory that attempted to interpret axiological good *sub specie finis* would be the question whether finality itself tended to develop into and to explain axiology (as it would do, for instance, if axiological good were in reality the most satisfying sort of satisfaction). And certainly we may speak if we choose of a purer, a wider, a more solid, and a more lasting satisfaction. We may also suspect that most of the satisfactions that we call evil are apt to be commingled with disgust, or to be narrow, fleeting, and shallow. Nevertheless, the possibility at least would remain that lust or malice need not have these unsatisfying accompaniments, especially in warped or brutal minds, and contrariwise that there may be dissatisfaction in the attainment of many ends commonly accounted worthy, or even that men of the finest character may be among the miserable. In short, even the most satisfying kind of satisfying satisfaction would not necessarily be axiologically good; and the sensible thing to do is to admit that axiological good does have a distinctive meaning.

The next step in this attempt at analysis should be the endeavour to examine whether goodness has a meaning outside the process of expetition, and, if so, what meaning or meanings. To clear the way for such a step, however, it is expedient to devote some attention to the range of expetition.

When we speak of end and of means, of seeking and of the seekable, we are thinking, in the main, of some *conscious* process, and it seems exceedingly unlikely that consciousness is a *mere* epiphenomenon having no more significance for the substance of the facts reported in consciousness than a news-paper account has for a boat-race. Accordingly, the terms sub- or un-conscious should be used with much more cir-cumspection than is fashionable at the present moment. There is, for example, no intelligible probability that an "unconscious wish" (so-called) really is a *wish* at all; for wishing is something with which we are acquainted in personal conscious experience just as exasperation is, and unconscious exasperation, whatever it might be said to be, is not really *exasperation*. On the other hand, it is not at all unlikely that something very like wishing or exasperation, like it in its effects and in its mode of tension, should occur sub- or un-consciously.

These remarks are readily applicable to the entire field of expetition. Seeking and striving, in our conscious experience, are closely allied with appetite, impulse, and instinct, and, in very many of their instances are psycho-biological processes illustrating vitality quite as much as thinking or enjoyment. They cannot indeed be de-mentalized and remain unaffected; but vital occurrences at a sub-mental level may be very similar indeed to psycho-biological occurrences (and the relations between consciousness and mentality require fuller discussion than can be given here). Indeed, the natural units of expetition of which we have spoken are matched and may even be dominated by biological rhythm and restoration of vital equilibrium.

Therefore, although it is possible to maintain that there could be no *goodness* (although there might be something rather like it) at a sub-mental or sub-conscious level, there is little plausibility in such a view, at any rate so long as final goods and their instruments are in question. Which of us really believes that health is good *only* because we want to feel fit, or that there can be no injury unless it smarts? A fern may not literally be thirsty, because having no sensations (as we suppose) it cannot have the highly distinctive experience that we call thirst, but its behaviour is clearly, in a broad sense, appetitive. In short, final good is a teleological category, and should be presumed to occur wherever teleology occurs. To say that there is no teleological behaviour unless there is conscious choice of ends and of means is altogether opposed to the current and (I should say) to the proper meaning of teleology.

Indeed, it would seem reasonable to hold that teleological relationships do not suddenly appear (or, in the modish phrase, "emerge") when life appears, but that a similar relationship may be found in things that are not alive, whenever we may speak significantly of non-indifference in Nature, that is to say wherever there is any sort of affinity or selective action, either positive or negative. In this sense the indifference of the magnet to the silver churn, and its non-indifference to iron filings may suitably be compared with the fern's non-indifference to water and the Scotsman's non-indifference to ardent spirits. Following Francis Bacon we might call this principle the principle of Natural Election (the more obvious term Natural Selection having been pre-empted for another scientific purpose).

Passing now to the question whose consideration has been delayed in order to allow the above explanation, we have to examine whether, outside the process of seeking, there are senses of good (and of bad) similar to but distinct from the senses of good (and of bad) that are discoverable within that process.

In the first place, the sense in which we have hitherto used the term "instrumental good" seems to be inconveniently narrow. What is good "as a means" is something that is chosen because it is likely to lead to some desired end. Among many possible extrinsic relationships the particular extrinsic relation of causality here receives exclusive prominence and (what is more) the word "means" implies our *choice* of the thing we regard as the probable cause of a final good.

Plainly, this causal relation might exist if choice were not exercised and even if the causation were quite unknown. There may be undesigned instruments of a final good as well as designed instruments. Again, the causal relationship is usually held to imply a certain distinctness (at least temporal) between cause and effect, and there may be no such distinctness in many of the instances that are relevant in this matter. Thus in what are commonly regarded as goods of the body, and contrasted unfavourably (by many moralists) with goods of the mind, it would not be accurate to say that bodily goods are mere causes of mental goods unless body and mind were quite different things (although in partnership). If the truth were that bodies may not merely live, but may also think, there would be no better reason for saying that body and mind are different things than for saying that body and life are different things (although there are bodies that never think, and none that always think). Similarly, although all living bodies are spatial, we should not naturally say that space was a "cause" of life.

In general, then, there are conditions and an implied basis in many goods that are not mere causes of such goods, and yet are such that many goods would not exist without them. We might call them "conditioning goods," and therefore should extend the conception of an "instrumental" good, or of what is good "as a means."

Matters of greater importance arise when we turn our attention to final goods. As most hedonists have correctly noticed, it is not the case that all contentment or all happiness are the fulfilment of an appetite, desire or other appetitive process. A fragrant odour, for example, pleases without any antecedent seeking for it, and although, having once experienced the pleasure, we may well desire and seek after its repetition, this circumstance, while it proves that such pleasures may become ends, affords no justification whatsoever for the opinion that they always, or even normally, *are* ends.

Similarly, friendship and the affection of others are, by common consent, among the very best things in any human life. These goods may, indeed, be sought with fear, and tears, and trembling; but they largely come unsought; and statements of the order, "I'll make you love me," "I'll win your affection," and the like, ring foolishly and pathetically. It is one thing to propose and another thing to be accepted. No doubt we may desire what we cannot appropriately seek. The middle-aged may desire a renewal of their youth, but, as the illustration shows, there are goods that, like youth, are quite non-expetible and for all that may be very great goods. Similarly, when we turn to the side of evil, it is plain that very few things are *made* evil by being shunned, feared, hated, and sedulously avoided. On the contrary, totally unexpected evils are among the worst. When we subsequently take pains to avoid them, the reason is that we have already had experience of their evil.

Such goods, then, are very similar to final goods, for they tend very easily to become final goods. Having experienced them, we would seek them if we could, and we do seek them when we can. Again, it may be held that they are similar in other ways also. When the pleasures of fragrance arise unsought, it may still be contended that they refresh a dull or jaded organism and therefore, literally, are "final" goods, not in the language of conscious seeking, but in the language of Natural Election. They bestow unexpected favours and therefore are similar in kind to the expetible favours implied in the analysis of end and of means.

Because of the close analogy between contentment and pleasure in general, on the one hand, and, on the other hand, the particular species of contentment or pleasure which is the

fulfilment, or the fruition, of expetitive process, it is difficult
to resist the conclusion that contentment, as well as final good,
must be sharply distinguished from what is axiologically good.
The question whether or not the contentment is a worthy
contentment is always significant, and so is the question whether
one kind of contentment may not be finer, nobler, worthier
than another. Certainly it is usual to speak of evil pleasures
when we really mean taking pleasure in evil things. If, therefore,
the pleasure could be sharply separated from its occasioning
conditions, it would be possible to hold that the pleasure itself
was not evil although its conditions were. Similarly, when we
speak of mean and furtive pleasures we may really mean the
pleasure that is taken in ignoble and crepuscular practices;
and when we deplore the pleasures of malice or cruelty we
may really deplore the impulses that prompt the pleasure.
And on these lines a wary disputant might argue that pleasure
itself was always axiologically good, however much we deplored
many of its conditions.

I do not think, however, that "pleasure" thus prescinded
from all its occasions is either an event in nature or a part of
experience. It is only a common name for the fact that something is liked somehow by someone, and this attenuated sense
of the term is not what we mean when we say, for instance,
that the delight we take in another's suffering is the worst
part of the evil that we call cruelty. When a pleasure is said
to be good it is at least as concrete as any process of teleological
satisfaction, and in that concrete sense a thoroughly genuine
pleasure may very well be axiologically evil. The spectator's
delight in some harrowing spectacle is exciting, but is not
axiologically good, unless, indeed, it is purely an aesthetic
delight, or, like the modern delight in bloodthirsty "thrillers"
and the child's delight in ogres and in the disembowelling of
giants, is not affectively attended by any belief in the reality of
the so exciting horrors.

Pleasure and contentment, therefore, like satisfaction, may
be (axiologically) inferior and even positively evil, and may

be so, not extrinsically but intrinsically. Therefore axiological goodness has its own quite distinctive meaning here.

This conclusion is repugnant to many moralists, not merely because they dislike the idea that a single term "good" should have so many different meanings in its common use, but also because they believe that the essence of all goodness must contain an affinity with action and an influence upon action. Final good obviously has such affinity and influence. It is connected with our seeking in such a way that there is no point in asking *why* a final good should move us. Pleasure and contentment again tend to become objects of desire. They attract, and in their stronger forms (as in excitement, rapture, joy, and ecstasy) they attract us very forcibly. Therefore their affinity with action is not in doubt.

It is otherwise with axiological goodness. To show that a thing is axiologically good is to show that it is in some sense admirable; but why should we seek it on that account? Why should we not say: "It is a noble thing, but it is nothing to us"? Again, might we not hold that the goods of which we are speaking are in reality *human* goods, and that axiological goodness in general has no special reference to humanity? We should not expect a dog to be interested in the loveliness of Botticelli's *Primavera*, and we should not care whether the dog were interested or not. We would not even care whether he were interested in what we regard as the daily bread of beauty—a sunset, the starry heavens, the northern lights. Yet without absurd presumption we cannot suppose that nothing is axiologically good except what appeals to humanity. In short (it is said), we assume that axiological good should be the object of our passionate allegiance, devotion, and worship without reflecting that *de facto* admitted excellence has little effect on our action, and further that there may well be countless excellences that no human being can ever perceive, dream of, or aspire after.

These arguments, however, do not seem to be strong. If a man appreciates excellences that a dog does not appreciate, that, we should say, is evidence that the man is superior to his dog. If there are excellences that man can never appreciate, there is proof, in consequence, that man is rather a poor creature; and a man is a poor creature also if, appreciating some excellence, he proceeds to ignore it. The question is whether we have any knowledge of axiological good, and whether, having such knowledge, we ought to seek such good, and to rejoice in it when it comes unsought. It is a sufficient answer that we are (axiologically) better if we do.

Indeed, it seems clear that there is something very wrong indeed about any theory that makes goodness, in all its significant senses, entirely relative to some animate species. In the first place, the argument, "That may appeal to most of my species but it doesn't appeal to me," seems no less conclusive, in terms of contentment and final good, than the argument, "That may be axiologically good but it is not a human good." For, after all, it is men and women who strive and feel, not the human race in general. In the second place, we hold that one species may be better than another, not merely in the sense that it is "better" from the human point of view, that is to say more easily domesticated, or possessed of attributes like grace or agility that we admire in human beings, but also that it really is (axiologically) "better." In short, we do habitually speak of goodness in a sense in which it is not merely possible, but also likely that human goodness may be parochial and all too human, and in which the most that we want to maintain is that human goodness, if a small thing, is nevertheless genuine. That sense of goodness is just the axiological sense.

I submit, then (as many others have submitted), that axiological goodness is quite distinctive, and that it is distinctively different from goodness in any other sense. If this be granted it is plain, I think, that the axiological sense of goodness is the fundamental sense in ethics. For ethics attempts a critical evaluation of such goods as man may come to know, and may seek and aspire after when he knows them. Such critical estimates purport to be axiological, and they *are* axiological if there is any such thing as axiological goodness.

Nevertheless, it is contended in many quarters that the axiological sense of goodness merely seems to be but is not really intelligible; and although no one is bound to answer every conceivable objection to his views, or to renounce such views unless he is prepared to analyse all possible analyses in such a way that analysis itself expires, it would be unreasonable to dismiss these scruples about the intelligibility of axiological good without attempting any defence.

In the first place, then, there is the complaint that the axiological sense of goodness is merely a dictionary sense, and that the dictionary sense of words is frequently an abbreviation of much bad grammar. Thus we call many things (intrinsically) good when we should be forced to admit (if cross-examined) that they are only extrinsically good. For example, we might say that hotel advertisements by the roadside were a crime against natural loveliness, our meaning really being that these eyesores interfere with the wayfarer's enjoyment of the beauty that nature may cause in him. The suggestion therefore is that all so-called goodness is really an extrinsic goodness, something favourable to mankind.

Here, however, the objector overreaches himself. Suppose that what he says about natural beauty is correct, and that if we call natural objects good because beautiful we can only mean that they are extrinsically good on account of what they do to us. In that case we have still to ask whether they do not cause something in us that is good, not because it, in its turn, causes something else, but in some quite different sense. Certainly this other sense might be that of final good; but final good would be *another* sense of good. Indeed, as we have seen, the very meaning of "good as a means" presupposes and is contrasted with "good as an end." It is therefore impossible that *all* goodness could be extrinsic in the sense here supposed (and this without prejudice to the general question of extrinsic versus intrinsic goodness). Therefore, if final good (as has been shown) is not identical with axiological good, the objection (which presupposes the sufficiency of "good as an end, or as a means to an end") is itself quite inadequate.

In the second place it is said that the moralists who have recently laid most emphasis upon the uniqueness and intelligibility of (axiological) good, in particular Professor Moore in *Principia Ethica*, Sidgwick, whom Moore partially followed, and McTaggart, who accepted Moore's view, have claimed too much and have claimed it unwisely. For Moore maintained that (axiological) good was an indefinable, because a simple, quality, whereas, according to the objectors, it may not be indefinable and cannot be a quality.

In this context "indefinable" is taken to mean unanalysable or *logically* simple, and the objection is either to all logical simples as such, or also to the assertion of simplicity in this particular instance. If so, it should be conceded, I think, that if the claim of simplicity be a challenge it may be unfair, while, if it is asserted as a pellucid certainty, it may be rash. In other words, what seems simple may really be complex. Therefore it may be unfair to demand that either the complexity be shown or the objector hold his peace, and it may be doubtful whether any conceivable insight could assure us that the quality of goodness is wholly simple and uncompounded.

What has been argued in the present chapter, however, is only that axiological good has a distinctive meaning that cannot be dissolved by analysis; and any such view need not be perturbed by the objections mentioned.

The question whether (axiological) goodness is or is not a "quality" is even more technical, since the metaphysics of "quality" is highly disputable. In a general way, however (axiological) goodness should be called a "quality" if the proposition, "This is (axiologically) good," is ever literally true.

In this general sense I should suggest that axiological goodness is a "quality"; but many objectors allege that if it were a quality, it would be a quality so very peculiar that a cautious disputant would never call it by that name unless he were very inadvertent.

Thus Mr. Moore himself, as we observed,* suggests that axiological goodness must be a non-descriptive quality. Others would say that if it is a quality it must be a quality "of a higher order." A third party, as we also noted, would say that it is an ejaculation rather than a quality.

The first of these views, I remarked, occupies very dangerous ground. It is to the general effect that a thing's nature (using "thing" very widely to designate, for the most part, a conscious experience) must be distinguished from its worth, in such a way that it is possible to describe the thing's nature *completely*, without any mention of its worth, and that worth does not lend itself to any description at all. A thing's worth (it is said) is the worth of its whole nature, and not a part of that nature.

It seems to me, however, that any such distinction between a thing's nature and its worth, however convenient for certain purposes, cannot be absolute. If a thing *is* (axiologically) good it must have that property, and the contrary view either surreptitiously assumes that worth is some sort of reaction of a subject towards the thing, or else asserts some form of the theory that worth is a quality of a higher order than the usual descriptive properties.

This second view, viz. that worth is a quality "of a higher order," becomes intelligible only when the nature of the "higher order" is described. The phrase, in fact, is used in many connections, but two of its possible senses seem to be especially important in the present affair.

(*a*) It may be said that axiological goodness is similar to "excellence," that is to say is really a superlative. Again, it may be held that "good" is a derivative of "better," and bad a derivative of "worse." Good seems to be a direct positive quality but is not.

This view is usually expressed in terms of preference. A

* In the passage quoted on p. 90.

good thing is one that would always be preferred to an indifferent thing, and a bad thing is one to which an indifferent thing would always be preferable. I do not think, however, that the language of preference can be adequate; for it would not distinguish between axiological and final good. Apart from that, it seems clear that good and evil, like virtue and vice in the traditional comparison, differ as hell from heaven, not as either of these from earth. If so, each must be a genuine positive, simple if either is simple, and in any case not surreptitiously comparative.

(b) There are certain terms, like those of "modality" in logic, that appear to be straightforward although, in fact, they are devious. Thus, according to many logicians, if anyone asserts "S must be P," he is really asserting that the proposition "S is P" can be certified to be true by a certain type of evidence such that its truth is necessary. What appears to be a straightforward sentence, therefore, is very complicated and includes one or more sentences about a primary sentence.

It is possible, I think, that axiological goodness is "of a higher order" in some such sense as this. If so, the statement "X is good" would not, as it seems to do, apply directly to X, but to something vastly more complicated into which X enters. This fact, however, if it were a fact, would not prove that that axiological goodness is not a quality of something.

The third view, viz. that axiological good is really an ejaculation, is, as we saw (p. 92), a modern statement of a very ancient theory. In the old days it was affirmed that to call a thing good is to say that it evokes the sentiment of approval or admiration in some beholder. Nowadays a distinction is drawn between the "emotive" and the "referential" use of language. Words may be used, not to tell us anything, but to excite us. And "good" means "cheers."

Since in general the best way of exciting anyone is to *tell* him something exciting, it seems impossible (as we saw in Part I) to accept this supposedly absolute distinction between emotive and descriptive speech. The new theories, therefore, do not differ appreciably from the old, and the old, in the ethical way, are rather more subtle. Approval, according to the older moralists, was something very different from a grunt of agreement, although it was based upon sympathetic liking. It was a calm and detached sort of sentiment, a feeling about our feelings "on the general survey" and "in a cool hour." It was a dispassionate passion in which the moral critic occupied an emotional armchair.

Superficially, this theory may seem much more adequate than most that we have considered. For instance, it enables us to distinguish quite clearly between mere contentment or satisfaction, on the one hand, and, on the other, the approval of a moral (or other) connoisseur. Axiological good, on this theory would indeed mean "Bravo" and nothing more; but the plaudits would come from refined persons in the exercise of their refinement, that is to say after a careful scrutiny of all relevant facts and at an appropriate "psychic" distance. Again, there would be little or no sense in asking whether this "Bravo" was itself (axiologically) good. It would not require another and a still more refined "Bravo" in order to be authentic. Furthermore, these highly sophisticated plaudits really do occur; for the critics really are moved in their detached way, and evince their refined emotions with a genteel clapping of discreet hands. They may even become enthusiastic.

Nevertheless, it is doubtful whether the "Bravo" of critical approval is in itself anything other than a simple "Bravo" having complicated conditions, in short, whether there is such a thing as a specifically aesthetic, moral, or other boniform emotion; and if there are such specific emotions it is surely strange that they and the ejaculations they arouse should be *all* that is meant by axiological goodness. Is the "careful survey," the appropriate "psychic distance," and so forth, a mere preliminary to the critical plaudits, and if so, why? Is it not much more reasonable to hold that the (axiological) goodness that is discerned arouses these emotions, and that the critics are good critics precisely in so far as their taste corresponds to the excellences they appraise? Without insight the critic perishes.

Axiological goodness, then, is a thing of insight, not a thing of mere feeling. And, by the same logic, axiological badness is a thing of insight too.

XV

CLASSIFICATION OF GOODS

WITH or without express intention, most attempts to classify goods are attempts to classify final goods. Anyone therefore who maintains (as we have maintained) that axiological goodness is a conception wholly distinct from the conception of final goodness (or of a means to final goodness), is disposed to walk delicately along the beaten tracks in this region. In particular I would suggest that there are at least two general presumptions, inevitable (or almost so) when the talk is about final goods and the means to them, which seem rash when axiological goods are being debated. These are the presumptions that extrinsic goodness is negligible in comparison with intrinsic, and that all genuine (axiological) goods must in some sort be mental.

The first presumption is natural when the only extrinsic relation contemplated is that of the means to an end, but need not be at all convincing when other extrinsic relationships are contemplated. The second is less obvious even with respect to final goods, since, granting it to be true that we seek satisfaction, and indeed our own satisfaction, it does not follow and is not obvious that the satisfaction in question is wholly or principally mental. Nevertheless, when we think of conscious expetition, that is to say of the pursuit of a consciously proposed end, and of the means that are chosen with this end in view, it may seem rather obvious that a conscious experience is being sought. Even the man who makes his will, it may be said, that is, the man who designs something whose fulfilment cannot be a personal experience, is really satisfying himself with the dispositions he is making during his lifetime. He has to trust others, just as he trusts others when he posts a letter; but in both cases he is thinking of *his* part in the affair, and has no intimate concern with anything else.

Remembering, then, that these general presumptions may wear a decidedly altered look when we keep strictly to the standpoint of axiological good let us proceed to examine some of the better-known classifications of goods.

Here a suitable point of departure may be found in the traditional Stoic position. Many, indeed, would dispute the Stoic view that the only great human excellence was independence of spirit and serenity of mind, a reasonable, tranquil, and imperturbable "acquiescence in oneself." Some would add jollity and all high spirits, some would call attention to loveliness and aesthetic sublimity, some would demand sanctification and deiformity, some would say that the barriers of self should be overthrown and a superpersonal union with humanity in its entirety be somehow effected. Therefore the Stoic's account of the *only* great human good may well be challenged. On the other hand, the Stoic ideal indicates *a* great human good, and is apt to commend itself very strongly to anyone who, like Spinoza, disputes the Aristotelian view that a great good must be a final good, while retaining the other Aristotelian view that a great good must be self-sufficient (although not necessarily isolated), at any rate if such a good is personal.

The Stoics, however, maintained that there were subordinate goods, "things to be promoted," which, although incomparably smaller than the imperturbability of spirit before mentioned, were good in their own petty way; and although the stringency of this contrast may again be disputed, some such discrimination in detail commends itself to most of us. The list of promotable things that were not of the highest worth was threefold. In the realm of the mind there were such qualities as cleverness, skill, and intellectual power; in the sphere of the body there were life, health, strength, fitness, beauty, and completeness of members; in the field of "detached things" there were wealth, reputation, and gentle birth.

It may be complained, no doubt, that this list of promotable things is rather an indication of the provenance of these excellences (reputed to be so small) than a classification of different excellences. Even in the second class, however, the list of minor excellences was not a list of mere means to excellence, and in the other classes something more was at issue than simply a question of origin. I think, then, that the list offers a useful basis for discussion, and shall proceed to examine this classification of promotable things, as a first approximation, without assuming that their excellence, when compared with the worth of settled self-mastery and acquiescence in oneself, is necessarily so very small.

We have first to consider the question whether it be not true that all goods (although not all contributions towards good) must be mental, and, to be more precise, must be states of consciousness.

This view is sometimes assumed, sometimes argued. Among the arguments, the most striking appear to be those offered fairly recently by McTaggart and still more recently by Professor Moore.

According to McTaggart, "It is generally agreed that only the spiritual can have value. This proposition is ultimate and synthetic. It is impossible to prove it. But it is very generally, if not universally admitted" (*The Nature of Existence*, ii, p. 399).

An ultimate synthetic proposition, that is to say a proposition (*a*) that asserts that properties quite distinct must necessarily and always go together, and (*b*) that is based upon insight into the properties themselves, has achieved metaphysical respectability since Kant's day; and some such truths, I suppose, really are evident. This particular proposition, however, does not seem to me to be evident, and, of course, like all others of its kind, it may be denied without self-contradiction or other patent absurdity.

It should be noted that McTaggart's term "spiritual" is rather wide, and would include "whatever pertains to a spirit" as well as "a spirit or its states." Inter-spiritual relations would not therefore be necessarily excluded (a point on which McTaggart had his own metaphysical observations to make); and the "spiritual" according to McTaggart himself need not be consciously so.

McTaggart's "ultimate synthetic proposition" is therefore considerably wider in its scope than, say, the view (which is also quite commonly held) that some conscious experience, such as a pleasure, can alone have any value that is not merely contributory. I doubt, however, whether the proposition would even appear to be plausible if it were not based either on induction or upon an imaginative experiment; and although induction and imagination deserve well of logicians, they do not seem to be convincing on the present occasion.

The induction is: Make an inventory of human goods (principally final) and you will find that all the great human goods are "spiritual." This seems likely, but its application to axiological goods in general is not apparent. The imaginative experiment is: Think of any great human good (principally final). De-spiritualize it, and what have you left? The answer is (I think) that a good deal might be left, and that, in any case, the experiment is something of a sham. A parallel would be: "Imagine yourself consciously valuing something without being conscious, and where are you?"

Professor Moore, on the other hand, maintains that the connection between spirit and intrinsic value is analytical, that is to say that there would be flat absurdity and sheer contradiction if anyone held that anything non-spiritual might have intrinsic value. His argument in substance is (*Aristotelian Society Proceedings. Supplementary*, vol. xi, p. 124) that an intrinsic good must be one that is "worth having for its own sake" and that only the experiences of a self can be "had" in this special sense.

The reply is simple and (I submit) sufficient. The phrase "for its own *sake*" strongly suggests teleology and even actual seeking, and there is no such implication in an "intrinsic" good. Apart from such question-begging explanations, however, it seems clear that there is no need for "having" in the special sense on which Mr. Moore's analytical argument turns. As a critic has shown (Mr. Duncan-Jones in *Mind*, October 1933, p. 493) it is quite as legitimate to speak of "worth doing for its own sake" as of "worth having for its own sake" and such "doing" need not be the "having" of an experience. What is more, a self cannot "have" itself in the sense in which it "has" its experiences. Mr. Moore's argument would therefore imply that a self cannot *be* (intrinsically) good although its conscious states may be good, indeed that there would be utter absurdity in supposing that selves could be intrinsically good. In short, he has misplaced the absurdity.

There may, of course, be other and better arguments of this kind, but I do not believe that there are. I shall therefore decline to assume that there is either logical absurdity or manifest wrong-headedness about the mere idea that there could be goods (other than simply contributory) that were not goods "of the mind." To say this, however, is not to deny that the greatest human axiological goods of which we have any experience *are* spiritual, in some general sense of that word. On the contrary, this more moderate view would seem to be true.

If, then, we ask what the major goods "of the mind" are, the usual answer would be "the (morally) Good, the Beautiful, and the True," a pertinent but not a very satisfying answer. Again (as we saw), the Stoics had their list, but their list is usually condemned, not quite fairly, because cleverness, skill, and intellectual ability may be almost as readily (morally) bad as (morally) good. It seems preferable, therefore, to look for some other division, and I propose to examine McTaggart's list of "spiritual" goods.

He says (*op. cit.*, ii, p. 412): "I think the following list will include all that have received any support. Firstly, it has been held that knowledge is good and that error is bad. Secondly, that virtue is good and that vice is bad. Thirdly, that the possession of certain emotions is good, and that the possession of others is bad. Fourthly, that pleasure is good and that pain is bad. Fifthly, that amount and intensity of consciousness which we may call "fulness of life" is good (to this characteristic there is no converse which is held to be positively bad). Sixthly, that harmony in consciousness is good, and disharmony, I suppose, bad." He rejects the sixth class "because I can see no good or evil under this head which does not come under one of the other five"; but he accepts the other five.

Let us, then, examine these classes *seriatim*.

(1) Knowledge may be good as a means because it is power, and it is good as an end because it fulfils a strong, although variable, natural impulse of curiosity, and because there is genuine satisfaction in conquering intellectual obstacles and in clear vision "for its own sake."

These facts may certainly have an important and a relevant bearing upon the axiological worth of knowledge; but why should *knowledge* be singled out among similar mental employments? In a general way we distinguish, in this kind, the senses, memory, imagination, belief, opinion, reasoning, and intellectual vision. Is "knowledge" a general name for all of these, or is it intended to apply, principally or even exclusively, to science, philosophy, and intellectual insight? In the former case, the inclusion of "knowledge" among the great axiological goods is only a preliminary suggestion that needs to be followed up. In the latter case, the doctrine seems to be indefensible. Is there no worth in the senses, no treasures in memory, no splendour in imagination? Is it truth and error only that count in these regions, and, if so, why? And if truth and error alone count, why should happy guess-work, bold unproven speculation, true beliefs that are matter of faith rather than of sight be ignored, and *knowledge*, in its strictest sense, alone accepted?

Again, if the contention be that knowledge is a great axiological good *to its possessor and within his soul*, there is surely a serious difficulty. Omit the point that when knowledge is concerned with trivial, evil, or ugly matters—when, for example, it is a gossip's knowledge, a blackmailer's knowledge, a dilettante's knowledge—its axiological value is more than doubtful, and the fact remains that knowledge, in any of its senses, is essentially a relational thing, since it is or implies the correct apprehension of facts. The facts so apprehended obviously cannot be regarded as mere means to knowledge; for it is the knower's business to know, and truth as opposed to error is the doing of this knowledgeable business (for to say that a proposition is true is to say that if it were apprehended it might be *known*). Knowledge may indeed be a great privilege, in respect of which the knowing far excel the unknowing. Nevertheless, the thing itself is as much a relation as a possession, and its worth seems to be relational as much as "intrinsic."

(2) McTaggart may be presumed to have chosen the word "virtue" to describe moral goodness in general. What the term primarily suggests in this connection, however, is the value of a moral character to its possessor; and morality is, in the main, interpersonal. Indeed, although some moralists would maintain (as we have seen) that the moral relations between persons, particularly the relation of justice, should be described as right and not as good, there seems no sufficient reason, unless axiological goodness is confused with final goodness, for denying that the relations between persons as well as the qualities intrinsic to personal character, may be admirable, noble, and, in a word, good.

This subject will be resumed later. At the moment it should be noted that just as the value of "knowledge" would be commonly supposed to be a wide commendation of all man's cognitive functions in their successful employment, so there should be a similar wide commendation of the active part of man's being, his "will," his expetition, his impulses, and appetites. In this regard, virtue and all moral goodness are plainly far too narrow, and a great variety of possible goods, other than merely moralistic ones, discloses itself before man's mental vision. Since axiological good may not be confused with final good, we should not, indeed, commend axiologically all that teleological moralists commend; and we need not even accept the prevalent opinion that all man's natural or fundamental impulses are healthy and sweet, although they may be perverted into evil forms, may be ruined by excess or distorted by some malign twist of example or of circumstance. There is nothing inconceivable in the doctrine of original sin, and there is much special pleading in Butler's contention* that such an apparently natural impulse as envy is a form of rivalry and emulation which *may* enable the clear spirit to rise.

That, however, is another story. In a general way it is plain that the active part of man's being may be worthy in many employments, and that moral goodness no more exhausts the range of its potential values than intellectual insight exhausts the potential values of memory, imagination, and sagacity.

(3) McTaggart's third class of goods, "the possession of certain emotions," contemplates a wide variety of emotional goods, and therefore presents no parallel to the unaccountable restriction in his opinions concerning the goods of "knowledge" and of volition. On the other hand, it is necessary to ask, "What emotions?" and it would be permissible to ask whether some pattern of emotion, rather than this or the other particular emotion, might not be among the greatest goods of this species.

It seems likely that many philosophers would include under this head (*a*) the Stoic and Spinozistic personal ideal of serenity and free acquiescence of spirit, especially if such an ideal were touched with religious peace and awe; (*b*) that many others would include beauty in all its forms; (*c*) that the values of love and of personal affection would certainly be included; and (*d*) that McTaggart's reasons for treating pleasure as a class apart must be largely technical.

Postponing the treatment of pleasure, therefore, in deference to McTaggart's opinion, we should consider at least three varieties of emotion, or, at any rate, of emotional pattern.

(*a*) While the strictly *emotional* part of a free and sane self-mastery, indeed while the emotional peace of renunciation,

* In a footnote to the first Sermon.

may be prominent in the value so generally attached to these conditions of the spirit by men whose experience has been deep and broad, it would not be correct, I think, to regard such conditions as wholly or predominantly emotional, and to suppose that the sanity, power, and restraint that they imply are mere means to a profound emotional experience. On the contrary, the dominant good, in these cases, is, surely, to *be* sane, to *be* immune from the gustier vicissitudes of circumstance, and to *be*, in that sense, free.

Even the consciousness of these conditions of the spirit (I should say) is less of an axiological good than the reality of them, whether or not we rejoice in that reality; and if, being in error, we had only the consciousness without the reality, believing ourselves immune from fortune's arrows when her shafts were already on the wing or, for that matter, if we were insanely tranquil and treated as such by our fellows, there would either be nothing good about our state, or else a good so small as to deserve a chuckle at the best. Again, a defiant imperturbability, since it is not sane, is truly an occasion for pity. The experience, at its highest, is called "acquiescence," precisely because it is assumed to be a true and justified acquiescence, not simply a brooding although heartening emotion that may be found in madhouses as readily as in the Stoic's porch. In short, the good in question is much more than an emotional possession, is relational as much as intrinsic, and is a firmer thing than any wind of emotion, however steady.

(*b*) Fine art and aesthetics form a subject so wide and at the same time so disputable that any cursory account of them, set down with brevity in the course of a general discussion of the goods that men may discern, has perforce to be reprehensibly slight.

In so far as fine art is concerned, the question seems to be a question of *making*, that is, of a kind of production that somehow is *fine*. In such making, mind and medium seem to meet, so much so that there is always a doubt whether, on the one hand, the plasticity of the medium (despite the problems that are set by its relative stubbornness), or, on the other hand, the way in which the medium, metaphorically speaking, seems to the craftsman to dictate a perfection of its own, is the major influence in art. However that may be, and however great the craftsman's anxious, preoccupied but entrancing emotional experience while he is a-fashioning, it still seems impossible to maintain that the worth of artistic production is simply the possession of a certain emotion, or that "art for art's sake" could be intelligible on any such assumption.

Even those who insist (whatever they may mean) that fine art is fine because it is creative, could hardly defend the opinion (if they were challenged) that their divine creativeness is good simply because it is a high private emotion. Grant (what is unlikely) that they create out of their heads, that is to say out of nothing, that their spiritual freedom, their power of "disimprisoning the soul of fact," is what they truly prize as one of the greatest of all axiological goods, and it would still be plain that this metaphysical proof of their redemption is something far more considerable and far more complicated than a mere emotional condition.

Moreover, the fine craftsman has plainly to produce *something*. He is producing, not for the sake of producing, but for the product's sake. Such statements, of course, are in terms of final good, and there are senses in which the product, and also those natural beauties that Bacon called the art of God, may be only a means to aesthetic experience. (For it is always possible to say that a painting is, in one sense, a mere material object in which moist oils smeared upon a taut canvas have become dry.)

If, however, we turn from final to axiological good, and also refrain from attributing potential worth to a painting that remains for ever in a forgotten cellar, we still have the principal aesthetic problem on our hands, that is to say the problem of taste and of the aesthetic worth of fine things whose fineness can be sensed. This matter (one may opine) is not in any intelligible sense a sort of participation in the process of production, as if Rembrandt were saying, "Come, paint along with me." (We are not Rembrandts, even for the nonce and in a little way, when we admire his *Saul*.) It is just the aesthetic appreciation of his work, and Rembrandt himself must have combined two natures in his own person, i.e. the maker's nature and the critic's.

If we make the very disputable assumptions that beauty resides only in the sensual show of things, and that the senses, in strictness, are always the private modifications of private men's souls, we should certainly obtain the conclusion (having previously inserted it) that beauty must be a private possession, and that talk of beauty in any other sense (especially of the alleged beauties of nature and of the material results of a painter's brush) is an elliptical way of describing the mere physical causes of the sensual experiences that alone can have beauty. Even on these extreme assumptions, however, beauty would not be simply an *emotion*. There is probably no peculiar aesthetic emotion (although there are peculiarly aesthetic attitudes of soul that are fired by emotions in their own distinctive way); and if there were such an emotion its mere possession would not be the experience of beauty. Let beauty be for every man something exclusively *his*, something that must occur within the private world of each man's self if it occurs at all; and beauty would still be largely a relational thing within each private world. Let emotion (perhaps, although improbably, some quite distinctive emotion) be a part of beauty's essence, and the problem remains of correlating any such emotion with the private shows of private things in the private sensory theatre of each particular mind.

Beauty, by common consent, is one of the great axiological values accessible (in some measure) to man; but it is not simply "the possession of a certain emotion." If it is correctly described as a "good of the mind" it seems to be rather a good of the whole mind, very complexly related within itself, than a distinctive transient emotion.

236 AN ENQUIRY INTO MORAL NOTIONS

(c) Few would deny that friendship and personal affection are among the greatest of goods that life has to offer to mankind, in any of the senses in which the word "good" is significantly used. There may, indeed, be amicable disputes on the question whether 'tis better to love or to be loved; some have complained that the penalty of an engrossing friendship is an unlovely indifference to the rest of the world; and a few, very unwisely, have complained that there is too little *merit* about friendship, opining (it would seem) that friendship should be proportionate to moral esteem, that it should exclude publicans and sinners, and that it should not, as in fact it does, make yoke-fellows of persons who are dissimilar morally and in most other ways. These niggling reservations, however, are of little moment, and scarcely so much as dim the gleaming shield of friendship and of love.

Nevertheless, if the contention be that the personal and private emotion of love is the whole of this noble good, it should not be accepted at all. On such a view a man's friend would be merely a means to his own private delectation, and if his mind were clouded so that he loved as if they were living imaginary friends or friends long dead, the emotion, if it were genuine, would be not at all inferior to the love of real people for one another. Love and friendship, in reality, occur only when there are at least two lovers or friends, each acutely aware of the other's existence; and love and friendship, in their full sense, imply the knowledge on the part of each of the other's reciprocation. These matters belong to the essence of love and of friendship regarded as axiological goods. They are not merely indispensable occasions for arousing private emotions in the parties concerned. Consequently, this shining good is misdescribed if it is called "the possession of a certain emotion."

(4) Many moralists have maintained (or, should I say? have proclaimed) that man's animal pleasures have little or no axiological worth, and have been driven by their own logic to proclaim also that animal pains are not axiological evils.

It is not surprising, however, that their following has been relatively small, especially in the second part of this thesis. It is not a little thing for mankind that childbirth and surgery have become so much less grim than they used to be, or even that the commercial cult of sport has raised the pleasures of the body in popular estimation.

Again, even when animal pleasures and pains are officially scorned, it is rare to find that *all* pleasures and pains are likewise scorned. An Augustinian like Malebranche, who despised all sensual pleasures (after the Fall) and contrived to bring pleasures of imagination and of civil fame under his ban, believed, nevertheless, that the highest good was just the pleasure of union with divine power and wisdom. Similarly, those who regard the fear of bodily pain as an unworthy weakness of the flesh (being comforted, we may suppose, by the dubious Epicurean maxim that such pain, if acute, must be short) usually stop short of proclaiming the absurdity that wretchedness and despair are not most miserable evils.

Therefore we may agree that while pleasures may not always be axiologically good and pains may not always be axiologically evil, there is, in general, much axiological good in pleasure, and much axiological evil in pain. Accepting the fact, I should like only to offer a pair of comments.

(*a*) As we have seen, pleasure and pain, when regarded, as by hedonists, as the only good or evil, seem to be interpreted in a sense so abstract that their application is doubtful. They extol a life rich in enjoyment and exempt, so far as may be, from misery; but their theory is based upon "pleasure" in the abstract, and the conceptions of pleasure and of pain are stretched and tortured in consequence with the object of showing that anything reputed good is in some sort a "pleasure," and anything reputed evil, in some sort, a "pain." The critics of hedonism, therefore, have an easy task. The good we applaud, they say, must be something more solid than a series of agreeable, ephemeral feelings. "Voluptuaries" and other pleasure-seekers are vapid fellows who mistake the frills and furbelows of their existence for its authentic reality. And so forth (with rather less plausibility regarding pains).

It should be remarked, therefore, that the hedonistic tradition in ethics, encouraged, no doubt, by certain current physiological ambiguities, was not, in its own eyes, concerned with biological frills and furbelows, but believed, on the contrary, that pleasure was always a vital motion, pain a vital obstruction. In the view of many hedonists (such as Hobbes) the heart was the hub of vitality, and physiologically much stronger than the head (as all might see, after Harvey's discovery of the circulation of the blood). Accordingly pleasure was scarcely to be distinguished from vital force and power. Similarly Spinoza regarded it as a "transition to greater perfection" although felt and not understood.

Such views exaggerate the extent to which pleasure is symptomatic of vital efficiency and pain of weakness and physical decay. Apart from that, they would be more successful if they attempted to prove that pleasure was an indication of vital well-being than if they tried to show (as they did try to show) that it *was* such well-being.

(b) Pleasures and pains are the best examples that could be chosen of a merely "intrinsic" good or of a merely "intrinsic" evil. Let nothing come of them, let them be fleeting, let them be detached as well as evanescent, and, for all that, they may be good or evil without any reasonable doubt whatsoever. A hedonistic doctrine, therefore, is peculiarly suited to the attempt to estimate the magnitude of benefit by the summation of "intrinsic" goods. When non-hedonistic ethical theories are planned on the same lines they may easily neglect to notice that very few axiological goods are obviously "intrinsic" in the sense in which pleasure is.

(5) The phrase "fulness of life" in McTaggart's view describes a certain opulence of conscious experience, and has two dimensions, the intensity and the variety of such experience. It does not, however, imply that we must be conscious of this opulence, congratulating ourselves upon its amount and

intensity, but only that the opulence should exist within us, and be our possession. Indeed, there seems to be no good reason why the phrase should not mean what it says, that is, fulness of *life* as well as of conscious experience (unless McTaggart's "ultimate synthetic judgment" is the reason).

Hence it seems odd that McTaggart should have denied the existence of an equally clear but opposite evil. For surely we deplore poverty of life and experience on the same grounds as we commend opulence in these matters. Again, when we condemn a stunted, poor, narrow, contracted human existence, we condemn it, not so much because the man who lives such a life is aware of its poverty, but more usually because he is *not* aware of it. It is a poor life, we say, largely because its poor owner knows no better.

Accordingly, the poverty in question cannot be reduced to discontent, and it may be doubted whether the narrowness that is condemned is only some form of narrow-mindedness.

There is also some doubt whether "fulness of life," regarded as an axiological good, is a separate good, distinct from the other axiological goods we have already examined. Its most obvious meaning is to express more of these goods, not to add another good to the list.

Again, the "fulness" is a rather vague indication of what should be meant. According to some authors, the desirable opulence of the existence expressed by the term is directly proportional to the number of impulses that are satisfied without a disastrous clash, and this view would seem reasonable if we were speaking of final goods, and could employ a system of reckoning that could reduce the impulses to comparable units. If, however, our impulses, natural or acquired, may be axiologically bad, no such standard of axiological good could be prudently used.

It is also to be remarked that in these affairs much of the gold may not glitter. The apparent opulence that consists in versatility (even when there is gusto and intensity in the versatility) need not be of high axiological value. The narrow existence of a scholar, say, may be richer than the unscholarly suppose, even granting that the scholarly are sometimes aware that it is better to do great things than to describe them greatly, and are far too apt to suppose that the noise of many type-writers bestows a genuine benediction on their craft. Again, classics and romantics argue for ever regarding the *pros* and the *cons* of discipline *versus* range of experience. We need not join the fray, but cannot help remarking that harmony seems to be at least as important as variety and intensity.

(6) As we saw, McTaggart denied that harmony was a separate good, distinct from the other five; and he may have been right. Certainly, harmony seems to enter into all the other classes including the fourth. For pleasure may be a harmony, and a mere succession of agreeable thrills would seem, even to most hedonists, to be a meagre ideal in comparison with what they were contending for. It is even more apparent that a succession of flashes of insight, a few good deeds glowing fitfully in a naughty world without any harmony of moral character or of social stability, the possession of "certain" transitory disconnected emotions, or a jarring and distracted "fulness of life" would not have a high axiological rank.

The truth is, however, that few if any of the goods in McTaggart's list are wholly separable from one another. There is passion as well as vision in truth, joy and beauty in moral goodness, and (to be brief) a similar commingling in the other cases. Each of these goods is distinctive enough to deserve separate attention; but most of them do not exist in isolation.

After this prolonged discussion of the "goods of the mind" it is excusable to be rather curt concerning the "goods of the body," since the discussion itself, in various places, was as much psycho-biological as psychical. I shall, therefore, only remark that I do not believe that bodily health and fitness, when regarded axiologically and in their proper place in the secular existence of living men and women, are mere means to goods of the mind. In a metaphysical sense the description of "the mind and its machine" may indeed be defensible; but other views are also defensible, including the doctrines of the consubstantiality of mental and physical in a human mind-body and of the *minding* of the normal human body when alive and also not asleep. Indeed, there seems to be no special reason why moral philosophy should be committed to any one of these metaphysical hypotheses, or to any other among the seven or seventeen or seventy legitimate metaphysical hypotheses that might be excogitated in psycho-physics.

Therefore, if the relation of our bodies to their minds is not simply one of means to end, it is permissible to believe that some more solid and more vital connection may achieve an appreciable axiological value on the side of a living and vigilant body, unless, as McTaggart thought, we can see by inspection that the finest human organism, *qua* body, has as little worth as desiccated soup that remains desiccated. If others can see this I can only say that they are different from me.

On the other hand, the Stoic list of goods in the sphere of "detached things" requires further discussion. Wealth, it is true, is a means to a means, that is to say, an instrument of purchase, the purchase itself being the acquirement of possessions that, in the main, are themselves but instrumental goods. In so far, however, as a man's wealth may legitimately be regarded as the index of his power over his environment, social and physical, it is also the index of a possible relational good. The strength of individualism, in ethics and in politics, is that human enjoyment, and the greater part if not all that we mean by final good in the human species, is personal, not collective, and it seems likely that the greatest axiological goods of which men have any knowledge are to be found in this region also. Nevertheless, the view that axiological good is to be found exclusively in a man's own soul is in no way evident of itself, and seems to be a peculiar view in the case of a being that, like man, is so very obviously not self-sufficient. A man's biological existence, it is true, is a certain kind of dominance over the physical environment that serves and obeys him; yet he, in another sense, has to serve and obey it. His intellectual, aesthetic, and moral life, similarly, is an assimilation of the nourishment and atmosphere supplied by co-intelligence, traditional and contemporary, although it is something more than *mere* assimilation. In an extended sense, therefore, "wealth" may be both biological and spiritual, and in that sense is a relational good, rather than a simple means.

"Reputation," again (as we have seen), has been belittled by many moralists who have tamely followed Aristotle's lead (*Nic. Eth.*, i, p. 5). Certainly, fame is apt to be an inconstant, an exacting, and a disdainful mistress, and may therefore be unwisely sought as a final good. Moreover, the man who (as in Aristotle's depressing picture) seeks reputation in order to have evidence of his own merits, may easily attach a pathetically high importance to the tinsel of fashion, and so debase his own standards.

Aristotle's general argument, however, viz. that the higher goods should be a man's "very own," and should not depend on others, seems oddly weak. Anything that is good in a genuine partnership, friendship, or companionship plainly depends upon others, not only in the sense that these others must exist for the companionship to be possible, but also in the sense that each of the partners has to adapt his own aims to the aims of the others. The final good to each partner is therefore highly complicated, but should not be suspect on that account, even when regarded as a personal and final good. As an axiological good, the thing seems to be essentially (although not exclusively) relational, and to be no whit the worse on that account.

In a similar way "gentle birth" is a theme with interesting variations. Certainly, men do not make their own parents; but what is a man's very own if his pedigree is not? Therefore, if lineage is regarded as an axiological impertinence, the standard must be a good that each man *makes for himself*, not merely a good that is his "very own"; and it is not at all obvious that all axiological goods are of this nature.

If a man thanks God for his parents, his upbringing, his

traditions, and the like, he is being thankful for things that could not be his own doing. Yet there is no reason for maintaining that such things may not be, axiologically, very good indeed; and although it is possible to regard such things as mere means and opportunities for the personal achievements that alone are truly good, it is arbitrary and unconvincing to hold such views. Indeed, even the most extreme individualist might hesitate, in such matters, when he thought of his own posterity. From one point of view, he is simply a particular man equipped with generative powers, who, if he finds a willing partner, may beget children just to please himself. From another point of view he is but a link in a chain of personal succession. Eugenically, it may be better if his ancestors were tough than if they were either gentle or moral; but if his own worth has anything of potency in it, that is to say has axiological as well as merely instrumental value, it need not be confined to his own short life.

I shall not try to give a summary of the argument of this section. Its course has been too sinuous and too complicated to lend itself readily to condensation; but I should like to append certain reflections, some of them underlining what I have already said, others (I admit) unargued.

I have argued that there is no sufficient reason to suppose that all axiological value resides exclusively in someone's conscious experience, although it seems probable that the highest axiological values we know of are not at a sub- or unconscious level either in ourselves or anywhere else. This statement, however, is more readily applicable to "intrinsic" than to relational goods; and it seems to me that the axiological value of the latter has been deprecated or ignored largely because the critics thought of final goods (and of the means to them) when they should have thought of axiological goods. I have also argued that, even in the case of axiological goods that are both "intrinsic" and spiritual, there is no adequate justification for insisting that the highest goods should be self-made as well as, in some sense, our "very own."

Nevertheless, among the goods that man can discern it would seem that *acquiescentia in se ipso*, or, in other words, the Stoic imperturbability (not insensibility) of soul takes a very high place, and it is likely that the traditional trio called the (morally) Good, the Beautiful, and the True, are also among the very high things. We should also, I think, include the Jolly, even if we do not rank it quite so high, and should remember that in all this ordering of classes we are thinking rather of what *may* be very good than of what *must* be.

On the other hand, science, morality, loveliness, and happiness, when singled out in this way as pre-eminent axiological goods, commonly draw upon man's whole nature, or at any rate upon much more of that nature than is usually remembered by those moralists who speak as if mere bloodless intellectual insight, or an almost mindless succession of agreeable feelings were great (or the only) axiological goods. The truth of this observation is obvious as soon as we begin to consider the heights to which types of spiritual experience not included in the traditional list—compassion, say, or love, or imagination —may rise.

It is therefore understandable that many modern writers prefer to think and to write in terms of value-patterns either spiritual or incarnate or both, and that among these writers many should remember the Platonic Forms, finding these Forms both flexible and prophetic. In general, however, any such treatment of the subject tends to be an account of the habitat and penumbrae of the major axiological goods rather than a critical investigation into their axiological essence.

XVI

THE COMPARISON OF GOODS

AT an earlier stage of this discussion we saw that it was very difficult, if not downright impossible, to find any general principle, at once sufficient and intelligible, according to which an obligation could be pronounced *righter* or more obligatory than another. Indeed, the word "right" may seem to have no genuine comparative, although the word "good" obviously has the comparative "better." It is frequently argued, however, that there can be no sufficient and intelligible principle for deciding whether, in general, X is better than Y, and consequently that an ethics of benefit and well-being is not at all superior to an ethics of duty in this important particular.

The comparability of goods or of obligations is a question distinct from their multiplicity. It may be reasonable to argue that pluralism, not monism, is the truth regarding both, and yet that "better" is intelligible although "righter" is not. This argument is frequently used, and the substance of it is still more frequently assumed without explicit argument. The attempted comparison of benefits, therefore (which is now our theme), has a side reference to other theories. Again, if anyone holds (as Mr. Ross does) that the obligation to produce the greatest possible benefit is *one* of our moral obligations—although not the only one—it is clear that the comparison of benefits is one of the questions that moralists have to examine.

In the classification of goods attempted in the last section, it was assumed, rather than explicitly argued, that there is a multiplicity of goods that cannot, in any plain sense, be reduced to a single set of axiological constituents, and I propose to retain this assumption, supposing it to have been verified in part by the discussion itself, and believing also that a further (although partial) verification is afforded by the failure of moralistic enterprises based on the opposite contention. The

246 AN ENQUIRY INTO MORAL NOTIONS

number of these, for aught I know to the contrary, may be legion, but the most usual and, historically speaking, by far the most plausible has been the dogma that all (intrinsic) goods and evils can be reduced to a common denominator of pains and pleasures which are comparable *inter se*.

At this time of day it is quite unnecessary (I believe) to re-demonstrate what has so often been demonstrated, viz. that pleasure is not the only good *per se*, nor pain the only evil. The more moderate opinion, sponsored by McTaggart* with some reservations, and believed whole-heartedly (I daresay) by some others, that pleasure and pain yield an accurate *measure* of good and evil although they do not *constitute* goodness or badness, seems unlikely in itself and is opposed to much that has been argued and that will be argued in the present essay.

Anyone confronted with the general problem of the comparison of benefits would be inclined to suppose that goods may differ (1) in mere amount, (2) in degree, and (3) in kind; and that these three ways of differing are at least provisionally distinct. This natural view (if its provisional character be remembered) seems to me to provide a useful basis for discussion, and I shall therefore follow it for a time.

(1) There are at least two respects in which something may be said to be "better" than something else in the simple sense that it contains more good, that is, more of a good quite similar in kind and in degree.

The first of these respects is the number of persons who possess such a good, or, in the case of goods like pleasure, the number of sentient beings. A field in which ten lambs are happy seems to be a better place than a field in which only one lamb is happy, and if there were no other happy beings in either of the fields, I do not see why the first field should not be said to be a place precisely ten times as happy as the second field. In a similar way ten educated people, or ten artistic people, should theoretically attain ten times the good of one

* *Studies in Hegelian Cosmology*, ch. iv.

educated or of one artistic person, provided, as before, that there was no relevant difference in the degree or in the kind of their excellence.

So stated, the argument applies only to goods that may be regarded (or so far as they may be regarded) as private possessions. It does not apply to "better" in the sense of "more efficient," and it assumes that the private possessions in question are independent of one another. If the ten lambs were playing with one another, or if the ten educated men were raising the standard of education by conducting Socratic dialogues, other considerations would enter, although it would still be relevant to consider the number of persons who enjoyed any such benefit.

Most Utopia-mongers seem to think that the optimum world-wide human society should not be very numerous. If so, there would be sharp limits to the principle of "the more the better," and limitations of this order might (although they need not) cast a doubt upon *every* naïve application of moral arithmetic in this matter. The counter-principle of the Utopia-mongers, however, seems to be mixed and dubious. If they hold that our earth cannot support a high quality of human existence unless the human population is relatively small, on the ground, say, that a large population requires industrialism, in all its horrors, to a very marked extent, their argument is, in effect, that the quality of human life must deteriorate if its quantity becomes large, and so is irrelevant to the contention that a greater quantity *of the same quality* is a greater good. If they simply dislike the notion of a teeming humanity on aesthetic grounds, it may be doubted whether their objections are either clear-headed or clean-hearted. I do not admire the spectacle of a crowd at a football match or at a Royal Wedding, but I do not see why anyone should find the sight repulsive —unless, indeed, he is a misanthrope.

The second respect in which simple extensive quantity seems to enter, without any important qualification (or disqualification) is the time during which any good is lived through, experienced, or enjoyed. In this respect the argument is commonly developed with regard to the individual enjoyment or suffering of the same agent. If Jones has a bout of toothache for one hour, and subsequently a bout of toothache for two hours, it seems natural (and, I submit, it is correct) to say not only that the second bout was worse than the first, but also that it was precisely twice as bad. No doubt, if the memory of the first toothache affected the experience of the second, the above piece of arithmetic would not apply. It would apply only where there was no sufficient reason to doubt that the quality and degree of the toothache was the same during all the unpleasant hours. Such instances, however, seem to occur, and to occur in other cases than those of simple pleasure or of simple pain. If life be good, a long life, other things equal, is better than a short one. Any high employment of the mind is better in proportion as it can be sustained, or repeated, without boredom and without any weakening of its quality. There are some philosophers, it is true, who regard all the great "values" as timeless and, in that sense, "eternal." If so, our argument does not affect *these* goods, but it may and does affect a great many others.

Therefore the number of persons affected and the time during which any intrinsic personal good lasts are respects in which amount of goodness or of evil, in a straightforward sense, exists. There may be other straightishforward senses of which the same might be said; but most of them, I think, are not very clear. Some, however, should be mentioned.

(*a*) Amount of extension would seem to enter into relational as well as into intrinsic goods, both as regards the relations between persons and as regards relations more narrowly personal. Thus, in the case of inter-personal relationships, the *width* of justice has a certain relevance. In times of calamity, as in the agony of a great war, there is some alleviation of the general wretchedness if most of the unhappy people in the belligerent countries are convinced that an attempt is being made to apportion their heavy burdens fairly; and although this aspect of the matter is, in one sense, a private affair for each, its relational features seem also to enter. Similarly, the extent of a man's power over his physical environment is extensive, may be measurable, and may be axiologically good.

(*b*) Dr. Richards (*Science and Poetry*, p. 33) is responsible for the statement, "The best life for our friend will be one in which as much as possible of himself is engaged (as *many* of his impulses as possible)," and in his *Principles of Literary Criticism* (ch. vii) argues that a "greater good" is the satisfaction of "a greater number of equal appetencies," and that appetencies are unequal in proportion to "the extent of the disturbance of other impulses" when any given appetency is thwarted. His reasoning is therefore circular, but a part of it might be removed from the circle, and, in that case, would deal quite simply with number and amount. Similar arguments might be adduced if we spoke of the "number of perfections" instead of the number of satisfied appetencies.

(*c*) His argument concerning "more of oneself," however, has several possible forms, and many Hegelians would maintain that the higher is better than the lower principally because it includes the lower, yet transfigures the lower without relinquishing any part of it. It includes the lower and something *more*. Hegelians believe, however, that quantity itself is a very low way of thinking; and they resent seeing their views debased by the mere asking of vulgar questions. It is impolitic, therefore, to pursue the topic (which, in any case, is more appropriate to a discussion of the meaning of a difference in kind).

(2) Difference in degree is usually illustrated by intensive quantities such as a brighter light, a higher temperature, or a keener pleasure; and it is clear that many intensive quantities can be measured, as well as compared in some vaguer way, although the measurement may require special conventions different from (and less simple than) the conventions employed in measuring extensive quantities. Thus 60° F. in my bedroom and in my sitting-room do not together form a temperature of 120° F., and the temperature 60° F. in my bedroom is not

twice the temperature of 30° F. outside. On the other hand, the difference between 60° F. and 30° F. is precisely twice the difference between 45° F. and 60° F.

This question has been pretty thoroughly debated with regard to pleasures and pains. The intensity of a pleasure, of course, must not be confused with the intensity of the stimuli that cause pleasure. Indeed, in most cases (but with many reservations concerning the range of the stimuli) increase in degree of pleasure seems to correspond to the logarithm of the increase in stimulation, according to the simplest formulation of the Weber-Fechner law. If, however, the goodness of pleasures and the evil of pains could be held to correspond precisely to the intensity of their pleasantness or painfulness, we should be able to compare and to measure the greater goodness of any pleasure in so far as such pleasure varied simply in intensity.

It is sometimes said, for example, by Mr. Collingwood (*Philosophical Method*, p. 73), that *every* difference in degree is also a difference in kind. If so, the conclusion would be that the comparison or the measurement of mere differences in degree selects a very abstract feature of the situation, not that it is either worthless or absurd if it recognizes its own limitations. Mr. Collingwood's argument, however (if I have not misunderstood it), applies only to conscious experiences, and even in that application seems exaggerated. It is surely possible to experience a sharper or a weaker twinge of essentially the same toothache, that is to say of toothache that otherwise *seems* the same, localized in the same area, having the same distinctive tang—in short, appearing to differ in intensity only.

Moreover, in so far as pleasure is good and pain evil, there seems no sufficient reason for denying that the increase of intensity in pleasure (or pain) is directly proportional to the increase of good (or evil).

Even supposing, however, that the mere intensity of many pleasures and pains were a comparable and, indeed, a measurable dimension of them, yielding a corresponding scale of their degree of goodness, it would probably still be objected that no other goods had the dimension in question, or, if they had it, had it in such an attenuated and wraith-like form that little instruction could enure to moralists.

This again seems to be an exaggeration. Keener insight, a livelier imagination, a sharper wit, a nicer virtue, a heightened sense of beauty, greater gusto in living, and the like, seem, in the main, to be matters of degree, and, indeed, of intensity of bodily and of mental existence. I do not say that it would be easy (it may even be impossible) to measure such differences, and I do not think that the difference in intensity in these cases is usually of a pure and uncompounded sort. Nevertheless, such differences exist; they can be noticed; and when good things are weaker or stronger, there is reason for calling them worse or better on that account. Again, I do not say that heightened intensity is always an advantage, even in cases not visibly evil. I do not much like "intense" people, and I may possibly have axiological reasons for this attitude towards them. These distinctions of keenness, zest, intensity, or gusto, however, are, very largely, what we mean by a difference in spiritual or in physical vitality; and I personally prefer intense young people to tired ones. This preference may indeed be a prejudice, or, at any rate, ap-axiological, but there is a possibility at least that it is not a prejudice. If so, moral theory should take account of it.

(3) It is frequently supposed that goods that differ in kind are for that very reason non-comparable. That supposition, however, is itself ambiguous and therefore needs consideration. Men and horses, for example, differ in kind, but they are comparable in some respects, as railway companies know when they assign eight horses or twenty men to the same waggon. Things that differ in kind may be comparable in some respects, and the question that concerns us now is whether they may be comparable in respect of their (axiological) goodness.

In a well-known argument, usually supposed to be not conspicuously clear-headed, Mill argued that dignified or noble pleasures were qualitatively better than sottish ones, and he explained, in a way that (for a hedonist) was obviously muddle-headed, that noble pains might be better *per se* than swinish pleasures, so that Socrates dissatisfied was better than a pig satisfied.* The dignity-dimension, in short, might contradict and override the pleasure-dimension.

If Mill had not been a hedonist there would have been no contradiction in this position, and he could have consistently retained a part of his hedonism by holding that nothing except joy of the one part or suffering of the other part could have any dignity at all. Any such view could accommodate itself to extensive differences in quality. Fine art, Mill might have said, differed in kind from the higher sciences. Simple honesty, for choice in "an humble plain man," differed in kind from Balboa's emotion on that peak in Darien; and so forth. Nevertheless, all these experiences, despite their differences in kind, were comparable in respect of being pleasant and also in respect of being dignified. There might well be a scale of dignity as well as a computation of amounts of pleasantness; and if axiological worth attached both to pleasantness and to dignity, there need be no objection in theory to the view that, despite all differences in kind, the axiological problem is simply one of degrees of worth.

Accordingly, it is *possible* that the most diverse goods are comparable in this important respect, and since differences in degree may sometimes be measured, it is worth while enquiring whether all goods, however heterogeneous, may not, in some wide sense, be commensurable in respect of their goodness.

If a good q were incommensurably greater than a good r, it would follow that no amount or intensity of r could match or surpass the least conceivable amount or intensity of q; and it has sometimes been held that goods that differ in kind are incommensurable in this way. Thus, according to Cardinal Newman in the familiar passage we have already mentioned

* The philanthropic d'Argenson, Louis XV's minister, wished to see in the common people "a menagerie of happy men."

(*Anglican Difficulties*, p. 190), it were better for millions of men "to die of starvation in extremest agony" than for *one* human being "to steal one poor farthing without excuse." The alternatives in Newman's statement are, on the one hand, a peccadillo, and, on the other hand, the utmost conceivable wretchedness; but Newman would presumably have also held that the most venial sin was incomparably worse than an infinity of ugliness, imbecility, or other evil.

I think we may say, quite curtly, that few would uphold this extreme position, regarding either sin, or ugliness, or error, or non-acquiescence with one's soul. If, however, we reject the extreme position, there is no alternative but to admit a certain comparability in the magnitude of all goods and of all evils. If a Demiurge, for instance, had the choice between permitting a single venial sin (otherwise than as an occasion for the exercise of grace), and permitting the agony of millions (for no ulterior purpose), I do not see that he could be morally commended for choosing the latter; and his choice *ex hypothesi* would be governed by a comparison of the magnitude of all the goods and evils he could effect or permit.

Certainly, it might be argued that the Demiurge, in this theological illustration, could not make certain comparisons of this order, even if he were omnipotent in any intelligible sense of that word. He might not, for example, be able to make a numerical reckoning of these axiological magnitudes, since goods and evils, although comparable in respect of their magnitude, might be non-numerically so. Again, it might be said that (consistently with the other designs of the Demiurge) there would be a metaphysical impossibility in bringing into existence more than a smallish number of beings capable of knowledge, morality, pleasure, and other goods, and that, within this limited range, certain kinds of knowledgeable or aesthetic experience were, *de facto*, incommensurably better than, say, the maximum possible suffering within that range.

The second of these objections has no considerable theoretical importance, since, presumably, the Demiurge could contemplate illimitable possibilities of goodness in the worlds he might create, but abandoned on account of technical demiurgic difficulties. The first objection, however, is important for our purposes.

If we ask what could be meant by a non-numerical axiological calculus, we can reach some sort of answer without great difficulty. In the first place, if by a non-numerical calculus we meant one that could not be computed, with complete accuracy, in whole numbers, we could point to a series like $1, \sqrt{2}, \sqrt{3}, 2, \sqrt{5}$, which, in this sense, contains incommensurables. In the second place, it would be reasonable to remark that a numerical calculus can be applied only where appropriate units can be discovered, such units being exclusive, equal, and together exhaustive of any sum-total that is reckoned. It should theoretically be possible to have an order of greater-and-less in which the gaps could not be filled, quite neatly and quite fully, by suitable units.

These possibilities, however, do not seem to be of great importance in the present connection. The first of them is obviously a genuine possibility even for a Demiurge, but (retaining the illustration) it is possible, by the use of fractions, to obtain an indefinitely close approximation, in whole numbers, to the surds in the series. The second of them may have considerable practical importance for *us*. Few suppose (and these few not very wisely) that any human being has hitherto discovered, or is likely to discover, a workable set of axiological units in terms of which he can employ his moral arithmetic and obtain results that are other than amusing. For the most part, therefore, we have to compute in these matters in a way that is largely non-numerical, if we compute at all and also remain sensible. The Demiurge, however, could, if he chose, employ the method of margins, that is to say he would be able to perceive that a certain amount of good V was just inferior to a certain amount of good U and just superior to a certain amount of good W. Thus, given a great variety of conceivable comparable goods, the gaps in the reckoning (if they existed) would be negligible; and this result is important for the general problem whether in the nature of things an axiological series must be non-numerical, although it may be indifferent for the practical purposes of would-be human computers who cannot even pretend that they have constructed an adequate numerical axiological series.

Accordingly, we should conclude (I think) that although a certain comparability of all goods, however heterogeneous, in respect of their axiological magnitude should be conceded, it is very unlikely indeed that a high degree of precision in such comparisons can be attained over the whole field of values. This conclusion, of course, does not deny the possibility that some of these comparisons, and, more generally, certain areas within the total field, can be compared, and even measured, with a pretty high degree of accuracy; and I shall return to the point. At the present stage in the discussion, however, I have to point out that the matter has been over-simplified in the last few pages, and that certain further reservations have to be made.

For, firstly, I have spoken of a good q being superior to a good r, these goods differing in kind, and this might readily be taken to mean that every q is axiologically better than every r. In general, however (as the incidentals of the argument showed), the affair is much more involved. The man who says that knowledge, for instance, differs in kind from simple pleasure and is superior in its kind, need not be understood to mean that every instance of knowledge is superior to every instance of simple pleasure. He would concede, I suppose, that the pleasure I obtain from smoking a certain tobacco may be a greater good than *certain* pieces of knowledge—for example, than the knowledge that I purchased the tobacco from such and such a tobacconist and received two coppers in change. What he would mean would be that knowledge could attain a degree of excellence that no simple pleasure could match; and even then he should admit that in all probability no single person's knowledge could be as great a good as a really extensive contribution to human happiness.

Secondly (and in consequence of the above), if our moral arithmetic were multi-dimensional, as it often has to be, there would be a serious difficulty even if each separate dimension were quite readily measurable. In the estimation of pleasures, to say nothing of other goods, we have to take account both of extensive and of intensive magnitude. Let it be granted that two minutes of toothache in Jones is precisely twice as great an evil as one minute of the same toothache in Jones, and (what is perhaps not quite so plausible) that if Jones and Smith experienced the same kind and intensity of toothache for a minute, there would be precisely twice the amount of evil that would occur if Jones were the only sufferer. Let it also be granted that we can give a perfectly good sense to the statement that Jones's toothache, now, is precisely twice as intense as it was five minutes ago. We should still have to enquire whether the increase of intensity could be equated with the increase of extension, whether, in short, a doubled intensity during one minute is precisely equal to two minutes of the given intensity. It is not at all clear what the correct answer is.

Despite these supplementary difficulties, however, I think it is worth our while to pursue these problems a little further, keeping, so far as possible, to types of comparison and of (vaguish) commensuration that are likely actually to arise. I shall try to put some of the main points in a very simplified form.

Let us suppose that A, B, and C are major goods, differing in kind from the minor goods P, Q, and R, and that they are such that it is very unlikely (as an empirical possibility) that the goodness of any amount or degree of such minor goods could even approach the goodness of one of the major goods.

If so, it is clear that many of the problems of computation might actually be simplified. If there were opposition between a major and a minor good (in the above sense of major and of minor) the minor good should be simply neglected. A major good plus a minor good would be better than the said major good alone; but so little better as not to matter much. And if our choice were restricted to minor goods (as above defined) we should have to do with a petty business.

The serious question would therefore be whether the *major* goods permitted of comparison, each in its own kind, and were comparable one with another. If they were comparable, there would be no serious problem of principle. If they were simply incomparable in respect of their axiological magnitude, we should have no means of deciding between A and B, if they conflicted, except the very unsatisfactory criterion that if, in the conflict, A would be very little damaged by the choice of B, although B would be gravely affronted by the choice of A, there might be some small reason for preferring B to A. If there were no conflict A + B would be better than A by itself, and greatly better, since, by hypothesis, B is a major good.

All such arguments, however, presuppose the possibility of assessing the axiological value of various goods in such a way that the values of A and of B respectively are not affected by the fact that in A + B they are taken *together*. This is reasonable when A and B do not enter into any effective combination or partnership. It would be reasonable, for instance, if we were considering the comfort or degree of education of a Chinaman as A, and the comfort or degree of education of a Scotsman as B. If, however, we were considering, let us say, the conscience and the secular knowledge in the same man, or the relations between the morals and the intelligence within the same nation, the factors would not be independent; and those who believe that good and evil have to do rather with the commingling of forms and patterns than with any sort of sum of values make precisely this criticism.

It is commonly said that the value of a whole bears no constant relation to the values of its parts, and consequently that most of this talk about A + B has little genuine weight. I do not think, however, that the objection is by any means so serious as many of its critics suggest. If they *know* the truth of the principle they advance so confidently, they must be able to assess the values of, at any, rate, a good many wholes and also the values of the parts of these wholes. Is it impossible, then, or even unlikely, that although they cannot find a single formula for inferring the value of a whole, given the values of its parts, they might still discover the principal types of combination relevant to these matters, and so be able to modify their moral arithmetic accordingly? And if they could not do so, what would be the result? It is admitted, on all hands, that there is a very great multiplicity of goods. Suppose, then, that we are forbidden to infer the value of *any* whole from the values of its parts. In that case certain wholes are good and certain parts are good, and *all* these goods are independent. Some wholes, say L or M, are much better than, say, the components *a b c* of L or the components *d e f* of M. Another whole, say, N, is much worse than its components, say *a b e*. There is no greater difficulty in dealing with a multiplicity of this order than with any other multiplicity of goods. There is only the need to guard against a plausible fallacy.

Regarding moral arithmetic in general, there is fair comment (I think) in the complaint of many authors that any attempt to arithmetize good and evil has been elaborated from various historical attempts, such as those of Bernoulli, Laplace, and Jevons, to arithmetize pleasures and pains; that all such enterprises are better suited to intrinsic than to relational goods; and that they persistently regard goods and evils as isolable *items*, not as structures, patterns, or forms. As Mr. Joseph remarks (*Some Problems in Ethics*, p. 86), the factors considered were held to be *simple* items, as "some pleasures, sounds, scents, very uncomprehensive actions."

We should all agree (I suggest) that if all comparisons between better and worse had to traffic in a sort of comminuted axiology, the ensuing computation, even if it were non-numerical, would be very jejune indeed in comparison with what its promoters contemplated, that is to say an appraisal of what is currently meant by a good life. I am not convinced, however, that this restriction to fragmentary items is inevitable in terms of the theory, and even if it were inevitable, it would not therefore condemn the theory altogether. There is surely a certain item-like character in the fact that knowledge, imagination, virtue, and the like are in some sense parcelled out among different people, and that within the same person there is so much interruption and so many abrupt changes of conscious experience, that even "items" have to be considered.

Therefore it seems to me to be important to observe that the possibilities of moral arithmetic are a good deal more promising than many moralists would have us suppose. According to Bradley (*Ethical Studies*, 2nd edition, p. 157 *n*.) there is only one moral law that should *never* be broken in obedience to a higher law, and that is "the universal law to do the best we can in the circumstances." If this rigidly "universal law" implied that one's best had to be computed quite generally by moral arithmetic in terms of commensurable items of good and of evil—which is not what Bradley would have said of it—we may agree, as a result of our discussion, that the computation would be very hazardous indeed, and would be likely to omit a great deal that should not have been omitted. We may agree, too, that a simple choice between two trains of consequences would also be very hazardous if it had to be attempted on these lines; for although the effect of anyone's choice frequently ceases to be appreciable when there is an intervening tract of history, the most trivial acts (in appearance) may be big with historical consequences. Nevertheless, it seems clear that even the despised method of moral computation is (as Mill said of hedonism) "tangible and intelligible," even if it is not sufficient for estimating comparative values.

That a greater number of persons is affected: that of two goods that seem very similar one is more intense, more lasting, or (we may add) purer than the other—propositions such as these are applicable to our comparison of values, and collectively have great significance. Again, it is unphilosophical to be contemptuous of "items." In the main, our views on these topics, if solid, have to be built up with pains and patience from simple and direct comparisons between better and worse, for such comparisons, together with direct judgments of good and of bad, are the alphabet of an ethics of well-being. If "better" in many of its ranges has an alphabet, and if "righter" has no alphabet at all, an ethics of well-being is to that extent stronger than an ethics of duty; and the extent is considerable.

I have tried to argue that such is in fact the case.

On the other hand, since many comparisons between better and worse do not lend themselves readily to computation (if they lend themselves at all), and since there are many pitfalls in apparently straightforward calculations concerning benefits, it is important to observe that plain men habitually make such comparisons without any thought of a calculus residing in them, and that the philosophers who scorn calculation in such matters nevertheless admit the possibility of many such comparisons. The plain man says that there is greater liberty, fineness, elevation, dignity, or some such quality in one course of action than in another; that someone whom he admires or respects would choose it; or the like. Such views may not always be axiologically sound, but, often, they are sound. And the philosophers who are much too philosophical to calculate are not too philosophical to indicate what they consider just grounds for an axiological preference.

At the present moment, for example, it is fashionable to say that the notion of Forms, elaborated by Plato, akin to the spirit of much in Hegel, and fortified by the *Gestalt* psychology of recent times, may provide the desired clue. In a Higher Form or Nobler Pattern there is a blending of opposites that transfigures both instead of (in a pedestrian way) retaining the better features of each. Distinctions are retained, but are made tractable and mild. There is a happy marriage between Degree and Kind.

Such views may be both true and relevant; but it should further be remembered that even the despised pedestrians on these highways were prepared to dispense with calculation.

Take, for example, the utilitarians of the traditional hedonistic variety. Bentham, it is true, believed that a "moral thermometer was required which should exhibit every degree of happiness and suffering." He therefore took pains over the theory of the thermometer; and Jevons, by employing the marginal method on Benthamite assumptions (in his *Theory of Political Economy*) professed to give hedonism all the advantages of the differential calculus in place of the homely arithmetic with which Bentham had struggled. Between these extremes, however, the intervening utilitarians (for the most part) preferred other methods. According to Austin (*Jurisprudence*, Lecture II) the rules of conduct depended, in the end, upon observation and experience of pleasure-giving tendencies, but there was, in general, no calculation of utility in particular cases. "Our rules would be fashioned on utility; our conduct on our rules."* J. S. Mill, again, although he believed that "the truths of arithmetic are applicable to the valuation of happiness as of all other measurable quantities" (*Utilitarianism*, ch. v.), was also quite prepared to dispense with calculation. To anyone who objected that, being a busy man in his moral affairs, he had no time to calculate the "lots of pleasures and of pains" that Bentham and his followers talked about, Mill replied that men had been learning the tendencies of actions during "the whole past duration of the human species" (*ibid.*, ch. ii).

This reply seems to me to be perfectly adequate. It is possible, I suppose, to prove by elaborate statistics that cancer is a more dangerous disease than measles, and that arsenic, bulk for bulk, is more poisonous than lysol. If, however, no reliable statistics were available (as, for aught I know to the contrary, may actually be the case regarding lysol and arsenic), it would surely be absurd to say that we had not learned these things by experience. Similarly, if the hedonists were right in supposing that pleasure determined what each man preferred, it would

---

* And a nice remark of Austin's may be quoted here, although it was made with a different purpose. "It was never contended or conceived by a sound orthodox utilitarian," he said (Lecture IV), "that the lover should kiss his mistress with an eye to the common weal."

surely be permissible to say that mankind had learned a great deal about human preferences, whether or not they had done much in the way of accurate measurement.

Knowledge of this kind would apply to what were great and what were small pleasures, as well as to the presence or absence of pleasure; and if, as we have assumed, the hedonists were wrong in maintaining that pleasure is the only good, there seems to be no sufficient reason why mankind could not learn a great deal about what is better and worse in this more general sense both from experience of the usual tendencies of things and by direct inspection of good and of evil. And all without accurate measurement.

Although our experience of the tendencies of things is obviously of great importance in this matter, the judgment of good and of evil, of better and of worse, is still more important, since the tendencies in question are tendencies to produce good or evil, that is to say, of what is either judged or known to be so. On this point some further observations seem to be necessary.

When Mill set about to answer the question why a dissatisfied Socrates was better than a satisfied pig, he replied that those only could judge who had had adequate experience of both types of pleasure, and that if such judges (or a majority of them) preferred a Socratic to a swinish existence there was no more to be said. The pig was disqualified from judging because he was incapable of appreciating the Socratic side of the question.

Mill's argument referred to certain conscious experiences, viz. to pleasures and to pains, however dignified. Consequently, it had the great merit of insisting that such affairs should be judged, not by hearsay, but by experience. On the other hand (and keeping to pleasures and pains), it had obvious defects. To a Socratic temperament swinish pleasures might be abominable; but they might nevertheless be very delightful to beings who did not have a Socratic temperament. It might happen that Socratic pleasures became enjoyable at a time of life at which disreputable pleasures had lost their zest, and so that the opinion of Socrates was suspect in the same way as that of a man who used to like claret but now had no taste for anything except brandy. Again, a majority verdict is very unsatisfactory, and there might be so few qualified judges that even a majority verdict could not be obtained. It might be the case, for instance, that hardly anyone has become really eminent both in fine art and in science. Leonardo da Vinci was one of the rare exceptions. But would anyone say that if Leonardo preferred science to art, all mankind should agree that science was better (or pleasanter) than art?

In principle these objections apply, not merely to pleasure-sippers relishing their favourite beverages, but to all judgments of good and evil that imply personal experience. We have to say, then, in this as in other matters, that our own opinions, however confident we may be, are the better if they are fortified by the assent of others. We have also to say that if we have reason to suspect some personal idiosyncrasy (as we may have regarding the relish of certain pleasures and also concerning many other goods), we should add some qualifying phrase, such as "to persons of my stamp." That very qualification, however, suggests the possibility of knowing that the qualification is frequently needless. We can distinguish, in fact, between goods that are peculiar and goods that are common. In doing so, we have to accept (although not uncritically) the usual inferences from the speech and behaviour of other people. If they say that they like watching football, or find high aesthetic value in the spectacle of a bull-fight, we should admit (for the most part) that they do experience these hedonic and aesthetic values, even if we personally are bored by football and if a bull-fight simply makes us sick.

Mill's argument, if fully developed, would appear to involve the conclusion that all comparisons of values were negligible unless they were made by the vanishingly small number of human beings who had adequate personal experience of all human values. We cannot assume that a man's artistic sensibility, say, is independent of his intellect, or his intellect of his moral character, or his moral character of his physical health. Therefore, it would be imprudent to pool the verdicts of an inartistic A who could compare health with morality, of a sickly B who could compare intellect with fine art, and so forth. We should need to have universal experts.

His claim must, therefore, be abandoned, but its abandonment does nothing to justify the suspicion that good and evil, better and worse, are unknowable. Men do not have infallible insight into such matters, but they do have genuine, fallible insight. They can test, compare, and purify their judgments on these as on other questions.

XVII

DUTY AND BENEFIT AGAIN

IN the penultimate chapter of Book II we discussed a part of the problem of the relation between duty and benefit, and concluded that one of the requisites of any right action was that it should either be or be meant to be beneficial, that is to say, not maleficent and not futile.

To prove this, however, was certainly not to prove that the *only* reason why a right action is right is the benefit, or the probable benefit, it brings. For there may be other requisites. It also does not prove that "doing one's best in the circumstances" is ultimately the sole rule of righteousness. "Doing one's best"* would be such a rule if benefit, actual or prospective, *alone* could justify conduct; for if benefit is the sole relevant consideration, it follows that the pursuit of a lesser good when a greater good might be reached is a sin. In Mr. Ross's language the "optimific" action would *ipso facto* be the morally right action. Obviously, however, we cannot infer this proposition from the verity (if it be one) that the conferring of some benefit (i.e. being simply "bonific") is *an* essential constituent of every right action.

Mr. Ross, indeed, believes he can prove that in many instances the "optimific" action is *not* the right action, and other moralists, such as John Grote and Bishop Butler in his *Dissertation on Virtue* have said the same thing. In the present section, then, I intend to conduct a further examination of these objections to the sufficiency of an ethics of benefit, but still to examine only a part of the field. It is best to track the quarry stage by stage.

At the present stage, then, I shall construe the thesis of

* If the man who "does his best" is asked why his best was not better, he can reasonably reply that if it could have been better it would not have been his best.

an ethics of benefit in a narrower sense than that ethics is entitled to claim; and one of my reasons for doing so is that this narrow interpretation seems in fact to have been the contention of traditional utilitarianism and also of certain theories of non-hedonistic or "ideal" utilitarianism. (Indeed, it is this narrow sense of the theory that Mr. Ross and other critics seem to have principally, if not exclusively, in their minds.)

The narrow sense of the theory with which I am now concerned is the view that the rightness or wrongness of a moral action should be judged entirely by its probable *consequences* in the way of benefit or disservice. Nothing is to count in this matter except what is likely to come of the action; all the probable consequences are relevant; and the maximum probable benefit *in the way of consequences* is the standard of right and of wrong.

To avoid misunderstanding, certain definitory observations should be given.

(1) It may obviously be impracticable to attempt to assess *all* reasonably probable consequences, and the remote consequences of certain decisions may be such that the given decision is only a negligibly small part-cause of these later events. If so, the method is proportionately circumscribed; but it does not follow that any other method is possible, or that, within its limitations, the method is not very useful.

(2) I shall not assume, with the traditional utilitarians, that pleasurable and painful consequences should alone be considered, or that an effective moral arithmetic can be undertaken. I shall assume only that we can often speak significantly of the best probable consequences and of better and worse probable consequences. This being understood, I shall retain the liberty of arguing in terms of algedonic consequences (i.e. of comfort or of misery) where this seems appropriate.

(3) By the consequences of an act I mean all the results to which the act contributes, in so far as it does so contribute. This includes the effects of which the action, as we should

commonly say, is the decisive part-cause, and also those of which it is a contributory, but minor, part-cause.

This observation may seem superfluous, but there is so much ambiguity in the usual talk about consequences that some such explanation seems unavoidable. Thus the present Lord Chief Justice of England, Lord Hewart, on a very serious occasion (for it was a trial for murder) said:

"Then I would ask you to consider this, whether it is better that a guilty man, if he be guilty, should be punished, or that a sane man, on a false allegation of insanity, should be detained for a long time in a criminal lunatic asylum? Please do not consider consequences at all. The question for you is much simpler, much more direct, much more free from any consideration of that sort" (*The Times*, March 9, 1935).

The "consequences" that his Lordship had in view when he made this statement must have been collateral consequences, consequences in the way of public policy, or the like, for it is plain that the execution of the accused man, on the one hand, or his incarceration in a criminal lunatic asylum on the other hand, *were* consequences of the jury's decision. I want to make it plain, then, that when I speak of "consequences" I *mean* consequences, and not some special sort of collateral or oblique consequences.

The question we have now to consider was stated with considerable precision by Bishop Butler in his *Dissertation* in the passage beginning, "Without enquiring, how far, and in what sense, virtue is resolvable into benevolence, and vice into the want of it; it may be proper to observe that benevolence, and the want of it, singly considered, are in no sort the whole of virtue and vice," and I think it will be profitable to follow Butler's argument in some detail, with special regard to the reasons he gave, and to his illustrations.

I have heard Mr. Ross say in public that he was contending, in essentials, for what Butler contended; and Mr. Ross (independently) gives the same sort of examples. In many respects, however, Butler spoke in a much more guarded way than Mr.

Ross does, and was much more sympathetic towards what we now call a utilitarian view of these matters. It is probable, indeed, from Butler's later reference to "the constitution of our nature" as being morally decisive, and for other reasons, that he supposed he was able to prove that virtue could not be reduced to benevolence (or to benevolence and prudence combined). I should point out, however, that what Butler specifically undertook to prove in this passage was that, whether or not virtue could ultimately be reduced to benevolence, there was a great deal more to be considered than mere, simple, *prima facie* benevolence, especially in particular instances. This cautious statement (I suggest) was obviously correct; but I should like my readers also to be interested in the further question whether the resources of utilitarianism are exhausted when objections are raised simply in terms of "benevolence, and the want of it singly considered."

In detail, Butler's reasons were as follows:

On the hypothesis that virtue could be reduced without remainder to simple benevolence or philanthropy, we ought to conclude that nothing mattered to a moral man morally engaged except the degree of benevolence he could exercise.

But (*a*) we do approve of *preferential* benevolence;

And (*b*) although falsehood, injustice, and "unprovoked violence" are reprehensible on utilitarian grounds (because, in general, they tend to produce an "overbalance of misery") they are *also* reprehensible on other grounds.

In illustration of (*a*) Butler said that a moral man should prefer a friend or a benefactor to all others who were "competitors for anything whatever," irrespective of the admitted utility of friendship.

Again, partly in illustration of (*b*) he said that it would plainly be wrong to purloin from A what A had justly earned and to bestow it on B, even if B's pleasure would probably be greater than A's annoyance, and if "no bad consequence would follow."

Moreover, (*c*) if a man, by an act of injustice could procure a greater benefit for himself than any inconvenience he would thereby procure for his society, there would be no vice in such an action. (Indeed, Butler might have spoken more strongly, for, since by hypothesis this unjust act is optimific, it must, on the theory, be *right*, not simply permissible, and anyone who wilfully neglected such an overbalance of profit would be a knave as well as a fool.)

Let us examine these contentions.

(*a*) Butler's argument appears to be that pure benevolence looks only to the amount of the probable benefit, and does not discriminate between the recipients, although certain (probably insufficient) utilitarian reasons might be discovered for such discrimination. The admission in the second part of this statement seems greatly to weaken the first part of it.

His illustration was unfortunate, but not uninstructive. Accepting the ideas of his century and occupation regarding patronage and preferment, he argued that a moral man, out of friendship, should give his friend preferment, but should be rigidly impartial if he had to deal with strangers.

There would not seem to be any difficulty at all in dealing with such questions on utilitarian lines. For example, the civil service in any community might be recruited by lot, by competitive examination, or for party reasons. There are historical precedents for all of these (even, in the case of the last of them, for an extensive change-over in minor administrative appointments after a presidential election), and it might very well be argued that it is for history to decide which of the plans works best. It is a logical consequence of each system that persons of a certain class should be selected, and persons of other classes rejected. If there are more general reasons than the empirical test of history for preferring one of these systems to the others, there is no good reason for supposing that these are not *general utilitarian* reasons.

Consider again why (rightly or wrongly) we should nowadays be disposed to deny Butler's view regarding this particular obligation of friendship. We should usually say to-day that in every competition the best man should win, and consequently that neither friendship nor gratitude should be allowed to interfere, unless they supply special evidence of fitness (and even then they are suspect). I do not say that we always live up to this ideal; but most of us profess it.

Why has this change occurred in our sentiments? Among many reasons, one of the chief, surely, is that the biassed friendly system interferes with efficiency. Our historical evidence in favour of this view may not be entirely satisfactory; but we assume that it is.

It does not follow, of course, that there may not (as Butler says) be non-utilitarian moral grounds for our convictions upon such subjects; but it does follow that the utilitarian grounds are stronger than Butler here suggested.

The views of the new intuitionists may be compared with Bishop Butler's. Mr. Prichard (*Mind*, No. 81, p. 27) seems to deny that probable results afford any sort of reason for moral rightness or wrongness, for he holds that if a benevolent act is right, it is right because benevolence suits a given situation, and not because any good is likely to be done. Mr. Ross's position is nearer Butler's. Probable future benefit, he says, is one possible ground of right action. He also holds, however, that this ground "ignores or at least does not do full justice to the highly personal character of duty" (*R.G.*, p. 22), i.e. that benevolence is in principle undiscriminating and consequently cannot justify the highly special obligations attaching to friendship, gratitude, being a son, being married, and the like.

On the contrary, it would seem to me that it is not only possible, but also easy and frequent, to justify special obligations on utilitarian grounds. Why should we not say that it is for the general good that the payment of debts should have priority over donations to charity? Is it not constantly argued (correctly or incorrectly) that it is better for a community if parents are responsible for the upbringing of their children than if the matter were left to State educators as in some red system of public non-family responsibility for youthful Comrades? It is quite a mistake to say that utilitarianism is at all helpless in such matters, although, of course, it *may* not be wholly successful.

(*b*) Butler's next argument is to the general effect that the (perfectly sound) utilitarian reasons against injustice, false-hood, etc., are insufficient since there are many particular cases in which wickedness would *not* be condemned on utilitarian grounds; and Mr. Ross (*R.G.*, pp. 34 *seqq.*) relies on such instances to *demonstrate* (as he says) that wrong actions may, quite frequently, be optimific.

Let us choose as forcible an instance as possible and suppose that A purloins from B (who is rich and does not notice the loss) something that he gives, by stealth, to C (who is poor and values it). Suppose further that A keeps the matter a secret to his grave.

In that case there is *no* loss (at any rate no sensible loss) to B, and there is a net gain to C. C, moreover, is an innocent beneficiary, and cannot be troubled by conscientious scruples. Again, A may be supposed to be a utilitarian who sincerely believes (under the conditions aforesaid) that this particular action is optimific and therefore right. There is therefore no reason to hold that A's conscience should trouble him (i.e. Butler and Mr. Ross need not assume, as they do, that A's common sense must tell him that he is doing wrong although for a philanthropic purpose). No doubt the secret might be hard to keep, but the hypothesis is based upon probabilities, and it may be highly probable that such secrets could be kept.

It seems to me to be quite plain that such cases might occur and that, if they occurred, there would be an overbalance of pleasure or other similar advantage in favour of the successful theft or falsehood. If such considerations exhausted the relevant meaning of "optimific," Butler and Mr. Ross would have proved their point, and we must regard this conclusion as a fixed datum for further argument.

(*c*) In the above argument, A was supposed to be an impartial philanthropist who benefited C in an antinomian way without appreciably injuring B. Butler points out, however, that the same conclusion would follow if A benefited *himself* by some act of fraud, adultery, etc., without appreciably injuring others (or in the case of adultery if A and C gratified themselves B and the rest of the world remaining unsuspicious).

On the assumptions we have provisionally made in this section, Butler's conclusion follows. A benefit to the agent is just as genuine a benefit as a benefit to anyone else. If benefit alone justifies action it would be wrong to neglect anyone's benefit, even one's own. The man who says, for instance, "I am prepared to sacrifice a great deal for my brother's education, but I am not prepared to ask any member of the family to sacrifice a farthing for *my* education," is speaking foolishly and unethically, unless the brother is the clever member of the family.

Certainly, if we held, as some moralists do, that "all moral good must be positively altruistic,"* it would follow that the greatest benefit would not necessarily determine moral obligation; for the benefit in question might be principally one's own, and so would not be "positively altruistic." I do not think, however (any more than Butler did), that this view can be sustained. Yet since Mr. Ross, as well as Brentano and some others are sympathetic towards it, I shall try to give my reasons for rejecting it.

If a man has greater opportunities for achieving his own good than any one else's, that, I submit, is a moral reason for seeking his own good. According to Kant, our own perfection was a moral end, although our own happiness was not. The first part of this view was based upon the false ground that we could improve ourselves and could not improve others morally; but Kant's point remains even if we allow (what is the truth) that we ourselves have a special responsibility and opportunity for fashioning our own moral characters and only

* A quotation from Eaton's account of Brentano's views in *The Austrian Theory of Values.*

an indirect potency of this order towards others by instruction, advice, example, and the removal of gross temptations. In the second part of his view, Kant (I suggest) was simply wrong. If the happiness of others is an object of moral endeavour, the reason is that it is a good. If so, the agent's own happiness is also a good. (I do not say that Kant gave this reason; I say it is the correct reason.)

Even if an elderly philanthropist could give great enjoyment to others (say, by promoting a "youth movement") and could experience but little himself, it would not follow that he was justified in neglecting his own small happiness either morally or in any other way. Indeed, it would be quite logical (and not immoral) to hold that a certain degree of "push" and self-assertion is commendable in everyone, and permissible, e.g. in a candidate who does not necessarily think that, if appointed, he would be the best man for the job.* What is not logical, and is not moral, is either to assume that one's own good, as such, is superior to anyone else's, or to act, intentionally or unintentionally, as if we did make that assumption.

So far as I can see, the counter-arguments in this matter are very weak. It is said, firstly, that we are so prone to invest our own doings with an aura of virtue that the only safe rule is to take no account whatsoever of personal advantage in moral affairs. To this I answer that it is very unsafe to ignore what is obviously true, and that the argument, in a lesser but still in a considerable degree, would apply to our friends as well as to ourselves. Is a man to ignore his friends, just because he is quite likely to be biassed in their favour?

It is said, secondly, that each man is strongly moved to consult his own interests, and therefore does not need to make a duty of doing so. To this the usual reply is that he may not be *wise* in such matters; and again that he may fall into acedia or despair and *then* may require conscientious reasons for taking proper care of himself. Any such reply, however, although

* Cf. Westermarck, *Ethical Relativity*, ch. i.

valid in its way, seems weaker than is necessary. Has a man no duty to defend his rights, that is to say, to insist that he shall not subordinate himself to others without sufficient cause? And why should morality be regarded merely as an *additional* motive to action, useful only when our inclinations would lead us to act immorally? Even if, in certain cases we may *have* to do the right thing, I for one cannot see that such actions cease to be right in consequence.

I conclude, therefore, with Butler, that personal as well as philanthropic consequences should be included in an "optimific" action, and this, not merely in accordance with the special assumptions provisionally made at this stage of the argument, but for general moral reasons.

The question then is whether such particular cases of optimific actions that belong to a class generally accounted wrong is or is not a proof that utilitarian theories of moral obligation are necessarily insufficient. This question needs more elaborate discussion.

Among the utilitarians John Austin (I think) gave his mind most closely to the problem (*Jurisprudence*, Lecture II). According to him, what fell to be considered was "the probable effect on the general happiness or good" if acts of a certain class were generally performed or generally omitted, and he explicitly asserted that "considered in themselves" exceptions to classes of action that were generally reprehensible on utilitarian grounds might be positively good. As instances he mentioned the act by which a poor man "assuages his poverty with the superfluous wealth of another," or tax evasion where the evader gained much and the loss to the revenue was as nothing in comparison with the total revenue.

In short, Austin fully accepted the type of illustration on which Butler and Mr. Ross rely so confidently, but he denied that such illustrations undermined the utilitarian position. His argument was, in substance, that utility fixed and justified the general rule; that it was better, on utilitarian grounds, that men should follow a few well-established rules than that they should try to calculate consequences in particular cases, since the calculation was much too difficult for ordinary, busy, and moderately intelligent human beings.

Nevertheless, Austin added: "There certainly are cases (of comparatively rare occurrence) wherein the specific considerations balance or outweigh the general: cases which (in the language of Bacon) are 'immersed in matter': cases perplexed with peculiarities which cannot be safely neglected, in short, *anomalous* cases. Even in these to depart from the rule is mischievous, but the specific consequences of the resolve are so important that the mischief of following the rule may outweigh the mischief of breaking it." An example would be a political rebellion (that had some prospect of success) against a thoroughly objectionable Government.

What is the force of such arguments?

The doctrine naturally appeals to legally minded moralists. The intention of a legal enactment is to ensure *general* performance or forbearance (admitting the judge's discretion concerning penalties, and the possibility of pardon or amnesty). In the extreme case, indeed, it is not even necessary that a prohibited practice should in itself be worse than the practice enjoined. What is socially expedient (e.g. in the rule of the road) is that there should be a uniform practice, although we should usually say that a legal rule was bad if it were frequently incommodious.

Even if it were assumed, however, that a good law is simply a law that is socially beneficial, it would never be necessary to prove that in every instance the law-abiding action must be optimific (although law-breaking would be made universally impolitic if detection were certain and a sufficient penalty were enforced). The law is proved benevolent if (apart from artificial penalties) it is a benevolent *rule*.

Lawyers are also entitled to argue that, in general, it is socially inexpedient for individual citizens to show an unhealthy curiosity into the merits of each particular case. Their main business is to learn what the rule is (preferably through a solicitor), and they should be prepared to find that theirs is one of the law's hard cases.

Obviously, however, this line of argument can easily be stretched to absurdity. If a law is generally incommodious, the subjects, unless they are very unenlightened, will soon discover the circumstance, and the law (like prohibition in America) will become a scandal. Indeed, most of the utilitarians regarded the general enlightenment of the people as a prime desideratum.

It is therefore probable that Austin's reluctant admission of "anomalous cases" was much too grudging. Holding that a legal sovereign must be legally absolute in all particulars, he seems to have thought that the only choice lay between the complete acceptance of a given sovereignty in all its works and explicit rebellion. It would be more reasonable to say that even if a good Government is always (legally) absolute, the type of Government in which intelligent criticism of the laws is possible and also effective is much superior to any other.

It would not follow, however, that such intelligent criticism should not be utilitarian.

It may further be argued that the reliance of the law upon fixed general rules may become something of a fetish. Granting that rules are necessary (e.g. regarding marital relations), it does not follow that special types of cases may not be excepted for sufficient reasons. Marriage laws that permit no divorce are simpler to grasp than laws that do permit divorce, and the rules permitting divorce may have various degrees of complication. It is possible, however, to buy simplicitly too dear; and it is absurd to suppose that all administrative regulations can ever become really simple. Revenue officials must have subsidiary regulations regarding what is and what is not "the same occupation"; land valuators must have rules for deciding whether or not a tenant who effects improvements at his own expense is or is not to be regarded as the "owner" of that part of the property. There are periodic simplifications of such things, but never complete simplicity.

Let us pass from law to morals.

Austin, like many other lawyers, would say that laws are promulgated and enforced by determinate persons who are the authorities duly constituted, but that morality depends more vaguely upon the decision and the "sanction" of public opinion. Yet few competent moralists would accept the public opinion of every place or age as the sufficient and unquestioned arbiter in moral matters. There is nothing easier to conceive than a wrong-headed but fashionable standard of morals.

No doubt we may be asked what alternative we can offer to mere public opinion. It will not do to say, "Each man's conscience"; for conscience, too, can be wrong-headed. And moral infallibility is nowhere to be found. Insight and clarity, however, appreciable if imperfect, may very well be discovered —sometimes among the experts (however much they may overlook through becoming bespectacled by their theories) sometimes by persons who are not experts (however unskilful they may be in theorizing). The qualified opiners in this field may be very numerous, since everyone has to face moral problems and to think about some of them; but what is wanted in these matters is the force of reflection combined with experience, not the vicissitudes of fashion and custom, or (in that sense) "public opinion."

This being granted, the question, in terms of our present provisional assumptions, is how law differs relevantly from morals, if both are justified by the probability of benefit.

A sovereign legally absolute can frame any law he chooses and attempt to enforce it. He may therefore legislate about moral matters and also about matters not usually considered moral (although everything connected with the public interest may have a general and indirect connection with morality).

On the other hand, few Governments (even in a theocracy) attempt to enforce *all* the generally admitted moral rules; and, for the most part, there is much that a wise Government prefers to leave alone. This would be so whether or not a Government professed to limit its function to keeping the peace at home and threatening war abroad, indeed it would be so if the Government educated all its subjects, provided them with medical attention and otherwise busied itself about their comfort and efficiency. Legal machinery is relatively cumbrous, legally permissible evidence is not wholly satisfactory; a plethora of regulations is expensive. Therefore excessive Governmental interference does not pay, however good (morally or otherwise) its object may be.

Hence (it may be said) there is a very relevant difference between legal and moral standards. Let us assume, in substance, that the law aims primarily at decisions; that these should be prompt and effective; and that although its machinery may be cumbrous, it is, on the whole, more serviceable than nicer, juster, but slower and more intricate methods. No doubt our laws are very intricate; but it may still be held that the ordinary citizen can know quite enough about really serious matters (such as burglary or murder) without having to consult a solicitor, and that professional people can similarly learn most that they need to know about mercantile, commercial, or other special classes of legislation.

If so the simplicity and, indeed, the inflexibility of the more fundamental legal regulations would be a condition of their utility; and there would be sound utilitarian reasons for adopting a device that might involve much real hardship in special cases.

In ethics (we may be told) precisely the opposite holds. A wise confessor (if not himself trammelled by some sort of canon law) need not adhere to the rigid inflexibility of legal generalities, and an enlightened private conscience need not do so either. Moralists can afford to be bold where lawyers are afraid to admit too many exceptions (publicly). There should be *nothing* clumsy in ethics, and *no* apprehension that laxity would result if iron generality were tempered. Why then should moralists deny that the optimific course is right even if, in particular cases, it conflicts with what is generally optimific in cases of the sort?

Per contra, it might be argued, again on utilitarian grounds, that ethics is just as much concerned as jurisprudence is with the utility of what is serviceable *if it is generally performed*, and that ethics is very specially concerned with the simplicity of moral laws, since it is essential to any sound morality that the commoner and more fundamental rules should be intelligible to ordinary people who have no academic or other expert acquaintance with moral theory. (This might not be so if men were content to leave such matters to a specially trained priesthood, but, at present, for most men, it is so.)

A drawn battle, therefore, may seem to ensue; but let us examine the matter further on utilitarian principles.

(*a*) It may be argued that such and such a principle is beneficial in most cases, and consequently that it should be followed in *this* case.

This argument seems contemptible. No doubt, if a principle is generally beneficial there is a certain presumption that it may really be beneficial where, superficially, it does not seem beneficial. The argument should warn us to be wary. If, however, after careful scrutiny it seems quite clear that a principle usually beneficial is mischievous in certain special cases (for sufficient cause shown), there seems to be no good reason why we should follow the principle when it is mischievous.

(*b*) Certain types of argument that are instances of the above should be distinguished with some care. The chief of these are the arguments, "Right for most people but not for X" and "Commendable in the long run, but not in the short run."

Regarding the first of these it seems clear that if there is a relevant moral difference between X and others, X should *not* do what others *should* do. There may, for example, be very good reasons (perhaps medical) why X should not attempt to have offspring although most people (perhaps) should. The mere fact that most people should try to become parents need have no bearing at all upon X's case.

The second formula is a little more abstruse. The phrase

"in the long run" may be taken to mean "in a high percentage of cases, given a long series." If the sum of our knowledge about a given action were that it belonged to such a class, then we should infer that we ought to follow the probability so indicated, although the improbable *might* happen. On the other hand, if we knew that, in a given instance, mischief would probably result, we should not be justified in performing the action, despite the probability of benefit that would correctly be inferred in the absence of such special information.

The phrase, "in the long run," might, however, be interpreted to mean "taking its whole (probable) subsequent history into account," i.e. temporarily profitable but unprofitable in the end. If so, we should not be misled by temporary advantage, however genuine.

It is sometimes complained that utilitarianism confuses the right with the expedient. Indeed, this complaint has come from the highest quarters, for the late Queen Victoria affirmed: "I have been taught to judge between what is right and what is wrong: but expediency is a word I neither wish to hear again nor to understand."

Utilitarians certainly hold that the balance of advantage (i.e. the *total* expediency) determines the rightness of action; but there is no reason in the world why they should not distinguish between temporary and total advantage, and so condemn the makeshift devices that are usually condemned as "merely expedient" with the same vigour as other people. It should be added, however, that utilitarians (or other people) need not reasonably object to every kind of opportunism, for the truth may well be that the greatest benefit on the whole may be obtained by a series of devices (or even of makeshifts) each designed to be temporary and each abandoned as soon as its utility becomes dubious. Even Queen Victoria might have been compelled to admit that something at some times was to be said for an *Interims-ethik*.

That, however, is a digression. The main point that has emerged from this general discussion is that, on utilitarian principles, the mere fact that a given sort of action is usually beneficial affords no sort of reason why it should be performed in a particular case (or in a particular subclass of cases) in which it is clearly probable that the action would be mischievous. One might as well argue that because, if a married woman is murdered, the murderer is usually the husband, therefore it would be right and expedient to hang the husband of any murdered wife, on principle, even if it were proved that he had been a thousand miles away from her at the material time.

(*c*) The really important utilitarian argument is quite different from the above. It is in substance the argument that the *general* performance of certain actions, and the *general* abstention from others may be of immense utility.

As we saw, uniformity of behaviour (as in the rule of the road) may be a great advantage, especially when it can be counted upon in advance, although the individual advantage of each such act, on its individual merits, may in comparison with a contrary act be negligible or non-existent.

The principle of the utility of uniformity, therefore, is quite different from the principle that most instances of a certain kind show individually an overbalance of advantage without regard to uniformity, although the two may often go together. Thus a punctual train service is a great social advantage. It will generally happen that if a train is late more passengers will be inconvenienced than the few who, arriving too soon, may have a dreary wait before they can go about their business. But the point is that the trains should run to time without any enquiry into the wishes of the passengers, and without any regard to the possible fact that in some particular journey most (or all) of the passengers might prefer the train to be late.

Trains, no doubt, are sometimes late. Nobody supposes that they should be accelerated, to make up for lost time, if there is a fog, or if the permanent way is being repaired. Their timely arrival is not a fetish or an absolute rule; but it is and should be independent of the special conveniences and aims of the individual passengers, except for some grave reason such as the sudden and serious illness of one of them (who may pull the cord). These special conveniences or inconveniences may be perfectly genuine, but they are irrelevant.

I have chosen this illustration because it is simply utilitarian, and because it can be discussed without any special reference to morals. But it does apply to morals also, and a utilitarian moralist is fully entitled to say that society will reap great positive advantages if certain things "simply aren't done," that is to say if most decent people habitually follow certain moral rules without considering the individual merits of a particular action unless some *very* serious consequence obtrudes itself upon their attention. Minor advantages and disadvantages, in such cases, fade into their proper insignificance.

Such a principle, of course, may be abused. The duel and other points in a code of honour need not be commendable. Class loyalty, patriotism, fanatical adherence to the Mahdi, an obscurantist conception of rules supposed to have been enacted by the deity, may indicate a conscience that should be obsolete, but in fact is not even obsolescent. It cannot be inferred, however, that all ethical uniformities are unenlightened simply because some are. We are dealing, in the end, with the sort of ethical uniformity that can withstand enlightened criticism.

It seems to me that this principle is amply sufficient to deal with the sort of instance that Butler, Austin, and Mr. Ross discuss so seriously—that is to say, successful tax-evasion when the revenue is ample, giving other people's money to a useful charity by neglecting to pay one's legal debts, and so forth. Mr. Ross and others suggest that we *know*, on non-utilitarian grounds that debts should have priority to charitable contributions, even if the charitable contribution would plainly do good and if the payment of the debt would do very little good or none at all. I have tried to show that there are good utilitarian reasons for such priority in all cases of the kind, reasons so good that they might well appear to be a simple intuition regarding the merits of the case, although they did not, in fact, have that sort of simplicity or sempiternal absolute evidence.

In other words, if we follow up Butler's hint in a way he did not himself do, and ask whether utilitarianism "singly considered" might not, if it were more fully developed, deal satisfactorily with these *prima facie* objections to *mere* utilitarianism, we find that it is capable of doing so. And this conclusion is of some moment. I do not say that there are no non-utilitarian reasons for moral duty, or that it cannot be proved that there are; but I do say that the type of reason we have considered in the present section is quite incapable of proving anything of the sort.

It should be remarked that the utilitarian argument, as I have stated it, is independent of one of the arguments commonly used in this connection (although this argument may have some weight). This is the argument that if a man is disposed, say, to break a promise (e.g. to pay a debt) on the ground that he can use the money to greater advantage, he should remember that his example would undermine public confidence, and tend towards general mischief. This indirect maleficent tendency, it is said, should therefore be included in his moral reckoning as well as all direct effects.

To avoid this complication, I was careful to select examples, at the critical point of the discussion, in which the affair could probably be kept secret, so that there would be no force of example, unless upon the agent himself, with regard to other secret actions.

If we assume that the example would have some force (and there is always the risk of such an occurrence), then it is quite true that this item should be included in the reckoning; and if the example had a mischievous tendency, this consideration might be sufficient to outweigh some tiny balance of advantage that might result apart from the bad example.

The reply is that the bad example, although bad and an example, need not be effective. If so and so breaks his word, other people, for the most part are not encouraged to break theirs. They know that the things that "simply aren't done" are done every day—but not by the people they respect; and even if they are done by persons they respect, they admit that their idols are not immaculate. They know that a small amount of tax-evasion will not seriously affect the revenue, and that very few tax-payers individually pay a sum that does seriously affect the revenue; but they also appreciate the fallacy of arguing in consequence that it doesn't matter whether one pays one's taxes or not (apart from the peremptory measures of legal compulsion). In short, a bad example, need not corrupt anyone. It is only dangerous when it is likely to be generally approved.

The utilitarian argument, however, may be stated without any reference to the force of example for good or for ill. It is simply that there may be great utility in the general observance of certain rules, and in the circumstance that men may usually count upon such general observance. When such general observance is enforced either by legal penalties or by public opinion the object is to prevent particular individuals availing themselves (or others) of a specious (or genuine) advantage in some special case; and an imperfect enforcement may be better than nothing. The point is that the rule should *be* generally observed, that is to say that most people in most circumstances should observe it without regard to the special merits of the particular case, and should form the habit of doing so. The fact that some people, with or without excuse, do not observe it, and that there may be quite special cases in which few (if any) reasonable persons would observe it, is irrelevant to this contention.

XVIII

FURTHER DISCUSSION OF UTILITARIANISM

As in the preceding section, I propose to define utilitarianism as the view that whatever is morally commendable in conduct or in character is commendable simply because it is a means to probable benefit, and, in the strictest sense, to the maximum probable benefit that may be attained by a given agent in a given situation. Our question now is whether there are more, and perhaps more serious, objections to this view than we have noted hitherto (for the previous bombardment left utilitarianism in effective occupation of its lines, although it may have been a little damaged). It seems best, however, to introduce these new considerations in the course of a general review of the situation as it might be seen by the intelligence department of the utilitarian forces.

(1) In itself, the circumstance that benefit is probable does not imply moral commendation of the instruments of such benefit. For sunshine and rain convey such benefits without therefore being moral at all.

(2) Morality, again, may be absent if the doctrine be restricted to human agency that is probably beneficial. Most moralists would object to such a theory on the ground that a man's moral conscience is quite *sui generis*, possessing unique authority and perhaps being even sacred. Our moral standards, they say, should not have to compete with other standards, as if a man's sense of duty were simply one reason, among others, why he should do this or that. Hence they would dissent from the view that morality was simply one beneficial agency among others, being a name for the species of beneficial action in which the agents happen to be human beings.

This particular objection may be disputable, and it may also be disputable whether there is any moral agency other than human. (For sub-human agency may be necessarily sub-moral, and super-human agency may be either super-moral or doubtful with regard to its very existence.) On the other hand, the view that morality or immorality are simply names for human beneficence or maleficence, in the literal matter-of-fact meaning of these words, is altogether opposed to any reasonable conception of the affair. On such a view unintended probable evil would be indistinguishable from intended, and a "typhoid carrier" or other unfortunate human being who quite unintentionally was likely to disseminate disease would be morally on the same plane (or on a lower plane) than the most pertinacious and evil-minded sinner. No such opinion could be reconciled with morality as commonly understood. The aetiology of benefits probably accruing from human agency is an interesting and important subject of study; but it should not be mistaken for ethics.

(3) As we have frequently seen, the explanation given by most moralists when these difficulties become apparent is that moral commendation or reprobation applies only to intentional voluntary actions (usually assumed to be human), and to character or disposition regarded as the permanent possibility of such voluntary action.

We have also seen, on several occasions, that there are serious ethical objections to the sufficiency of such a view, however true it may be that moral character and conduct are always to some extent voluntary, and, in the main, are directly and obviously voluntary. Kant (to repeat), by drawing the correct inference that on any such view (which was his) the New Testament would be talking nonsense by commanding us to *love* our neighbour, since the voluntary part of us could only act as if we loved him, showed how deep the abyss was that separated Stoic or Kantian ethics from Christian ethics; and I have suggested that in this matter Christian ethics is the truer. Moreover, it is difficult to see why the hedonistic utilitarians committed themselves to a voluntaristic ethics, unless the truth be that they thought of ethics in terms of law (whose threats and sanctions extend only to actions that are legally presumed to be voluntary), the theological utilitarians thinking in terms of divine commandments, designed for the happiness of God's creatures, and the secular utilitarians, like Beccaria or Bentham, being primarily reformers in the matter of legal draftsmanship and methods of punishment. A man's influence for good is not by any means confined to his voluntary efforts to make good come to pass, and the later hedonistic utilitarians (e.g. J. S. Mill) built their hopes upon the association of ideas and impulses (largely non-voluntary) rather than upon volition. If men's souls, by any means soever, became permeated by philanthropy and by public spirit, the social and the moral problem, they thought, would be solved in all governing essentials. In short, they were not consistently voluntaristic in their moral outlook.

Nevertheless, although a voluntaristic ethics tends to deny more than it should deny, there is less objection (and there may be none) to what it affirms. The view that ethics is concerned with voluntary actions and commends or deplores these with sole reference to the good they propose and are likely to effect, comes near to an accurate definition of the subject-matter of ethics as currently understood, and would be quite capable of suggesting the beginnings of a reason why men should regard their "conscience" with quite peculiar reverence. For action in accordance with settled and careful moral conviction, although it may not be very high, seems very definitely higher and more authoritative than most other human things.

(4) As it stands, however, the statement that ethics deals with the beneficial or maleficial aspects of voluntary actions, could but approach and could not reach accuracy when regarded as an attempt to define voluntaristic morals. A voluntary action is simply one that an agent can perform if he chooses to do it, and although, in a forced and oblique way, some degree of moral responsibility might be said to attach itself potentially to all such actions, there are many of them that (in any ordinary sense) could not be accounted moral at all. Thus I suggest that, for the most part, few would affirm that blowing on one's

hands to keep them warm or blowing on one's soup to cool it are, in the normal way, moral actions. Yet they are voluntary and designed to produce a certain benefit. I concede that the first of them might have some moral relevance. It might be a conspirator's signal, and it would have a bearing upon the wickedness of asceticism for ascetism's sake; but such possibilities, as I have said, are forced and oblique. The second is rather less forced, for it has something to do with good manners; but it is only quasi-moral, with very strong emphasis upon the "quasi-."

(5) Indeed, efficiency in some public service would appear to be the likeliest sort of action to produce considerable benefits. Tilly's victory at the White Mountain, Marlborough's at Blenheim, Wellington's and Blücher's at Waterloo, by settling many political disputes for about a century each, conveyed, and were likely to convey, more benefit than many millions of righteous actions. Improvements in food supply, in sanitation, and in surgery have been more philanthropic, in a plain, pedestrian way, than most instances of copy-book morals. They have enabled humanity to multiply, to live longer, and to live in considerable comfort. Even if technocracy should not supersede private ethics, it may be capable of being a more effective agent in the promotion of human welfare.

It need not be denied that such enterprises could be undertaken, have been undertaken, and (it may be) should be undertaken as a moral duty. Wilberforce, Ronald Ross, and Haig may have acted in that spirit, and so may many other doctors, soldiers, town-planners, and other public-spirited men. This would occur wherever the benefit of one's fellow-citizens or of all mankind were either the decisive motive or the principal intention in someone's character and conduct. If, however, the tendency to promote some great benefit, such as the enduring peace of a continent, the utter extermination of some horrible menace to health and of life, or the sweetness of general liberty were the standard of moral excellence (with the proviso that only voluntary actions having this tendency are included), the essential point would be that such actions should be undertaken whatever their motive. There would be little or no difference, from this point of view, if personal renown, or the pickings of office, or mere meddlesomeness canalized into philanthropic channels were the effective agency. If so, we should have a "moral" system on very different lines from what is traditional, and yet should be dealing throughout with voluntary actions and with the probability of benefit.

I suggest, therefore, that with regard at least to what may be called pedestrian benefits, such as the health, liberty, populousness, and happiness of mankind—and it is nonsense to say that these are negligible benefits—the direct and normal implications of utilitarianism do not march with morals in the usual sense of that word. It may well be true that veracity, fidelity, equity, and other moral rules may be justified on utilitarian grounds and are also preconditions of effective and lasting philanthropy. That, if it could be shown, would be a proof that utilitarianism *included* ethics, but would not even suggest that utilitarianism did not include much more than ethics. If the theory be that any voluntary action likely to produce greater benefit than any other is *de facto* the morally right action, much that is usually considered non-moral would be inevitably included.

This may not, in every sense, be an objection to utilitarianism, or even to the "pedestrian" species of utilitarianism we are now considering. Most, although not all, moralists say that they do not dispute the received standard of moral conduct, granting, of course, that it may become more enlightened both by retrenchment and by supplement. They are anxious neither to subvert nor to transform, but to explain. They want a premiss, or perhaps a hypothesis, that supplies an adequate reason for conclusions they do not (in substance) dispute.

Consequently, most moral systems present themselves as quarrels about the premisses, not about the conclusions of ethics, and they usually succeed pretty well in showing that they can adduce plausible principles in support of veracity, fidelity, toleration, and the like. If they did not do so they would not even appear to explain what nearly all of them profess to explain.

It is not true in fact, however, that "ideal" and hedonistic utilitarianism (let us say) justify precisely the same thing, still less that either of them justifies precisely what is justified by Kant or by the new intuitionists, or by exponents of any one of the numerous varieties of aretaics. What they all profess to justify may indeed include an extensive common region, and this may be identical with the ordinary moral rules. Very few of them, however, justify nothing else, and very few directly or properly imply that the ordinary moral rules have either the special and non-competitive authority that is commonly ascribed to them, or the internal degree of moral importance that, despite all perplexities, most moralists try to accept and to express.

Accordingly, it is not really a serious objection to utilitarianism that, if true, it would profoundly modify our beliefs concerning moral enterprise, although retaining a considerable part of what, for want of a less objectionable name, is called the morality of "common sense." The same, I think, could be said of most other moral systems, and they are none the worse for the circumstance. On the other hand, the theory that all serviceable actions, provided they are voluntary, are on the same moral level as saintly or righteous conduct seems to introduce a new world rather than to transform the old; and it does not seem clear that the new world is moral at all.

(6) Similarly, as has appeared in more than one of the world's great books (such as Plato's *Republic* or Hobbes's *Leviathan*), there is substance in the contention that the wisest thing men can do in order to achieve probable benefit is to band themselves together in an orderly political community. If so, the probability of benefit is principally an affair of ruling if one is a ruler, and of obeying if one is a subject, or, in other words, of performing one's function (or doing one's bit) under political regiment.

Such a theory may certainly be moralized in a way not obviously antagonistic to the ordinary moral conscience. The ruler, it may be said, should aim at *salus populi*, the security and well-being of his community. The subjects should co-operate by obedient submission and by equally obedient active help. A wise ruler may see that an enlightened people is better than a merely contented people. He may also see that he will be a better shepherd of his flock if he regulates their lives in accordance with the received ethical rules, enforcing covenants, forbidding sexual promiscuity, repressing the violence of housebreakers and robbers. For these are the ways of peace in *any* community, and if the ruler be negligent of them, the result will inevitably be friction and discord.

If we grant, however, that such a view may accommodate itself to the inclusion of received ethical rules (indeed, even if we grant this much more freely than the strict logic of the situation demands) it is surely obvious that the aims of a community planned on this principle, whether the corporative State of the Fascists, or the classless society that should supersede the proletarian phase of Lenino-Marxism in Russia, are not simply coincident with ethics in its ordinary sense. They include a species of applied ethics, but they are also in large measure extra-ethical, and the extra-ethical part of them is as much an affair of probable benefit (for that matter, of individual probable benefit) and of voluntary action as the ethical.

Allegiance, according to most ethical theories, is *one* moral obligation among others, and if the things that are our own, or our family's, or our friends', or God's could be clearly separated from the things that are Caesar's, it might be possible to discriminate clearly between political and moral probable voluntary benefit. It is hardly necessary to show, however, that a nicely balanced equipoise between morals and patriotism is the most difficult thing in the world to sustain, that most attempts of the kind are sedatives for the heart rather than stimulants for the head, and that the tougher-minded political theorists and rulers have with few exceptions preferred the maxim *Aut Caesar aut nullus*. There is no lack of logic in the view that probable voluntary benefit enjoins *salus populi* in its absolutistic sense, and includes ethics, at the best, as a subordinate part of this aim; and if anyone says that he votes and pays his taxes for utilitarian reasons *only*, he suggests that he conceives of non-utilitarian grounds for other parts of his conduct.

(7) The same difficulty is readily seen in the attempts of some later utilitarians (particularly J. S. Mill) to give an adequate utilitarian picture of justice and duty, by which Mill meant, not simply positive law, but impartiality, equality in certain important phases, keeping faith, and reward in proportion to desert.

Mill's view, in essentials, was that justice was more imperative in its demands than other forms of expediency; that it should therefore be enforced by law; and that *rightful compulsion* was the mark that distinguished justice and duty from the other forms of expediency. Such compulsion (or liability to punishment), he held, was in essence resentment moralized by its wide social advantage. "While I dispute," he said (*Utilitarianism*, ch. v), "the pretensions of any theory which sets up an imaginary standard of justice not grounded on utility, I account the justice which is grounded on utility to be the chief part, and incomparably the most sacred and binding part, of all morality. Justice is a name for certain classes of moral rules, which concern the essentials of human well-being more nearly, and are therefore of more absolute obligation, than any other rules for the guidance of life."

If Mill's view were sound the *magna moralia*, or fundamental moral duties, should coincide quite precisely with what either law or public opinion ought to enforce; for only the expedient should be enforced, and enforcement, *ex hypothesi*, is the distinguishing criterion of morals. It is clear, however, that there is no such coincidence in fact. In the common view, much of the finer essence of morality should *not* be enforced, even if such enforcement were feasible; and much should be enforced that is morally of little account (e.g. inadvertently parking a motor-car too near a hydrant). Public opinion, no doubt, ought to be on the side of morality. If it were not, the state of affairs would be morally reprehensible; but the question, as Mill argued it, is not whether public opinion should favour morality, but whether it should adopt some distinctive punitive method to enforce its attitude.

The problem of what is expedient to enforce either by the Government or by public opinion is interesting and important; but it is not, in any ordinary sense, the same problem as the distinction between moral duty and some other type of expediency, nor is it plain that an ethics of benefit has any right to exclude *any* piece of proved expediency from the province of morals. It is also highly probable (as has already been argued) that Mill's criterion of the expediency that it is expedient to enforce would yield results very different indeed from the usual ethical outlook. The sort of thing that a pedestrian utilitarianism at any rate would be most inclined to enforce would be vaccination, general education, and the notification of disease, in addition to the ordinary prohibitions of rape, murder, and the like. Such a view would be neither immoral nor unreasonable, and the shift in moral emphasis it implies may be due simply to the fact that we have different ideas now from the ideas of previous ages regarding the kind of private action that is likely to be noxious. It is *science* that has transformed our outlook. But there would be a transformation of duty and of justice as currently understood.

Accordingly (I hold), we should conclude that if morality alone be "sacred and binding" in Mill's sense, the utilitarian theory would justify much more than is usually accounted "sacred and binding" in this special sense, and is not entitled to lay exclusive or even very peculiar emphasis upon what Mill called "justice." In short, utilitarianism, regarded as a moral theory, proves a good deal too much.

This conclusion, however, has been reached by what may seem to be a question-begging route, since we have persistently assumed that we had to deal with a "pedestrian" form of utilitarianism, and have considered in the main only what Governments can kill or cure, that is to say the populousness, health, longevity, and the comfortable subsistence-level of a group of people or of humanity.

I am assuming that these are properly to be regarded as great benefits (although they may not *always* be benefits), partly on the ground of previous discussion, partly because the thing is tolerably evident in itself; but the "ideal" utilitarians seem also, quite obviously, to be right when they say that there are other and, in certain ways, greater benefits. In the eyes of any secular ethic, however, the pedestrian benefits, if relatively low, are also very wide and very deep. Most of them, indeed, are the pre-requisites of any others, as everyone knows, even if he is not a Marxist. If, then, other goods were much higher, but also much rarer and, so to say, much more volatile, an "ideal" utilitarianism might not differ so very much, in the end, from a pedestrian utilitarianism, although it would be bound to differ appreciably.

If, however, we were entitled to regard these pedestrian goods, in the Stoic way, as of negligible worth (except perhaps as a means or precondition), it is obvious that our ideal utilitarianism would be guided in the main by "ideal" (or non-pedestrian) benefits, and would differ profoundly if there were a serious difference in the value they put upon these other "ideal" benefits. If art and beauty were by far the greatest goods, our hearts should be set upon aesthetic attainment. If the pomp and circumstance of courts and armies were the highest end, a policy devoted to these benefits would be very different from the former. If knowledge is the greatest good, universities would be sacred like the slopes of Parnassus, and one need not even be a gentleman provided one were a scholar. If religious contemplation were the end we should aim at a monastic system of politics and of industry. Each such view would transform our ethical system, although each might present certain identical ethical features.

It seems to me, however, to be plain (and, indeed, to be plain without much argument) that "ideal utilitarianism" would not be likely to coincide with the received ethical standards, and to provide an adequate justification of these, unless it assumed that the goodness of moral character, disposition, and conduct was, in fact, the only or by far the greatest good. About this there is a good deal to be said.

Certain critics roundly accuse ideal utilitarianism of a formal logical circle. According to a recent Danish critic (Mr. A. Ross, *Kritik der sogennanten praktischen Erkenntnis*, p. 194) the circle is flagrant. "The striving after good is itself the good; and the good is to strive after good." Rashdall, Moore, and the present writer, among others, are alleged to be vanquished by this Scholar's Mate.

So stated, the onslaught can be met with comparative ease. According to ideal utilitarianism moral good consists in doing one's best, but ideal utilitarians do not hold that beauty, insight, happiness, and other non-moral goods should not be sought or included in the "best" that is striven for. For instance, they condemn cruelty to animals, principally because non-moral animal suffering is evil. They condemn devotion to bad art or to a vain or futile "science"—and condemn them morally—because of the misdirection of the effort, such misdirection being proved not by moral but by artistic or by scientific canons.

Therefore, in at least one important particular, the alleged circle depends upon a verbal misunderstanding. Moralists (and other people, too) occasionally use the word "good" to mean "moral good" and nothing else. This they do, for example, when they contrast the Good with the Beautiful and the True. In this sense it would be a tautology to say that " 'tis only noble to be good."

In the present work, however, I have consistently assumed that axiological good is not restricted to moral good. Whatever is fine, great, noble, or excellent may be such a good, and so may innocent pleasure. That, as I conceive, has always been the view of ideal utilitarians. It was certainly my own view in the book against which this critic is arguing; and, without begging the question, it seems impossible to prove that "good" ought to mean "moral good" either for utilitarians or for anyone else. Even Kant admitted that much might be "good" in addition to the "good" (or moral) will. What he claimed for the moral will was that it alone was intrinsically, unconditionally, and invariably good, adverbs that he seems to have thought equivalent. The adverbs, however, are not equivalent, and none of them, taken singly, proves very much. What is intrinsically good might be intrinsically a minor good, and much inferior to an extrinsic or relational good. What is unconditionally good might be a feeble good, not to be compared in excellence to many conditioned goods when the relevant condition existed. What is invariably good might be invariably a little good, of much less moment than another thing that was *very* good when it was good, although horrid when it was bad.

Nevertheless, if good consequences supplied the moral standard, and if these good consequences were held to include moral advantage, there would be grave suspicion of a logical circle in a part of the argument, viz. in the part that concerned moral consequences, and there would be the further inconvenience that moral consequences would be (or might be) competitors with other consequences, which is just what is denied by the numerous and important authors who hold that it is wicked to give a non-moral reason for moral conduct. It is therefore understandable, although inexcusable, that certain ideal utilitarians should have argued that excellence of moral character, and of equitable and righteous status was the greatest good of all.

If Mill was right in holding such matters to be "sacred and binding" in a sense entirely unique, and if he was utterly wrong in his attempt to generate this unique characteristic from vengeance and a punitive machinery, it is tempting to argue that these sacred and binding goods should be accepted as such on their intrinsic merits, and to go on to argue that the defects of a pedestrian utilitarianism ought to be remedied on precisely these lines. Morality (so this argument would run) is not the only means to voluntary social benefit, although it is always socially beneficial, but in so far as it has laid emphasis upon integrity of personal character, upon purity of heart, upon the governing importance of treating all other moral beings as responsible companions, and of trusting as well as respecting them unless (if ever) they forfeit all claims to such neighbourly treatment, it has brought into due prominence super-eminent goods that without it might well have been forgotten, and would very probably be neglected by those who strove for the greatness, opulence, or comfort of some particular community or, indeed, of all humanity.

The alleged circle, therefore, although it cannot strangle the entire theory, may threaten a very considerable part of the theory if developed upon these lines. Is there any defence?

(a) There is no circle in terms of *hedonistic* utilitarianism. According to that theory an agent is to be regarded morally as a pleasure-producing instrument and as nothing more. The fact that he is also a pleasure-consumer is irrelevant, and should not confuse a clear head. To be sure, the prospective pleasures of a good conscience must be included as well as other pleasures; but there is no circle in including them. Thus there is no circle in the commonplace selfish argument, "If I let my friends down in the present emergency I shall suffer a good deal in future from the recollection of my weakness, and I must expect to be reminded frequently and very unpleasantly of the matter. On the other hand, the risks of playing the game (as people say) are really terrible, and I will not take them even if my conscience troubles me for the rest of my life." I do not present this argument as a sound piece of utilitarian reasoning in ethics (for it plainly is not), but as a clear indication of the absence of a logical circle when the

K*

pleasures and pains of conscience are included as well as other pleasures and pains.

(b) There is no circle in an ethics based exclusively upon probable *consequences*, or upon exclusively *prospective* benefits. For when these prospective benefits occurred they would no longer be prospective, except with regard to some further prospect. They would be actual and not prospective.

(c) Indeed, there can be no circle in ideal utilitarianism, or in any utilitarianism, so long as it remains strictly utilitarian. A moral theory, in strictness, is *utilitarian* if and only if it regards moral action as a *mere* means to benefit. It is a producer's theory and nothing else, although the production aims at something quite different, viz. consumption. Even character and disposition are regarded as permanent possibilities of production.

Consequently, unless utilitarianism falls into confusion it is bound to avoid the alleged circle; for it cannot consistently regard moral qualities as *mere* means to benefit, and *also* as intrinsic goods that should be sought for their own sakes. If Mill argued (as he did) that virtue, once a mere means to happiness, had become a part of happiness, and if certain ideal utilitarians have argued similarly, they were one and all confused. No doubt much that is a means is also an end; but in that case it is not a *mere* means. No doubt (as in Mill's instance of the miser), what was once a mere means may come to be an end; but in that case it has ceased to be *merely* a means. A consistent utilitarianism *necessarily* avoids the alleged circle.

It has, however, to pay a very stiff price for its safety in this particular; for, except by inadvertence, it is impossible seriously to believe that a good moral character is not a most precious possession, that is to say, *not* a mere means to other benefit. I have argued, indeed, that the distinction between means and end does not suffice for all or even for most axiological purposes; but utilitarianism, in all its possible forms, is based upon that distinction, and must adhere to it or cease to be strict utilitarianism. The obvious fact, therefore, that virtue is not a mere means is a total refutation of utilitarianism regarded as a complete moral theory. Much in ethics may be justified on strictly utilitarian grounds—but not all.

The result of this discussion consequently is, firstly, that the impossibility of regarding moral good as merely a means is a refutation of all utilitarianism in its strict form; secondly, that (apart from the above refutation) utilitarianism tends to prove too much, since it would commend what would usually be accounted non-moral or quasi-moral action on the same principles as it commends moral action; and thirdly (partly in consequence of the second point), that it either denies what is usually regarded as a moral datum, viz. that there is something peculiarly "sacred and binding" about morality, or else, accepting it, palpably fails to account for it on its own principles.

These objections have very different degrees of seriousness. The first refutes the sufficiency of utilitarianism as an ethical theory, but it need not refute an ethics of benefit or of well-being, since such a theory need not assume that morality has value only as a means. The force of the second may be greatly mitigated by the reflection that most ethical theories, pursued with relentless logic, would transform the received code of ethics and would not merely supply a reason for it, and may also object with some reason that it is not always evident what the received code is. The third may raise the objection that if morality be rational and intelligible, it may afford to admit under pressure that its alleged "sacred and binding character" has been mixed with some superstition. Alternatively, it may argue that this sacred and binding character belongs only to certain moral duties, the great commandments or *magna moralia*, and that these do have a unique status when compared either with other moral duties or with what is non-morally profitable.

No moral theory can expect to make much headway if it simply attacks its opponents. If, however, the contention be that every moral theory should be able to distinguish with complete clarity between what is moral and what is not (since everything moral is visibly and impressively *sui generis*) it has to be remembered that aretaics and deontology have their difficulties in this particular as well as agathopoeics. These difficulties have been shown in their proper place, and it should not be necessary to recount them. I may remind the reader, however, that aretaics cannot consistently maintain that moral virtue alone is noble and fine, and may be driven to explain that its fineness is just the nobility and dignity that is shown in moral affairs, the said affairs having to be defined in some other way. The task of deontology, no doubt, is superficially easier. That theory *ex professo* confines itself to moral obligations. It has to admit, however, that beneficence, or the promotion of benefit, is one such moral obligation. Consequently, it cannot rid itself of any difficulties an ethics of benefit encounters in this direction, and, in the past, it has prudently refrained from distinguishing clearly between *magna moralia*, *parva moralia*, and *non-moralia*.

XIX

OF AGATHOPOEICS IN GENERAL

WE have concluded that utilitarianism, strictly interpreted, is not a tenable moral theory, since moral excellence cannot simply be one means among others for procuring benefit by voluntary action.

Many moralists appear to believe that if they have refuted utilitarianism they have also refuted the sufficiency of agatho-poeics in all its possible forms. In short, they suppose that utilitarianism and an ethics of benefit and well-being are precisely the same thing. Obviously, however, this view is mistaken. Utilitarianism restricts itself to beneficial *consequences*, and therefore excludes all goods that are not consequences from its consideration. If, however, there are such goods, an ethics of well-doing is entitled to include them, and is bound to do so if they have moral relevance. That is a deduction from the logic of the theory.

A further point of importance results rather from the habitual assumptions of moralists than from the strictest logic. This, in brief, is the assumption that in any estimate of benefits, intrinsic goods, regarded as each man's private possessions, are alone to be considered, all other goods being regarded as merely instrumental. Relational goods, if there are any such, are therefore excluded or ignored. It may appear, however, that there is no good reason for neglecting relational goods, if they exist, and it is clear that an ethics of well-doing which included them would differ appreciably from one that did not.

When we speak of a benefit we always speak of something conferred or conveyed, that is to say, of something passive; and when we commend moral qualities as having a value that is not the value of a mere means, we think of them not as passive benefits, but as instances of *active* goodness, commend-able in their own right as activities. This distinction (as

Aristotle and Kant in their various ways both saw) is as important as any in moral theory, and I want to make it quite clear that in the remainder of this discussion I propose to restrict the term "benefit" to passive well-being, to use well-being as the generic term, and to include active well-doing under it. I admit that the boundaries between active well-doing and passive benefit may sometimes be finely drawn, for instance when the "benefit" is the removal of temptation, the provision of special moral opportunities, the strengthening of moral character, or again in all education whether artistic, scientific, or moral. Even in these cases, however, the boundary *can* be drawn, although it may need close attention.

Our question, then, is whether an ethics of well-being, freed from the restrictions that are either inevitable or customary in a utilitarian ethics of benefit, may be a tenable moral theory.

As I formerly observed, it is abundantly clear, I think, that there is a vital omission in consistently utilitarian arguments. If the moral criterion be the maximum goodness of any action, then, even if we reckon in terms of intrinsic good, the good *in* the action should be included as well as the good designed or expected to come *from* the action. A voluntary action, no doubt, is designed to effect some change, and the future alone can be changed. The action, therefore, is future-regarding, prospicient of consequences. To ignore its direction towards probable consequences is to ignore an essential part of its very nature and intent. Nevertheless, *it* may *also* be good; and if virtue be a good, not merely as a means but in itself, there *is* a goodness in virtuous action other than its direction to probable beneficial consequences. The virtuous act would not be good and would not be itself unless it were so directed, but its instrumentality towards these consequences is not the whole of its value.

I think we may agree that virtuous action does have this additional value. Indeed, if we desired corroboration on the point from the utilitarians themselves we might find it readily enough. As we have seen, J. S. Mill maintained (irrelevantly) that virtue was *now* sought for its own sake although it *used* to be sought as a means only, and he also distinguished between the worth of an agent and the morality of his actions when he examined the instance of the rescue of the drowning man from sordid motives. If Mill had been consistent he would have been bound to maintain that the worth of moral character is only a name for a relatively permanent means to benefit. The man of good character is likely to produce benefits habitually; weaker characters are likely to produce benefits intermittently when they follow moral rules; but they do not habitually do so. And that is the sole relevant difference on utilitarian principles. When Mill referred to the "worth of the agent," however, he may have thought of it, like nearly anybody else, in a way not exclusively utilitarian.

Again, we may remember that Bentham objected to the "few exceptions made" by his predecessor Hume to a theory of complete ethical utilitarianism. Bentham thought there should be none (see my *Hume's Philosophy of Human Nature*, p. 219). Hume's principal and very significant "exception," however, was just that utility, in itself, might be non-moral. It was only moral when it instructed *virtue*, that is to say when there was a humane, generous, or public-spirited motive present in the action itself, some "particle of the dove" that could be trained to vanquish the wolf and the serpent in us, some spark of benevolence that could be fanned to a very flame of philanthropy, and taught, scientifically, to be serviceably directed to man's needs. The "exception," instead of being a punctilious triviality, was fundamental to Hume's entire theory.

In any case the point should be admitted, whatever the history of domestic utilitarian squabbles concerning it may have been. And it involves a highly significant correction of strict utilitarianism.

The present as well as the prospective goodness of an action is therefore relevant to moral estimation, its active goodness as well as the passive benefit it is designed to bring about.

And must we not go further? Is it not plain from much of our earlier discussion that morality has to be retrospective and circumspective as well as prospective? Surely we must admit what unguarded accounts of utilitarianism often conceal, viz. that moral obligations and moral virtue do not (to use a vulgarism) start from scratch. It is not true in morals that we should always, or usually, press on towards the mark, forgetting the things that are behind. Even if the best men, in general, should not have too long memories, they are frequently, and rightly, morally bound by their past, and by the past of others. They have to keep faith, show gratitude, and so on, and such debts may be their father's or their friends', and not their own.

In view of so much earlier discussion we can now afford to be brief, although the point is much more complicated than it seems.

No action can be wholly retrospective, since every action, from its very nature, is prospective. It does not follow, however, that such prospicience is independent of the past. On the contrary the prospective fulfilment of past commitments, although future-regarding, is also most decidedly retrospective. The statesman about to sign a treaty is about to make a future movement of his fingers which shall have many future consequences much more remote; but he is also completing a long series of past negotiations.

The new intuitionists and, I suppose, the old intuitionists also, appear to hold that retrospective obligations, as such, are necessarily non-utilitarian, but it is hard to see why they think they have proved the *necessity*. For if utilitarianism be true its logical implications must be true along with it. Suppose, then, that promise-making-and-keeping (say) could be justified on utilitarian grounds, being a fiduciary device necessary for social continuity in any society that is at all highly developed. This device logically implies a certain temporal span. What is promised at time t_1 is that something will be done at a later time t_2; and the device said to be so useful cannot be less than the entire transaction, including its temporal span. If utilitarianism justifies such transactions, it need not attempt to justify some mutilated part of them, e.g. making a promise and then breaking it. What it is concerned to justify is promise-making-and-keeping. The keeping of a promise that has been made is a logical implication of the existence of the transaction in its entirety. It implies no special moral obligation (whether or not the entire transaction demands such an obligation), but is a matter of part and whole. There is no promise-making-and-keeping if the promise is broken. If the *series* be what utilitarianism justifies, the mere fact that the series involves several distinct actions made at different times makes no logical difference.

Accordingly, the simple circumstance that many moral obligations are at least as much retrospective as prospective (when single actions alone are considered) is not a sufficient disproof of utilitarianism, much less a disproof of an ethics of well-being. But it may be possible to find other and better reasons.

What the new intuitionists claim is that they can see by inspection that certain retrospective *relations*, such as the return of good for good in gratitude, the return of evil for evil in the special and peculiar case of a just punishment, the bestowal of benefit in proportion to past services, and the keeping of an old promise, are "right" or "fitting" in themselves, are moral, and are not to be confused with anyone's benefit (although the consciousness that such "rights" are respected, and even the unconscious acceptance of one's rightful status are quite genuine benefits). If such relations are necessarily and absolutely *different* from benefit or well-being (however closely connected with the same), it follows at once that an ethics of well-being (whether or not it take the special form of utilitarianism) is an incomplete ethic. The essential difference being granted, there would be no need to try to prove the *utter* helplessness of an ethic of benefit regarding such matters. Agathopoeics *must* fail, however brave its attempt.

That is the last considerable question I propose to examine

in this book. As a preliminary to it, however, we must consider circumspective as well as prospective moral relations.

It is obvious that morality may be concerned not only with what is present, prospective, and retrospective in an uncomplicated way, but also with mutually dependent and contemporaneous obligations and purposes. Thus while it is usual to illustrate, say, by A's promises to B, it would be equally pertinent to adduce instances in which such promises were made only on condition that C's assent should be obtained. In international politics multilateral as well as bilateral treaties have to be considered. In short, illustrations abound.

In the main, this circumspective aspect of morality is a relational affair, principally between the agent and at least two persons or parties other than the agent. The relations, moreover, to use technical language, may be polyadic and not resolvable into a set of dyadic relations.

No one, I suppose, would dispute the existence of this circumspective aspect of morality, but there might be a good deal of dispute regarding its importance for moral theory. I would submit, then, that its importance is considerable for any moral theory, and of critical moment for some moral theories. Certain moralists, for example L. Nelson,* have maintained that the essential business of morals is to regulate and limit desires,† principally with regard to the claims and neighbourly status of all other men. If so, the circumspective relation of justice is the core and the seed of ethics; and on any theory, fairness and equity with regard to all relevant interests is a very essential part of morals.

Utilitarians, or other believers in an ethics of well-doing, may legitimately employ the same arguments regarding circumspective matters as regarding retrospective. In the case of justice, for instance, they may say that what is beneficial is the maintenance of an entire circumspective pattern, that the pattern should not be mutilated and must be allowed to possess its own logical implications.

* *Kritik der praktischen Vernunft.*   † Nelson says "interests."

It may be doubted, however, whether our commendation of such circumspect relations can reasonably be regarded as a mere means to widespread personal or intrinsic benefit, and if it cannot be so regarded it follows that the relations as such are commendable, provided, as we have seen, that they have an essential regard to benefit. (A maleficent or malignant equity is not commendable.) It would seem, therefore, as the new intuitionists affirm, that there are direct positive grounds for commending such relations morally, although not without certain necessary provisos. As an *argumentum ad hominem*, it may further be noted that the English utilitarians, I think without any exception, included at least one proposition of abstract non-utilitarian justice in what professed to be a purely utilitarian theory. They held that "each should count for one, and no one for more than one," not because this maxim describes an essential means to the attainment of maximum pleasure (which is plainly false, since men differ in their capacity for receiving pleasure as much as cows differ in their capacity for storing milk), but because it seemed to them to be manifestly fair and right.

Summing up the results of the argument in this section, we may say that an ethics of benefit, i.e. of the (passive) good consequences of action, is subject to two important sets of qualifications, both of which have clear moral relevance. The first is that active goodness in the moral way (and also more generally) cannot properly be regarded as a mere means to passive benefit. The second is that there seem to be certain governing *relations* of moral action (always morally relevant although not always morally decisive) which are certainly not identical with *intrinsic* goodness, either active or passive. If the latter are not *good* at all (but, instead, "right" or "fitting"), an ethics of well-being, and *a fortiori*, an ethics of benefit, is necessarily inadequate.

Let us examine these two points separately in their relation to well-being.

With regard to the first we may provisionally assume that

the active good in question is an intrinsic good. This is what is commonly meant by those who affirm that virtue, or virtuous motives, are good and fine in themselves, not simply as a means to benefit, and any further explanations that may be necessary come under the second of our headings, viz. moral relations.

This being assumed we may, I think, formulate the following propositions.

(*a*) Regarding benefit or passive good:

A voluntary action is morally commendable only if it aims at benefit.

Ceteris paribus, it is morally commendable only if it aims at the maximum probable benefit.*

(*b*) Regarding active *and* passive good:

Putting aside the question of the moral relations hereafter to be considered, the total moral worth of a voluntary action is a function of its intrinsic moral goodness together with its optimific prospects.

Certain observations concerning these propositions should be appended.

(1) They affirm that voluntary moral action, if morally commendable, must necessarily attempt to be optimific in respect of probable passive benefits, and I do not think that even Mr. Ross would object to this proposition when it is made subject to reservations regarding moral relations and is restricted to passive good. The proposition does not assert that the optimific projects of voluntary action are the whole of its morality. Again, in asserting that morally commendable voluntary action must try to be optimific, it does not assert the converse, viz. that all optimific aims are, as such, moral. The possibility of doing or trying to do one's best in non-moral or in quasi-moral enterprises is not excluded.

(2) Their affirmations concern voluntary action, or morality

---

* The phrase "ceteris paribus" is introduced in order to leave room for later discussion concerning moral relations. I do not propose to return to the problem of actual *versus* probable benefit.

in so far as it is voluntary. On any theory ethics is very largely voluntaristic, but, as we have seen, it is not exclusively so. One's moral influence and example, for instance, are not confined to the consequences one wills or (I should say) *could* will to bring about. A complete theory of passive benefit in the moral way, therefore, would have to enlarge these voluntaristic propositions. So would a theory of active moral good, for, as we have seen, it is not true that men *do* nothing except what they perform voluntarily.

(3) The propositions do not affirm that the benefits sought must themselves be moral benefits, and they would be absurd if they did. As we have seen so often, there is a moral obligation to alleviate physical suffering, although such suffering need not be moral at all. Indeed, if (in the common way) we think of moral good as always *active* good directed towards (passive) benefit, it would be inconsistent to include *such* moral good among the benefits at which a moral action should aim; and it seems reasonable to affirm that if we promote morality we do so only by removing obstacles, providing opportunity, and the like. Even the strengthening of character might in this sense be described as passive, not active, an effect rather than an activity. If we adhere rigidly to this standpoint there is no possible circle in the view. A requisite of active moral good would be to promote passive benefit, including certain favourable conditions for the existence of active moral good.

(4) The propositions do not state that all active good is moral. On the contrary, there is or may be much active goodness in art, science, and in the liberal play of the imagination. They affirm only that there is such a thing as intrinsic active good of moral character. I agree that such a theory is not more successful than any other that I know of in distinguishing with complete accuracy and finality between what is moral and what is not. All moral theories are able to indicate matters that are definitely moral, and the difference (rather more vaguely) between a moral and a semi- or non-moral point of view. More than this they seldom attempt to do, and, much as I

regret the circumstance, I am not prepared to try to offer anything better. So much, then, for the relation between active good (more especially active moral good) and passive benefit. Let us now pass to the second main question we have to consider here, the status of certain relations in moral theory.

Since we have agreed that none of the ethical theories we are examining in this essay, that is to say neither aretaics, nor deontology, nor agathopoeics is able clearly to demarcate, at all points, what on the one hand is completely moral and on the other hand wholly non-moral, there is no place for the criticism that it may be hard if not impossible to tell which of these relations are moral and which are not. It is fair to remark, however, that the difficulty does exist, for it is not unusual for the new intuitionists and others to speak of "right" or of "fitting" in a moral way, without giving any sufficient indication that these terms have a wider significance than the moral one, and that this wider significance may affect action and whatever is admirable in human nature.

In reality, as we have seen, "right" is just "*it*," what is *comme il faut*, and moral rightness is but a species of "right" in this general sense. The same is true of terms like "fitting" (Professor Broad's favourite),* "meet," "due," or "appropriate." Much may be appropriate in a non-moral way, and a glance at the history of ethics is sufficient to show that any difficulties of this order that attach to the concept of "good" are matched by similar difficulties attaching to "right" or "fitting." The Stoics, for example, drew a line, not by any means an agreed line, between what was morally *good*, and what was only advantageous, i.e. between ἀξία and προηγμένα. But similarly they drew a line, not by any means an agreed line, between the things that were morally obligatory (κατορθώματα) and the things that were only meet and fitting (καθήκοντα) either for men, or animals, or plants.

Let us, however, omit such difficulties, since parallels to them are universal, and allow that deontologists are able to

* In *Five Types of Ethical Theory*.

give obvious examples of moral relations, such as justice, veracity, the keeping of covenants, and the like. This being assumed, we have, in the main, three questions to examine. The first is whether these alleged relations really are relations; the second is whether, if they are relations, they constitute an independent part of moral theory that has been widely and improperly neglected; the third is whether, being relations, they may not be *good* relations and therefore correctly included in an ethics based altogether upon the conception of *good*.

(1) Certain moralists have denied that there are any specifically moral relations, and Hume (e.g. *Treatise*, Bk. III, sect. 1) tried to prove the point by showing that there was the same relation between a seedling that destroyed the parent tree in its natural growth as between a human parricide and his victim. This illustration, like many similar ones, certainly proves that such bare relations abstractly considered are not enough to demonstrate the presence of morality. There must be at least one moral term to the relation if there is, in any intelligible sense, a moral situation. On the other hand, where such a term exists, or (as in the instance of justice) where the relation would be meaningless unless it applied to a moral agent, the relation may well have an independent function in the moral situation, and Hume reached the contrary conclusion by a flagrant *petitio principii*, i.e. by asserting that mathematical and physical science exhausted all possible relations, and did not include any of the alleged moral relations.

(2) I have tried to show, on various occasions, that agathopoeics in general and even strict utilitarianism in particular are not nearly so helpless in face of these moral relations as the new intuitionists say they are, and that it is necessary that all such relations, if morally commendable, should occur within the ambit of the beneficent. I have, however, also indicated the probability, which I now fully accept, that an ethics of benefit, even when combined with an admission of active intrinsic good in addition to passive benefit, is unable to accept or to account for the full moral significance of such

relations. This being assumed, we are left with the third point.

(3) According to the new intuitionists, these moral relationships are simply (morally) *right* and are not good at all. These authors admit that there are obligations to do good, and to be good, but even then some of them would hold that such goodness is not a ground of rightness, but, on the contrary, that every obligation to do or to be good follows from the fittingness of goodness to certain situations. And they all agree that many moral relational obligations are either wholly or in great measure independent of goodness, whether of character, of motive, or of consequences.

If all goods were either intrinsic personal goods or mere means to such goods, it seems necessary to admit that the relational features in much that is morally commendable cannot be included in goods so defined. To revert to a favourite (because a very strong) example, it is not true that justice is morally commendable simply because men's sense of injustice rankles in their souls, and because their enjoyment of a status they believe to be just brings deep inward content. It is true that these inward (or intrinsic) goods are correlated with a correct estimation of an equitable status, but they do not exhaust what is morally commendable in that status.

On the other hand, it is very hard to believe that such relations are independent of goodness, active or passive. For either, as in the instance of justice, they have no meaning at all except when applied to a moral agent, morally engaged, or else, as in Hume's illustration of parricide, they are not reprehensible unless a moral agent, not insane, cherishes evil designs. Again, as I have frequently tried to show, no such relation is morally commendable unless it applies to actions neither maleficent nor futile. In view of these circumstances it is impossible to hold that such right or fitting relations have nothing to do with active moral good or with contemplated benefit; and if (as I hold to be evident) goodness does justify conduct, this fact, combined with the circumstance that no relation independent of goodness could justify it, makes it tempting at least to hold that there is no justification of conduct (moral or otherwise) *except* on account of some goodness pertaining to it.

If this were so, and if it were also true that the moral relationships we are now considering are commendable on account of something more than all the goods intrinsic to any man's soul combined with the causes of such goods, the necessary consequence would be that such relations must be *relational goods*. And that is what I think they are, although I should like to speak with all becoming diffidence.

According to this modest suggestion, an ethics of well-being is an insufficient ethics if it insists that the goods that constitute well-being are either the private possessions of this or the other man, or mere instruments of such intrinsic or inward goods. For much that is morally obligatory, much of duty, that is, and of right and justice, is relational in its nature. The new intuitionists, by calling (and *holding*) ethical attention to the special relational implications of many moral obligations, have revealed what should always have been obvious but frequently has not been noticed; but they have not refuted an ethics of well-being, if inter-personal relations as well as personal experiences and characteristics may be included in well-being.

The reasons why this matter has been neglected, or but partially remembered in so many theories of ethical agathopoeics are, I think, chiefly historical. Hedonistic utilitarianism reckoned in terms of certain quite private, inward, and intrinsic goods, viz. pleasures and pains, counting all else as mere means. Ideal utilitarianism, perceiving clearly that pleasure was not the only good *in se*, nor pain the only evil, modified its contentions accordingly, but, intent on its quarrel with hedonism, did not take sufficient pains to examine certain other assumptions in the doctrine it transformed, particularly the assumption that goods, unless quite subordinate, must be non-relational. Since there are no such entities as relational pleasures (although pleasure may result from certain types of inter-personal relations) this assumption hardly needed to be stated when hedonistic utilitarianism was the theme, but it became a most disputable assumption when non-hedonic goods were admitted to exist. And if (as frequently happened) "ideal" utilitarianism (so-called), ceased to be a strict utilitarianism and admitted active moral good as well as probable passive benefit, the same neglect of relational goods tended to linger.

There is, I believe, no reason why there should not be relational (axiological) goods, and it seems to me to be clear by inspection that justice (say) is not only "right" and "fitting," but *also* good. The question, therefore, although it involves names, is not simply one of names. It is real as well as verbal, and the view I am diffidently suggesting should not have to meet the taunt that it accepts the substance of the deontological criticism of agathopoeics, but rechristens the relational moral obligations of the deontologists by the name of relational goods. The new intuitionists affirm that such moral obligations have nothing to do with goodness, and this view seems to me to be wholly intolerable and absurd.

In previous argument I have maintained that axiological good should not be confused with final good (or with the correlatives end and means), and it is the *axiological* goodness of these relational moral goods that is now under discussion. If, however, it were held that axiological goodness is always a species of final good (for it is absurd to say that the two are identical), I should still maintain that the establishment of a just inter-personal status or of some other moral relational good is a worthy object of human enterprise.

INDEX